BILINGUALISM AND MALAY LANGUAGE

Planning in Singapore

Dr. Mohamed Aidil Subhan

PARTRIDGE

To order additional copies of this book, contact
Toll Free 800 101 2657 (Singapore)
Toll Free 1 800 81 7340 (Malaysia)
orders.singapore@partridgepublishing.com

www.partridgepublishing.com/singapore

Contents

Glossary xiii

Foreword xvii

Preface xxv

Chapter 1 – Bilingualism and Language Planning

Introduction 1

Bilingualism 2

Bilingual Education 7

Language Planning 12

Singapore's bilingual language policy and Malay language planning 21

Conclusion 39

Chapter 2 – Bilingualism and Malay Language Planning

Introduction 41

Reviews and Reports Enhancing Bilingualism and Impacting the

Malay Language 43

Report of the All-Party Committee of the Singapore Legislative

Assembly on Chinese Education 1956 47

Report on the Ministry of Education, 1978: Assessment of the

Bilingual Policy 55

Improving Primary School Education Report 1991 60

Malay Language Steering Review Committee, 1999 65

The Mother Tongue Language Curriculum and the Pedagogy

Review Committees...69

Report on Primary Education Review Initiative (PERI) 75

Mother Tongue Language Review Committee 2011....................78

Conclusion...83

Chapter 3 – Status Planning

Introduction.. 84

Status Planning 84

Status Language Planning for Malay... 88

Status of Malay...98

Impact of Bilingualism on Status Planning 99

Conclusion.. 102

Chapter 4 – Corpus Planning

Introduction.. 104

Corpus Planning.. 104

History of Corpus Planning for Malay 111

The Role of MABBIM in Corpus Planning................................. 119

Standardization of Malay.. 122

Need for Standardization 124

Issues with the Standardization of Spoken Malay 125

Sebutan Baku and its Implementation in Singapore 128

Corpus Planning for Malay in Singapore's Bilingual Framework....130

Conclusion.. 132

Chapter 5 – Acquisition Planning

Introduction.. 133

Acquisition Planning.. 133

Process of Acquisition Planning for Malay................................ 137

Overt Language Planning Goal 137

Method Employed to Attain Language Planning Goals............ 156

Conclusion.. 170

Chapter 6 – New Malay Language Pedagogy

Introduction 171

Language shift 172

Nurturing Active Learners and Proficient Users 176

Issues Pertaining to Language Acquisition Planning 191

Conclusion 193

Chapter 7 – Further Directions in Malay Language Planning

Introduction 194

An Accounting Scheme for the Study of Language Planning 195

Accounting for Malay Language Planning based on Cooper's Framework 198

Effect of Bilingualism on Malay 202

    Positive Effects of the Bilingual Policy 202

    Negative Effects of the Bilingual Policy 205

Pedagogical Approach to Supporting the Teaching and Learning of

Malay in an English-knowing Bilingual Context such as Singapore 209

Mother Tongues as "Cultural Ballast" 209

Overall Effects of the Bilingual Policy on the status, corpus and

acquisition planning of Malay 210

    Effects on the Status of Malay 210

    Effects on the Malay Corpus 211

    Effects on the Acquisition of Malay 213

Conclusion 214

References 219

List of Tables

Table 1   Haugen's (1983: 275) revised language planning model, with additions 16

Table 2   Phases of educational policy and reports, and effect on Malay 46

Table 3   Cooper's Acquisition Planning Model 135

Table 4   Dominant Home Language of Resident Malay Population Aged Five and Over.. 173

Table 5   Language Used by Malay Parents with their Children 174

Table 6   Student Use of Malay with Relatives and Friends........................... 175

Table 7   Differences between Deep and Surface Learners............................ 188

Table 8   Accounting scheme for the study of language planning.................. 196

Table 9   Accounting scheme for Malay language planning........................... 198

Table 10   Fishman's Graded Intergenerational Disruption Scale (GIDS) 203

Table 11   Percentage of Students Who Prefer to Read and Write in English....207

List of Diagrams

Diagram 5.1   Differentiated Instruction Model 165

 # Glossary

Acquisition planning – Language-in-education planning and matters pertaining to language teaching and learning.

Bilingualism – the ability to converse or communicate in two languages. In Singapore, this normally consists of English and one mother tongue, namely Mandarin, Malay, or Tamil.

Cambridge General Certificate in Education Advance Level (GCE A Level) – Pre-requisite for entry into university.

Cambridge General Certificate in Education Ordinary Level (GCE O Level) – Pre-requisite for entry into pre-university education.

Corpus planning – The planning of a language in terms of its written form, spelling, grammar, a key component of terminology and other linguistic matters.

Cultural ballast – The mother tongue, namely Mandarin, Malay, or Tamil acting as cultural defence against the ever-widening use of English.

Institute of Language and Literature (Dewan Bahasa dan Pustaka) – Institute dedicated to language and literature set up under the *Dewan Bahasa and Pustaka* Act to promote the use of Malay within Malaysia.

National Language and Cultural Institute of Singapore (Dewan Bahasa Kebangsaan dan Kebudayaan Singapura) – Institute set up in 1960 under the purview of the then Ministry of Culture, Singapore. Tasked with promoting the Malay language and strengthen Malayan culture among Singaporeans. The Institute ceased operations in 1970 due to the changing emphasis on English.

Diglossia – A situation where two language varieties (a high variety and a low variety) are used within a country or region.

Domain – A sphere of activity representing a combination of specific times, settings and social roles.

Heritage Language – A language spoken in homes where it is not the dominant language of the country or region.

Junior College – Two-year pre-university education equivalent to US 12th grade.

Language Planning – The development of policies or programs to direct or change language use.

Language Policy – Means by which government agencies or interest groups set out their intentions to safeguard, develop, or promote a language.

Malay Language Council of Brunei, Indonesia and Malaysia (Majlis Bahasa Brunei, Indonesia dan Malaysia – MABBIM) – Regional organization tasked with preserving, protecting, and promoting the Malay language. The three official members are Brunei, Indonesia, and Malaysia, represented by their respective Ministers for Education. Singapore sits as an observer, represented by representatives of the Malay Language Council of Singapore (MBMS).

Malay Language Council of Singapore (Majlis Bahasa Melayu Singapura – MBMS) – Government agency under the purview of the Ministry of Information, Communications and the Arts, tasked with advising the government on issues pertaining to Malay and to helping preserve and protect it.

Malay Language Learning & Promotion Committee (MLLPC) – Government agency under the purview of the Ministry of Education Singapore set up to plan the learning and promotion of Malay and to disburse funds to that ends.

Models of bilingualism - Constructs devised to help us understand the effects of bilingualism.

Mother Tongue – Pre-determined ethnic language, based on the father's ethnicity.

Parity Theory – Policy whereby what is given to one ethnic language (mother tongue) is also provided for in the other languages.

Primary Education – Basic 6-year education equivalent to US 1st-6th grade.

Standard Pronunciation (sebutan baku) – A form of pronunciation of Malay that emphasizes a single sound for each letter and pronouncing the language as it is spelled.

Secondary Education – Intermediate 4-5 years high school education equivalent to US 7th-11th grade.

Status Planning – Planning level of usage of and attitudes toward a language.

Types of Bilingualism – Categorization based on the different characteristics of bilingualism.

# Foreword

Looking at nations of insular Southeast Asia, one gets a picture of their search for language-derived identity at the time they became sovereign nations. Malaysia, Indonesia, Brunei and the Philippines found within their own native milieu one which became their national language. The first three countries happened to share the same language, Malay, but in different varieties, with Indonesia giving a new name in consonance with the name of the nation, *bahasa Indonesia*. The Philippines had Tagalog, which is now better known as Filipino, a name change analogous to that of *bahasa Indonesia*.

The national language in each of these countries is given a major role in the governance of the nation and in its education system, even in countries (Brunei and the Philippines) where bilingualism consisting of national language and English rules the day. But in terms of the status and role of their national language, these four countries can be grouped together in one and the same category. At a glance, in choosing Malay as the national language, Singapore appears to belong to the same category as her four neighbours. However, the difference lies in the fact that her concept of "national language" is not equal to that in those of these other countries. In Singapore "national language" really means only the language of the national anthem, whereas in the other countries "national language" is given a broader role than that.

With the national language appropriately placed in a nationalistic role, i.e. in the wordings of the national anthem, Singapore goes on to recognise four speech systems within her boundaries as official languages, these being English, Mandarin, Malay and Tamil. In Singapore as in Malaysia, in terms of conceptualisation, "national language" is a different entity from "official language", but the meaning given to each of these two concepts in one country is not necessarily repeated in the other. Another similarity is that Malay in both countries is given the status of official language, showing that in this very language there is a combination of two functions – one is symbolic (national), and the other is communication in officialdom. Here ends the similarity in the language policies of Malaysia and Singapore.

Each of the four official languages of Singapore has its own significance in the life of the citizens. It would be a cliché to say that English has the most highly rated standing in terms of socio-economic well-being of the people of Singapore, and there is little wonder why it is made the first language of Singapore, with the term "first language" having the signification of the "most important language" in the country. Applied linguists are baffled by this term, because in their academic discipline "first language" means one that is the earliest to be acquired by a child. And the meaning as given in applied linguistics may not have been the objective of the policy when it was formulated, as the policy also provides for the teaching of the mother tongues of the three main ethnic groups – Malay, Chinese and Indian. And mother tongue is always understood to be a first language of the child.

Over the years it appears that English has evolved to be a first-acquired language by a Singapore child, regardless of ethnic group. The rigour in its implementation as the first (meaning the most important) language is supported by its role as the medium of instruction in the schools, and this particular role has made English no longer a non-native tongue but a first language in every sense of the word. The multilingual policy which also provides for the teaching of mother tongue and the acquisition of another language among the three mother tongues should result in school children having the ability to function in three languages, presumably with varying degrees of proficiency, with English getting the highest score, followed by the mother tongue, and in the third place the other language.

A couple of years ago when I was given the honour to conduct a course on Bilingualism at one of Singapore's universities for the degree of Master of Arts, I was not surprised to read in the assignments (based on students' field research on bilingualism among Singaporeans) that English had become a home language in a great many families of all the three ethnic groups, side by side with the mother tongue. Such families can claim to have two home languages, and this sort of situation is nothing new, as it exists in multilingual regions where ethnic groups with different languages live side by side, as in the border region of Kedah-Thailand where Malays known to the local people as Samsam have Malay and Siamese as home languages. Whether English will ultimately replace the original home language in Singapore families, which may eventually be a mother tongue in the family, will be determined through time given that the social factors causing the change are already at work.

Socio-economic factors seem to be a powerful determinant in instilling the belief that knowing English is a sure way to success for oneself as well as for the country. And English occupies that powerful position especially after the last world war due to it being the language of the world's superpower, i.e. the United States of America. But the politico-economic situation of the world may not be in that *status quo* forever. We now see the rise of China as a challenge to America. If language is concomitant with socio-economic power, it will not be long before the Chinese language becomes a goal to be achieved among countries of the world in their struggle to succeed in trade and commerce and in technology. This social and linguistic change in world order has been predicted generally by political watchers.

In this volume, *Bilingualism and Malay Language Planning in Singapore*, Dr. Mohamed Aidil Subhan, who has been researching on language policy and planning this number of years, shares his observation of the immanent spread of Chinese as a lingua franca, following the path taken by English over the last century. As far as Singapore is concerned, the implementation of Chinese in the schools as a mother tongue of Chinese students, as well as an elective by the non-Chinese, has already paved the way for the adoption of Chinese as another super-power language. When this happens, there would have to be planning for the acquisition of the language for students to reach an attainment level that will be adequate for the use of the language for whatever type of purpose suitable in reaching the nation's goal. If the academic disciplines currently taught in Chinese as a mother tongue and as an elective to non-Chinese are considered to be limited to "soft subjects" like literature and history, the extension of the use of Chinese in the teaching of subjects like the sciences, mathematics, economics, ICT and others would be a sure way to instill in future Singaporeans the ability to use Chinese at a higher level than they have now, that is if they have not done it yet. For the Chinese, whose first language is English, the extension of their proficiency in Chinese into new domains would be an opening into a new history in their bonding with the language of their ancestors. For the non-Chinese, for example the Malays, they will be in pursuit of a bigger challenge to attain the level of proficiency of the same level as the native speakers of the language.

This volume focuses on Malay language planning and the bilingual situation which Malays in Singapore have to be part of. Singapore had once been the centre of the spread of Malay literature, specifically the new type of literature like the novel, the short story, and modern prose form. The newspaper in Malay was given its beginning in Singapore, mainly due to the introduction of the printing machine, and it was also modern technology that introduced the radio and broadcasting to the Malay world, and it had its first station in Singapore. All this goes to show that Singapore was the nerve centre for the development and spread of Malay, and the variety identified with Singapore was that of the Johor-Riau dialect. Until today this is the variety still in use as community speech system in the Riau-Lingga islands and the eastern provinces of Sumatera, namely mainland Riau and the Province of North Sumatera.

Politics has changed the Malay language situation in Singapore, especially after 1965, as seen in its language policy planning, which has affected its significance even in the life of its native speakers. With English as first language, and Chinese as *de facto* second language, a reversal to its former role as a variety of Malay with its own standing in the region, will require a special effort both in its acquisition planning as well as in planting a conviction among the Malay population that it would not be an impossible task. The reason for my saying this is that Singaporeans themselves will have to be authors and creators of literary and intellectual artefacts in Malay as attestation to the target of the planning. At the same time, they will have to take cognizance of the presence of a continual linguistic and literary power of Malaysia and Indonesia. Although these two neighbours have a close working relationship in the development of their language and literature, they have respect for each other in maintaining their own identity in their own variety of Malay. When identity resides in linguistic form, it stretches on to literature as well as any other type of text produced by users of that particular form.

Malay language planning in Singapore is entering a phase of a renewal of its glorious past – or to quote Dr. Mohamed Aidil, a renaissance. What this means is that Malays will have to maintain their ability to function in their mother tongue, which should also be a vehicle of intellectuality and creativity, two qualities which are the hallmarks of Malay writings from the seventeenth to the nineteenth century. That was the period prior to the modern era which saw a phenomenal growth of the Malay language through its literature and other genres. And as these writings were rendered in the Jawi script, it is clear to us that the coming of Islam to the Malay world was the most important factor that brought about this development, that is by giving literacy to the Malays, a skill which was denied to them before they became Muslims. The Jawi script did not restrict them to texts of the Islamic faith. With the Jawi-based literacy Malays began recording as much as they could narratives of various genres – native folk tales, and stories from other religions which came to their knowledge, such as those from Ramayana and Mahabharata of Hinduism, and the Jataka Tales from Buddhism, to mention a few. The great number of *kitab* in Malay written by Malays themselves for the purpose of teaching the tenets of Islam to the common folks may no longer be known to present-day Malays in Malaysia and Singapore, but they are still in use as texts for the teaching of Islam to Malays in Thailand, Cambodia and Vietnam. The language of the *kitab* is simple, as they were written for the comprehension of ordinary folks, although the translation of verses in Arabic may be baffling due to the word-for-word translation.

Towards the end of the twentieth century, Malaysia with the recommendation of a group of linguists embarked on a complete standardisation of the national language, Malay. The thinking behind this was that a fully standardised variety of Malay would bring prestige to the language (which could be called King's Malay, analogous to Queen's English). Thus was born the *bahasa baku*. As far as grammar was concerned, there was already a manual-cum-reference text which was widely used in schools. What was left to be done was the pronunciation, which was based on the way the language was spelt. Thus the *sebutan baku* came into being. The school had to change overnight to *sebutan baku*, replacing the erstwhile standard pronunciation. This took place in 1988. Only one TV station complied with the ruling in using the *sebutan baku*. People were confused with what they termed "an outer space pronunciation". As for writers of creative literature, they were not happy in having to follow the rules of the grammar of the school manuals, which restricted their style, hence their creativity. However, the unnatural variety of standard Malay lasted for ten years, as its end came when the Cabinet Ministers made a ruling that standard Malay should revert back to the variety in use before 1988.

Today in the media, Malaysia adopts a pluricentric view, where TV and Radio stations can use the standard variety of the region where the station is located. And leaders appear to do well in their communication with the people when they are given this freedom of choice. This stance is an indication that Malaysia recognises that the Malay language could not have charted its history being a language of governance, diplomacy, and the spread of Islam, and having a large corpus of fine literary works and epistolary, if there had been only one centre of development. Just looking at the Malay Peninsula alone, there have been many centres of the development of the Malay language and literature, with each sultanate having its own, particularly before the formation of the Federation of Malaya in 1948. (See Asmah Haji Omar, "Pluricentricity and Identity in the Malay World", in Rudolf Muhr/Benjamin Mesnitzer (eds.), *Pluricentric Languages and New Dominant Varieties Worldwide: New Pluricentric Languages- Old Problems*, Frankfurt a. M/Wien u.a.: Peter Lang, 2018, pp. 45-60).

The *bahasa baku* of Malaysia during its short life span appeared to have brought a whiff of change in the linguistic form of the Malay language of Singapore. In an interactive radio talk on a working visit to Singapore in 2012, I was asked by listeners, mostly Malay parents of school-going children, why their children were speaking a language that was strange to them. They were in a sense correct in pointing to Malaysia for that linguistic influence. And I had to inform them that Malaysia had realised the mistake she made and had abandoned that form of speaking in 1998.

The attitude of these parents should be taken as a feedback in the development of a variety of Malay that is specific to Singapore. While most Singaporeans speak the Johor variety of Malay at home, the variety they use officially appears to be that of the *baku*-type. It is normal in interactions using Malay in any part of Malaysia for speakers to shift from one variety to the other, for example from the national to the local standard, and from the local standard to a non-standard variety of the same dialect area. The use of local standard varieties is given a slot in the five o'clock news every day on TV1. From the Malaysian experience with *bahasa baku*, one can deduce that a variety of speech system is one that evolves from the users themselves. It is not one that is artificially invented and handed down from the authorities to the user. If ever a standard variety is deemed necessary for whatever purpose, it should be chosen from among the ones that are already in use in the community. The national standard variety of Malay in Malaysia was based on the Johor dialect, due to its wide geographical spread through the language of the newspapers and radio broadcasting. But its current form has evolved on its own with constant influence from other varieties spoken in Malaysia. Such is the evolution of this variety that it now stands apart from the Johor dialect which was its base form.

In concluding this Foreword, I would like to congratulate Dr. Mohamed Aidil Subhan, for the publication of this volume, from which we are able to learn about the bilingual situation in Singapore and the planning for the use of Malay within this context. My story of the development of the national variety as well as localised standard varieties in Malaysia is an example of how standard varieties at any level come into being.

Asmah Haji Omar
11 April, 2018

 # Preface

Singapore's bilingual policy has been dubbed an English-knowing bilingual system, in which English is the main language followed by a choice of any one of the three mother tongue languages: Mandarin, Malay, or Tamil. Among the three mother tongue languages, there is a perception that the language policy is Mandarin-inspired, especially given the opening up of China and the growing economic importance of learning Mandarin.

There is also a worry among Malay speakers that in spite of its status as the national language and one of the four official languages, Malay has seen its role within Singapore diminish from that of a language of unity and wider communication to a language of cultural repository, which is largely symbolic in nature. This will in turn affect its stated role as a "cultural ballast" in Singapore's bilingual framework.

Thus, there is a need for academic research that would detail these concerns, both perceived and real, among the Malay language community against a background of language shift and changing attitudes toward the language as a result of the bilingual policy and to analyze the impact of the English-knowing and Mandarin-led bilingual system. This research will list selected educational review reports and relate it to its impact on Malay language planning and offer a response in terms of pedagogical approaches required to address the changing demographics and language shift among Malay learners.

Besides addressing these issues, this book attempts to audit the Malay language planning in terms of its status, corpus and acquisition planning using Cooper's (1989) theoretical framework and accounting scheme. By doing so the researcher aims to highlight the positives and negatives of the bilingual policy on Malay language planning in Singapore.

In the publication of this book, which based on my PhD thesis entitled Bilingualism and Its Effects On Malay Language Planning, it is a culmination of 13 years looking at the state of affairs in Malay language planning in Singapore after so many more years before that of being involved directly as an educator and a social activist. I have many people to thank in helping me find the 'truth'.

Firstly, I have to thank Emeritus Professor Allan Luke, the man who first brought me into the 'world' of language planning back in 2002, for his dedication to the cause and keeping an eye out for me at the beginning of my journey at the Centre for Research in Pedagogy & Practice (CRPP), National Institute of Education, Nanyang Technological University, Singapore. Your courage and motivational speeches are second to none.

Secondly, Associate Professor Viniti Vaish, my PhD Supervisor, who took up the challenge of supervising me halfway through the PhD process. She continued Allan's legacy of the soft touch and quiet words of wisdom as I travail through the nuances of getting the PhD done. Your patience and encouragement I greatly appreciate.

Lastly, I would like to thank Emeritus Professor Asmah Hj. Omar who took time out from her busy schedule to write me the foreword to this book. An icon of the Malay world of language policy and planning. Once ostracized by the Malaysian government for going against the standardization policy for Malay, but now back on her feet again as her ideas were proven right and the said policy was disbanded 10 years after its' implementation. I first knew Prof. Asmah 25 years ago when I attended her lecture at the University of Malaya, Kuala Lumpur Malaysia, as a not-so young undergraduate eager to learn from the best. Always enjoyed her 3 hour lectures. No notes. No powerpoints. Pure lecture! Thank you Prof!

To the readers of this book, the Singapore bilingual story doesn't end. The story continues. This audit is meant to show the impact of a policy on a certain minority. Most policies are meant for the good of the masses. Unfortunately, there are some that has unintended effects. When I started on this journey, there were some who ridiculed me by saying there's no future in studying the Malay language or there is no language planning for Malay. But now, there is a greater understanding of the need to plan the development and scope of the language especially in the context of multi-lingual Singapore. This book is meant to be the first comprehensive look solely on Malay Language Planning in bilingual Singapore. And I hope it will not be the last.

Mohamed Aidil Subhan
11 April 2018

1

Bilingualism and Language Planning

Introduction

Bilingualism is a phenomenon that can be affected by language planning. The choice of what language is to be taught, for example, is made during the process of language planning. Thus, there is an inextricable link between the two. In the context of the bilingual language policy of Singapore, much has been said about the state of bilingualism in relation to the use of English and Mandarin. Based on policy documents and speeches that set out the plan and the implementation of the bilingual language policy, it appears that much of it is motivated by the need to preserve the Chinese identity via the Chinese language and by the need to balance the use of English and that of Chinese in order to ensure that Singaporeans do not become pseudo-western. This point was reiterated by (then) Singapore's Deputy Prime Minister, Lee Hsien Loong in a ministerial statement in 1999. He said,

> "…the mother tongue gives us a crucial part of our values, roots and identity. It gives us access to our cultural heritage, and a world-view that complements the perspective of the English-speaking world."

There is therefore a need to widen the approach and to look at the bilingual policy in terms of its effects on the two other major vernacular languages, Malay and Tamil. This research will focus on bilingualism and its effect on Malay language planning.

Bilingualism

Bilingualism is generally referred to as the ability to converse or communicate in two languages. The question to be answered is then: What do we mean when we say "ability"? What does it entail? There are four basic language abilities, namely listening, speaking, reading, and writing. Thus, being bilingual could mean the ability not only to listen and speak in two languages but also to be able to read and write as well.

Bloomfield (1933: 55-56) famously defined bilingualism as follows:

> "In the extreme case of foreign language learning, the speaker becomes so proficient as to be indistinguishable from the native speakers round him....In the cases where this perfect foreign language learning is not accompanied by loss of the native language, it results in bilingualism, (the) native-like control of two languages."

Haugen (1953: 7) defined bilingualism as a situation where not only is an individual fluent in a particular language but in in which someone "can produce complete, meaningful utterances in the other language."

Mackey (1962: 51) argues that bilingualism

> "...must moreover include the use not only of two languages but of any number of languages. We shall therefore consider bilingualism as the alternate use of two or more languages by the same individual."

Mackey's statement is similar to that of Weinreich (1953: 5), who argues that

> "The practice of alternatively using two languages will be called here BILINGUALISM, and the persons involved BILINGUAL. Unless otherwise specified, all remarks about bilingualism apply as well to multilingualism, the practice of using alternately three or more languages."

Edwards (2004: 8) has suggested that "earlier definitions tend to restrict [bilingualism] to equal mastery of two languages, while later ones have allowed much greater variation in competence." An example is Grosjean (1999, cited in Butler & Hakuta, 2004: 115), who differentiates between bilinguals who use two or more languages in their daily lives and "dormant bilinguals," who retain knowledge of the different languages but do not use them any longer.

Butler and Hakuta (2004: 115) define bilingualism as "psychological and social states of individuals or groups of people that result from interactions via language in which two or more linguistic codes (including dialects) are used for communication." They further define bilinguals as individuals "who obtain communicative skills, with various degrees of proficiency, in oral and/or written forms, in order to interact with speakers of one or more languages in a given society."

Bilingualism in Singapore is promoted via a bilingual education policy. In this context, the policy promotes not so much the learning of any two languages but the learning of English and another language, namely English and a state-determined "mother tongue," namely Chinese, Malay, or Tamil. According to Skutnabb-Kangas (1988: 16, bilingualism and mother tongue can be defined on the basis of the following criteria: origin, competence, function, and identification.

Origin refers to a bilingual speaker who has learned two languages in the family or is able to use two languages with the same ability as means of communication from a very young age. Nevertheless, the mother tongue is the language the speaker learns first. Competence occurs when a bilingual speaker has complete and equal mastery of the two languages. In this case, the speaker has what is referred to as "native-like control" of two languages. However, the mother tongue is the language the speaker knows best. Function refers to situations in which a bilingual speaker uses (or has the ability to use) two languages in most situations based on personal or societal needs. However, the mother tongue is the language most frequently used. Identification can be subdivided into two subsets, namely internal and external identification. Internal identification is when a person identifies himself or herself as a bilingual speaker, whereas external identification refers to someone who is identified as a bilingual speaker by others. In both instances, the mother tongue is the most readily identifiable language among those used by the speaker.

Common Concepts in Bilingualism

In addition to theories, types (or the different characteristics of bilingualism), and models of bilingualism (a human construct that helps us understand the effects of bilingualism), there are some basic concepts underlying the study of bilingualism. Garcia (2009: 56) divides these concepts into two distinct groups. The first group consists of concepts that researchers use when they see bilingualism from a purely linguistic viewpoint. These concepts include semilingualism, language dominance, and mother tongue. However, if we were to look at bilingualism from the bilingual speakers' viewpoint, these concepts should include that of second language and that of the heritage language learner. Among these concepts, the most relevant in this study will be mother tongue and second language learners and speakers.

<u>Mother Tongue</u>

The term mother tongue is a common concept in the study of bilingualism. Lieberson (1969: 291) highlighted the United Nations definition of mother tongue as "the language usually spoken in the individual's home in his or her early childhood, although not necessarily used by him or her at present." In spite of this seemingly simple and straightforward definition, it is not easy to put it in practice. Skutnabb-Kangas (1981: 18) highlights the difficulty inherent in identifying one's mother tongue, based on four criteria:

- Origin: The language(s) one learned first
- Competence: The language(s) one knows best
- Function: The language(s) one uses most
- Identification
    - Internal: The language(s) one identifies with
    - External: The language(s) others identify one with

Thus, one's mother tongue can be based on either a person's first language, the language in which the speaker is most competent, the language the speaker uses most often, or the language the speaker most identifies with. Skutnabb-Kangas (1981) concludes that it is sometimes not possible to clearly identify someone's mother tongue as the speaker may have more than one based on the criteria mentioned above.

In the Singapore context, we can add a fifth criterion, whereby a child's "ethnic mother tongue" is pre-determined, i.e., based on the father's ethnicity and thus limited to three main ethnic groups: Chinese, Malay, and Indian. In this regard, a Chinese father will give his child's Mandarin as the ethnic mother tongue while a Malay father will give Malay and an Indian father Tamil (Beardsmore, 1998 cited in Garcia, 2009: 58).

Second Language Learners and Speakers

According to Garcia (2009: 59), most teachers assume that their students are second language learners or speakers if they learn or speak a different language when at home. This view is based on the literature on English teaching, which tends to divide speakers into three distinct categories: native speakers, second language speakers, and those learning English as a foreign language. Based on this understanding, Kachru (1985) has proposed a model of three concentric circles, each representing different types of speakers: an inner circle, representing native speakers, an outer circle, representing second language speakers, and an expanding circle, representing those learning English as a foreign language. However, Kachru's (1985) representation has been challenged, particularly by Pakir (2003: 67-68), who refers to Kachru's second group as "English-knowing bilinguals" and to the third group as "English-using bilinguals." Garcia (2009: 59) argues that there is a need to replace the use of the term "second-language learner/ speaker" by the label "emergent bilingual" so as to clarify the fact that there need be no language loss when someone learns another language.

Diglossia

The concept of diglossia refers to a situation where "two language varieties are used within a country or region and where one (the High variety) is used in more formal spheres ... and the other (the Low variety) is used in informal spheres" (Alsagoff, Chng, & Wee, 1998: 63). Thus, the concept of diglossia should not be confused with that of bilingualism. This understanding of diglossia is derived from Ferguson's classic definition,

> Diglossia is a relatively stable language situation in which, in addition to the primary dialects of the language (which may include a standard or regional standards), there is a very divergent, highly codified (often grammatically more complex) superposed variety, the vehicle of a large and respected body of written literature, either of an earlier period or in another speech community, which is learned largely by formal education and is used for most written and formal spoken purposes but is not used by any sector of the community for ordinary conversation. (Ferguson, 2003: 354)

Fishman (2003), went further and differentiated between bilingualism and diglossia as follows,

> Bilingualism is essentially a characterization of individual linguistic behavior whereas diglossia is a characterization of linguistic organization at the socio-cultural level (Fishman, 2003: 362-363).

Thus, diglossia is a situation in which two or more language varieties are used within a community depending on domains determined as formal or informal. This is distinct from bilingualism, which refers to the use of two distinct languages within the same community irrespective of domains of usage.

Bilingualism and Biliteracy

Hornberger (2003) takes the concept of bilingualism a step further by connecting it with literacy, hence biliteracy. She proposes a framework for understanding biliteracy that uses the notion of a continuum so as to provide an overarching conceptual scheme for describing context, content, media and development. According to Hornberger (2008), the model portrays the four continua as intersecting and nested, demonstrating the multiple interrelationships between bilingualism and literacy in the development of biliteracy.

Bilingual Education

Edwards (1984: 12 defines bilingual education as "education in which two languages are used within the school." He further elaborates that there are two major models of bilingual education. Firstly, transitional bilingual education, where the main aim is to enhance fluency in the majority language. In the transitional model, the main concern is that of assimilating the minority language users into the majority language group. The second model is referred to as "maintenance" or "enrichment" bilingual education. In this model, the main aim is to ensure that the child has good language ability in both languages. This model is very much concerned with matters of pluralism, language enrichment, language restoration, and biculturalism.

Gaarder (1976, cited in Baker, 1988: 47) views bilingualism along similar lines. He divides the types of bilingualism into two: elitist and folk, similar to that of Fishman (1977). According to Gaarder, elitist bilingualism refers to a situation in which the bilingual policy is meant to serve the interest of the dominant power group and members of the upper class. This approach encourages the acquisition of a good knowledge of two languages for the sole purpose of attaining high culture as well as economic value.

Folk bilingualism, on the other hand, is a product of necessity or borne out of compulsion. It is triggered to some extent by the survival instinct of the community involved. The main aim here is to gain access to employment, hence the reference to the survival instinct.

This distinction highlights the motives of children during and especially upon entry into bilingual schooling. The success or failure of bilingual education programs is partially dependent on the motives and commitments of the students, their parents, and the sub-culture.

Types of Bilingual Education

There are four main types of bilingual education, which all share the main objective of achieving bilingualism. These are: Immersion Bilingual Education, Maintenance and Heritage Language Bilingual Education, Two-way Dual Language Bilingual Education, and Mainstream Bilingual Education (Baker, 2011: 158).

Immersion Bilingual Education

In an Immersion program, the students, who are mostly monolingual, begin immersion education on a level playing field since they have similar inexperience in the second language. In countries such as Canada, immersion aims to achieve bilingualism in two majority languages, namely French and English. In Catalonia, the aim of an immersion program is to make the students become fluent in both Catalan and Spanish, thus enriching them cognitively as well as culturally. Immersion bilingual education is introduced gradually, with a phasing-in period and plenty of scaffolding as well as interventions by teachers to facilitate the process. The opposite is submersion bilingual education, where the process is forceful and mostly conducted with little regard for human or social factors.

Maintenance and Heritage Language Bilingual Education

This main objective of this type of program is to assist students in maintaining their mother tongue and culture and simultaneously integrating them with other languages and cultures. Therefore, the students' mother tongue is protected and developed alongside the developing second language. Thus, bilingual education of this type is meant for either pacification or empowerment purposes. It is meant for pacification purposes if the end result is not accompanied by an economic and structural provision ensuring equality of opportunities and outcomes. Therefore, a pacification program emphasizes the link between mother tongue and ethnicity to "the exclusion of societal questions of economic and political power"(Skutnabb-Kangas

& Cummins, 1988: 394). If economic and structural provision is made hand in hand with linguistic provision, then bilingual education is meant to empower these minority students. In the empowerment model, the focus is on the mother tongue as the right of the individual, thus providing a better medium to help students cope with the second language as well as other skills coupled with "analysis, understanding, evaluating, and action in relation to societal questions of economic and political power" (Skutnabb-Kangas & Cummins, 1988: 394).

Two Way/Dual Language Bilingual Education

As its name suggests, this model aims to produce balanced bilinguals based on a two-way model in which both languages are used for instruction and learning. Emphasis is also placed on the enrichment and maintenance of the mother tongue. In both curriculum and classroom execution, equal exposure is given to both languages, thus helping the minority students maintain their mother tongue while expanding their learning of the second language.

Mainstream Bilingual Education

This type of program essentially promotes enrichment and is meant for both bilingual and biliterate students. An example is that of Malaysia, where there is joint usage of two majority languages in schools: Bahasa Malaysia and English. The international language is used as a medium of instruction alongside the dominant indigenous language, which is accessed for utilitarian purposes. Thus, language here is perceived as a means to an economic end.

With this in mind, Lewis (1981: 262) highlights the attitude that has to be in place for bilingual education to be successful. He argues that

> "Any policy for language, especially in the system of education, has to take into account the attitude of those likely to be affected. In the long run, no policy will succeed which does not do one of three things: conform to the expressed attitudes of those involved, persuade those who express negative attitudes about the rightness of the policy, or seek to remove the causes of disagreement.

Aims of Bilingual Education

Various types of bilingual education can be implemented in order to achieve a variety of goals such as enrichment, pacification, empowerment, maintenance, or simply economic gain. It can help minority groups to learn their mother tongue and culture alongside the dominant language, thereby feeling less alienated or dislocated in a new environment. Bilingual education can thus become a form of empowerment for this minority group if it helps them gain economic and political power. Bilingual education can also be seen from an economic viewpoint if the learning of two languages becomes profitable and the languages learned are seen as resources that can help the speakers gain access to trade and communication. Therefore, bilingual education is a means of achieving social, political, and economic objectives in diverse settings.

Effects of Bilingual Education

Research has shown that bilingual education plays an integral part in the overall personal and educational development of the child. Baker (2000, 2001), Cummins (2000), and Skutnabb-Kangas (2000) found that the use of the bilingual child's mother tongue helps him or her attain higher educational standards. Cummins (2008) proposed six descriptors to show the effect of one's mother tongue on higher educational attainment.

First, bilingualism has positive effects on children's linguistic and educational development. Research shows that bilingual children develop a better understanding of language and its effective usage. Their extra exposure to language gives them a literacy edge and helps them use both languages in context. The research also shows that bilingual children are flexible thinkers as a result of processing information via two different languages.

Second, the level of development of children's mother tongue is a strong predictor of their second language development. Children with a solid mother tongue background develop stronger literacy abilities in the majority language at school. However, this will happen only if the child has been widely exposed to the mother tongue at home via parents and grandparents through storytelling, discussing issues, and helping the child build mother tongue vocabulary as well as concepts. Cummins (2000) also indicates that the development of concepts and thinking skills are in effect interdependent on the mother tongue and the majority school language. According to Cummins (2003: 62), "both languages nurture each other when the educational environment permits children access to both languages."

Third, mother tongue promotion in the school helps develop not only the mother tongue but also children's abilities in the majority school language. Evidence shows that the bilingual child performs better in school when the mother tongue is taught effectively and the child develops proficiency in it. Conversely, when the child is encouraged to reject the mother tongue, his or her development stagnates, thus undermining the personal and conceptual foundation for learning.

Fourth, spending instructional time through a minority language in the school does not hurt children's academic development in the majority school language. Studies have shown that "well implemented bilingual programs can promote literacy and subject matter knowledge in a minority language without any negative effects on children's development in the majority language" (Cummins, 2003: 63).

Fifth, children's mother tongues are fragile and easily lost in the early years of schooling. The rapidity of language loss is dependent upon whether the mother tongue is used extensively within the community outside the school. If it is, the extent and rapidity of loss is lower compared to a situation in which the language is not used extensively within the community outside school. This rapid loss can take two to three years from starting schooling.

Sixth, negotiation of identity is a crucial factor in minority children's academic success. Teachers' should be encouraged to promote active participation by accepting the child's linguistic and cultural difference. Bilingual signs and posters should adorn the classroom to create a more homely atmosphere that supports learning in the school majority language by integrating it with the home language. According to Cummins (2003: 64),

"When educators affirm the value of minority children's culture and language in the school context, they simultaneously challenge the societal discourse that devalues children's cultural and linguistic capital.

Language Planning

Cooper (1989: 45) refers to language planning as the "deliberate efforts to influence the behavior of others with respect to the acquisition, structure, or functional allocations of their language codes." Thus, language planning is generally aimed at changing linguistic behavior. Language plans are deliberately made by authorities such as governments and implemented through an official central agency. Haugen was the first to use the term "language planning" in his study of language standardization in Norway (1959: 8). This was followed by Kloss (1969), who popularized the use of a widely accepted distinction in the components of language planning: status planning and corpus planning. Cooper (1989: 157) then added a third component he called "acquisition planning." These three components of language planning remain in use today as important aspects of language planning and policy implementation by language planning agencies.

Language Planning in Singapore

In Singapore, where there is no such agency, language policy and planning is implemented through the educational system. Tan (2007: 76) highlighted this aspect as follows

> The evolution of the language ideology and language regime
> is poignantly manifested in Singapore's educational system, a
> critical resource in social engineering.

An important element of language planning in Singapore is the application of the principle of equity: what is planned and implemented for one particular language is, as far as practicable, applied to the other languages. This practice began in 1956 with the Report of the All-Party Committee of the Singapore Legislative Assembly on Chinese Education, which later became known as the All-Party Report. The report, which was meant to review practices and recommend steps to ensure the survival of Chinese language education, took into account the concerns of Malays and Indians with regards to their respective mother tongues, which are Malay and Tamil. This practice of parity had served the latter two well as they remain the two main minority languages.

In the Singapore context, there are four official languages: English, which is the dominant language because of its status as the language of administration, law and commerce, and the three "mother tongues" – Mandarin, Malay, and Tamil.

Definition of Language Planning

Before we go any further, we need to clearly define language planning. According to Kaplan & Baldauf (1997: 3),

> Language planning is a body of ideas, laws, and regulations (language policy), rules, beliefs, and practices intended to achieve a planned change (or to stop change from happening) in the language used in one or more communities.

This point is reiterated by Ager (2001: 5), who defines language planning as

> ...the ways in which organized communities, united by religious, ethnic, or political ties, consciously attempt to influence the language(s) their members use, the languages used in education, or the ways in which academics, publishers, or journalists make the language change.

According to Rubin & Jernudd (1975), language planning involves deliberate language change. The changes referred to are "changes in the systems of language code or speaking or both that are planned by organizations that are established for such purposes or given a mandate to fulfill such purposes" (Rubin & Jernudd,

1975: xvi). Thus, they highlight that language planning is focused on problem-solving and future-oriented.

Ferguson (1996) explains this further by indicating that any deliberate attempts to affect the course of language change, either by fostering innovation or preserving the existing state, is by itself language planning. Fishman (1977) defines language planning as covering a variety of activities that are roughly sub-divisible into two broad categories:

a. Language status planning – where governmental policy decisions concerning which language should be assigned or recognized for which purposes within a country or region, as well as the various implementation (enforcing, motivating, influencing) steps taken to support the policy that has been adopted, and

b. Language corpus planning – where efforts are made to alter or improve the language per se, whose status is the object of policy decisions and implementation attempts.

In short, language planning is an attempt by anyone to modify the linguistic behavior of any community for any reason.

Components of language planning

As indicated in the preceding section, there are two main components of language planning: status planning, and corpus planning. In status planning, the aim is to allocate the function of the various languages that are present in a multilingual community. With regards to the planning of language and literacy, status planning can also be thought of as "those efforts directed toward the allocation of functions of languages/literacies in a given speech community" (Hornberger, 2003: 451). Ager (2001: 6) describes status planning as the process of modifying the status and "hence the prestige of languages or language varieties within a society." Ager adds that this is done by modifying how the different language codes are perceived by groups or individuals along with the deliberate effort to influence the allocation of the functions of a language among its community of users.

Corpus planning, by contrast, refers to planning of the language itself, including graphization, standardization, and modernization. Ager (2001: 6) explains that it "is what communities do to the forms of the language." In general, corpus planning is carried out after the implementation of status planning so as to determine the status or prestige level of the language before forms of the language are modified to suit its use.

Cooper (1989: 33) adds another dimension to language planning when he introduces the term "acquisition planning," which refers to the strategies used to teach and learn a language. Spolsky (2004) equates acquisition planning with language education policy. In this study, the conceptual framework proposed by Cooper (1980) will be used as it is of direct relevance to the planning of Malay in the educational system in Singapore and covers all three important components of language planning, namely status planning, corpus planning, and acquisition planning. This framework will give us a clearer picture in terms of Malay language planning and how it has been impacted by the bilingual language policy.

Language planning is closely intertwined with the social and political forces that are present in a country, and Malay language planning in the educational system in Singapore is no exception. Hence, to better understand the planning of the language, it is necessary to look at Malay language planning within the local socio-political context. However, not only internal factors but also external factors partly determine Malay language policy as Singapore is situated in a Malay-speaking region dominated by two Malay-speaking "giants" – Indonesia and Malaysia.

Frameworks for language planning

This study will be based on three frameworks for language planning that are complementary. These are the frameworks proposed by Haugen (1983), Haarmann (1990), and Cooper (1989). These frameworks are considered complementary as they look at language planning from two important perspectives: from the viewpoint of those who want to modify the language and from the viewpoint of those who want to modify the environment in which the language is used. As outlined above, these two perspectives have come to be known as corpus planning and status planning, respectively.

Haugen, Haarmann, and Cooper have attempted to define the activities that make up the language planning process and to provide a descriptive model of these processes.

Table 1   Haugen's (1983: 275) revised language planning model, with additions

	Form (policy planning)	Function (language cultivation)
Society (status planning)	1. Selection (decision procedures) a. Problem identification b. Allocation of norms	2. Implementation (educational spread) a. Correction procedures b. Evaluation
Language (corpus planning)	3. Codification (standardization procedures) a. Graphization b. Grammatication c. Lexication	4. Elaboration (functional development) a. Terminological modernization b. Stylistic development c. Internationalization

Table 1 shows the model by Haugen, in which the language planning activities are viewed from either a societal or a language focus. The societal focus is what we call here status planning. This consists of decisions made by a society about language selection and the implementation involved in choosing and disseminating the language or languages selected. Meanwhile, the language focus is what we refer to here as corpus planning. This consists of linguistic decisions that need to be made in order to codify and elaborate a language or languages.

As can be seen from Table 1, Haugen includes under a societal focus (status planning) the policy planning selection procedures, which include problem identification and allocation of norms, whereas in the implementation process, there is a need to correct (3a) and evaluate (3b) as part of corpus planning.

Like Haugen, Haarmann (1990: 120-121) indicates the existence of both status planning and corpus planning but with the addition of prestige planning, in which the process of seeing through the work done in status planning and corpus planning actually takes place. For example, from Table 1.6, we can see that in the activities of governments, in order to see through both status planning and corpus planning, there will be an official promotion as the driving force. This can be done in the form of national campaigns or government-endorsed activities. Thus, Haarmann's typology of language cultivation and language planning involves this prestige planning component, which drives the two main components: corpus planning and status planning.

However, Cooper's (1989) framework divides the process of language planning into three distinct phases: status planning, corpus planning, and acquisition planning. This study will be based on his theoretical framework.

Status planning – This modifies the status and hence the prestige of languages and language varieties within society, often by modifying through deliberate efforts to influence the allocation of functions among a community's languages the way the language codes groups or individuals use are perceived.

Corpus planning – This refers to what communities do to the forms of the language (graphization, standardization, modernization, and renovation), but is sometimes also subdivided into codification of the existing language together with its elaboration and modernization by adding new terms or styles and by controlling neologisms.

Acquisition planning – This affects the acquisition, reacquisition, or maintenance of first, second, or foreign languages.

Based on the above mentioned framework, Cooper (1989: 98) developed an "accounting scheme" to make it clear that analyzing language planning of these three types means tracking eight components, namely:

What <u>actors</u> attempt to influence what <u>behaviors</u> of which <u>people</u> for what <u>ends</u>, under what <u>conditions</u>, by what <u>means</u>, through what <u>decision-making process</u>, with what <u>effect</u>?

The actors here refers to the individuals or organizations involved in the policy-making, while behaviors refers to the planned behavior change. The people component refers to the target of language change, ends refers to language related or non-language related behaviors, and conditions is situational in nature or either structural, cultural, environmental or informational. By what means can refer to various forms of implementation, including via force, persuasion or promotion, and based on a set of rules where problems or goals are formulated. Lastly the effect refers to the outcome of the whole process.

Cooper's framework for language planning and its accounting scheme is widely used among language planning researchers as a guide to describe, predict, and explain language planning activities. This is exactly what Faiza Dekhir and Samira Abid (2011) did for their research on globalization and language planning activities. Their research was dedicated to describing the phenomenon of globalization from a language planning perspective. They describe Cooper's accounting scheme as follows:

1). *What actors*

These can be seen as working within four basic areas:

a. Governmental agencies involved at the highest level and having the largest scope in planning since government generally has the power to incite (or disincite) structures to enforce planning decisions (Kaplan & Baldauf, 1997: 5). Briefly speaking, government agenciesare those *"who get the most of what there is to get"* (Cooper, 1989: 88).

b. Education agencies usually acting under the force of higher level structures that often receive the entire burden of planning language change.

    c.   Other non-governmental organizations acting according to their own beliefs, including national and international language academies of great prestige.

    d.   All sorts of groups of influential individuals who create language policy as part of their normal activities. They are the people who promise, threaten advice, pester, or bribe but do not decide.

2). *Attempted to influence what behaviors*

    a.   Status: allocation of new norms and functions to a given language, identifying a language problem, managing competition between a national language and a foreign one.

    b.   Corpus: lexical elaboration, language modernization, or language revival.

    c.   Acquisition: teaching-learning processes and language choice as a medium of instruction.

3). *Of which people*

    a.   Type of target: individual vs organizations.

    b.   School vs university, private vs public sector.

4). *For what ends*

    a.   Overt: this generally includes making planning decisions as well as social changes such as language shift or linguistic assimilation. These can be classified under the impetus of language related behaviors.

    b.   Latent: this refer to non-language related behaviors, such as the satisfaction of interests.

5). *By what means*

    a.   Authority, force, power, persuasion, violence, or bribery.

6). *With what results*

    a.   Achievement of national unity.

    b.   Achievement of linguistic assimilation, linguistic pluralism, or language shift.

    c.   Achievement of educational, economic, or political advancement. (Faiza Dekhir and Samira Abid, 2011: 4-5)

Using this accounting scheme, the researchers described, predicted, and explained language planning activities that are meant as a driving force for change.

In his research on issues and prospects in language planning and policy, Bamgbose (2004) highlighted Cooper's accounting model or scheme as a descriptive framework for handling language planning situations and processes. He stresses that Cooper begins by looking at four alternative models that can be used for auditing language planning. These are,

> ...language planning as the management of innovations (who adopts what, when, where, why and how?), language planning as marketing (product, promotion, place, and price), language planning as the pursuit and maintenance of power (who gets what, when and how?) and language planning as decision-making (who makes what decisions, why, how, under what conditions and to what effect?) (Bamgbose, 2004: 77).

Thus, the basic premise of Cooper's accounting model is to make a comprehensive description of what happens in a language planning situation.

The basis of Cooper's theoretical framework has been used in Malaysia when discussing matters pertaining to language planning. In her study of language status and corpus planning in Malaysia, Asmah (1979) outlines the processes of Malaysia's language planning for unity and efficiency. She indicates that Malaysian language status planning consists of three main components, namely planning for the national language, planning for the medium of instruction, and planning for the official language. Thus, these three components effectively refer to planning for status, planning for corpus, and planning for the acquisition of the Malay language. Asmah also indicates that corpus planning is the deliberate effort to cause changes to language codes. She further highlighted that there is a symbiotic relationship between status and corpus planning. This point is reiterated by Fishman (2006) when he describes the link between status and corpus planning as being in touch with each other. Fishman states that "it implies that it doesn't do for one phase to be seriously out of touch with the other..." (Fishman 2006: 16). Cooper (1989) completes the link between status and corpus planning with acquisition planning, which is the planning for the teaching and learning of the planned language.

Thus, Cooper's accounting scheme is widely used because it answers the four difficult tasks that language planners always face, namely to describe, predict, and explain language planning outcomes and subsequently to derive valid generalizations about these processes and outcomes (Cooper, 1989).

Singapore's bilingual language policy and Malay language planning

According to Laitin (1992: 10), there are three models of language policy. These are: official multilingualism, language rationalization, and language maintenance policy models. Official multilingualism refers to a policy whereby all languages spoken within a community or country are given equal recognition. In this policy model, all languages are regarded as equal in terms of status and level of usage. In a language rationalization policy model, the advantages associated with certain languages are highlighted. These advantages may be in the form of social mobility, common identity, or just efficiency. Laitin further explains that this model involves the specification of domains of language use and the stipulation that a certain language can be used effectively within a given context. Subsequently, a language maintenance policy model advocates a principle of equilibrium between languages. The policy works towards an "equality of success" model that seeks to make all languages equally successful in their use. In the context of Singapore, the government practices a language rationalization policy model whereby English is promoted as the language of governance and commerce as well as education whereby the other three "official" languages are stipulated as carrying the burden of being cultural repositories. This will be further explained as part of Singapore's bilingual language policy.

In terms of its definition, Singapore's bilingual language policy can be considered "most restrictive and peculiar" (Pakir, 2004b: 254). According to Tay (1984: 5),In line with the official language policy of Singapore, bilingualism is defined not as proficiency in any two languages but as proficiency in English and one other official language.

As mentioned above, the official languages referred to here are Mandarin, Malay, and Tamil. This state of affairs has been referred to as "English-knowing bilingualism," a term first used by Kachru (1983: 42).

English-knowing bilingualism

Pakir (2004b: 258) indicates that there is no "central language planning organization or institution" in Singapore whose role is solely to implement formulated language planning policies. This role is undertaken by the Ministry of Education via ministerial statements that are translated into guidelines and subsequently implemented in schools. Thus, there is a symbiotic relationship between the language planning process and education, resulting in a language-in-education policy framework. Shohamy (2006: 76) defines language education policies as,

> ...carrying out language planning decisions in the specific contexts of schools and universities in relation to home languages (previously referred to as "mother tongues") and to foreign and second languages. These decisions often include issues such as: Which language(s) to teach and learn in school? When (at what age) to begin teaching these languages? For how long (number of years and hours of study) should they be taught? By whom, for whom (who is qualified to teach and who is entitled or obligated to learn) and how (which methods, materials, texts, etc.)?

Thus, in the context of language planning in Singapore, there is a clear delineation of roles and duties to be played by the four official languages, namely English,

Mandarin, Malay, and Tamil. English was chosen as the language of business, economics, science, technology, education and inter-ethnic communication. Meanwhile, the three "mother tongues" are expected to act as "cultural ballast," provide cultural identity, and facilitate inter-ethnic communication and unity. This functional polarization of language in Singapore (Bokhorst-Heng: 1999) gives importance to each language and rationalizes its use and learning in schools.

Principles of Singapore's Bilingual Policy

Singapore's first Prime Minister, Lee Kuan Yew (2011: 224) felt strongly that in building Singapore from Third World to First World status, his decision to implement a bilingual system of education was correct. In retrospect, he outlined eight principles that guided this policy and in his view, made it work.

Firstly, Lee felt that "language policy is a vital instrument for achieving national interest objectives and meeting the needs of governance" (Lee, 2011: 224). Singapore, being a multi-racial, multi-cultural, and multi-religious country, needs a language policy that can help unite the masses and "build a platform for communication with the outside world" (Lee, 2011: 224). Thus, English was chosen as the language of administration due to the fact that the "British colonial government ... had left behind a system of administration that used English as the working language" (Lee, 2011: 225). The key change implemented was in the education system, whereby all students had to learn their "mother tongue" as their second language.

A second principle stipulates that the "language policy can become a key to economic success" (Lee, 2011: 226). Lee felt that by choosing English as the working language of administration, Singapore would be spared the "political fallout" that would have ensued if Chinese or Malay had been chosen. Since Singapore's dominant population is Chinese and the country is situated in a Malay-speaking region, the choice of either language would have stirred strong communal emotions. Thus, English became the language of choice and Singaporeans' knowledge of English became a harbinger for "the multinational companies that set up their factories, research laboratories, and regional headquarters" (Lee, 2011:

226), leading to the employment of more Singaporeans, which in turn led to a growing economy and raising the people's standard of living.

Thirdly, Lee felt strongly that "language is more than a tool of communication: it transmits values too" (Lee: 2011: 227). The insistence that all Singaporeans have to learn English and one other language (their "mother tongue") is based on this principle of transmission of values. Although values can in principle be transmitted via any language, Lee was of the view that "each ethnic culture has its own unique heritage that is worth preserving and teaching" (Lee, 2011: 227).

Fourthly, based on his own personal experience, Lee was of the view that in learning a language, a start should be made from a very young age, preferably as a toddler. Citing his own personal experience of learning Mandarin, he found it difficult to learn the language as an adult. However, political imperatives had to override all other concerns. He thus reiterated that "bilingual education has to begin from Day One" (Lee, 2011: 228). He wanted all preschool educational institutions to teach both English and a mother tongue so as to start the child on the road of bilingualism early.

Fifthly, in most cases, a person can only master one language. This principle was borne out of Lee's own realization in the mid-1970s when the bilingual policy was only ten years old and still in its infancy. Lee first "demanded that our students master their second language to a level as high as that of their first language" (Lee, 2011: 229). Any failure was attributed to poor teaching standards. Later, he realized that the inability to cope with two languages was not necessarily linked to an intelligence deficit. Although there may be exceptions to the rule, this insight led to a slew of changes in terms of approach to the bilingual policy.

Sixthly, a sound foundation should be laid for the mastery of a language from young. Based on Lee's understanding that a person can only master one language, there is therefore a need for this person to learn the basics in order to gain linguistic competence and subsequently communicative competence in using the languaqe. This, it is important that schools lay this foundation well so that the students will have knowledge of "the rudimentary grammar and have a vocabulary sufficient for basic daily living" (Lee, 2011: 229).

Seventhly, due to varying linguistic abilities, there need to be "different courses tailored to those of different abilities" (Lee, 2011: 230). There should not be a one-size-fits-all curriculum, and the concept of differentiated learning should be the main thrust of any language program. Thus, students who show greater ability or interest in their mother tongue "should be given the facilities and opportunities" (Lee, 2011: 230) to learn it at the highest level possible.

Lastly, "language policy is a never-ending journey" (Lee, 2011: 231). Lee felt that with the ever-changing educational landscape coupled with demographic changes among language learners, further fine-tuning would be needed ahead. He highlighted the need for language policy to evolve in tandem with societal change and to remain relevant as "a vital instrument for achieving national interest objectives and meeting the needs of governance" (Lee, 2011: 231).

Mandarin-inspired language planning

There have been numerous studies of the bilingual language policy in Singapore. Notable among them is a collection of articles providing "a view of the language issue in Singapore from a range of relevant perspectives" (Gopinathan, Pakir, Ho and Saravanan, 2003: 5). The collection deals with Language in Singapore, Language in Society, and Language in Education. The section on language in Singapore examines the processes of policy making for language management in Singapore as well as the trends and issues that arise from such efforts at management. The section on the study of language maintenance discusses language shift and language variation. Finally, the book deals with the educational aspect of language use and reflects on the new understanding of the development of language and of bilingualism, the nature of language in the classroom, and the relationship between language and learning. Yet, despite the wide range of issues discussed in this book, there is only one chapter devoted to Malay, whereas three chapters are specifically related to Chinese. While the term "English-knowing bilingualism" aptly describes the system used in Singapore, research on its effect on Malay has not been sufficiently tackled. Most of the current research is geared toward the impact on Mandarin and on any adverse effects it may have and how these may be overcome, or it addresses the issue in general without being language-specific in terms of impact.

Pakir (2004b) outlines the goals and outcomes of the language policy in Singapore, with clear reference to its impact on Mandarin. Among the goals highlighted, one was to produce effective bilingual citizens by enhancing the use of English as a language of wider communication and by decreasing the use of non-official languages, that is, dialects. As regards outcomes, Pakir notes the unintended outcome of producing receptive bilinguals, that is, the ability to understand two languages but showing willingness to express oneself in only one, while the dominance of English has de-Asianized Singaporeans. Overall, the policy has led to an increase in the use of both English and Mandarin across all domains. This lack of reference to the impact on Malay in particular may be due to the ten-yearly Census of Population, which consistently shows that the use of Malay within the home remains high. This may have given researchers a false sense that the bilingual language policy as practiced has not had a detrimental impact on the use and development of Malay. Thus, studies of bilingualism have concentrated on the use of English and its impact on the learning of Mandarin and vice-versa (Pakir, 1993, 2003, 2004; Gopinathan, 1998, 2003; Borkhorst-Heng, 1999; Wee, 2003; Kuo, 1979, 1984).

Nevertheless, in 2004, the Ministry of Education initiated a comprehensive survey of the use of Malay among students in primary, secondary, and pre-university levels. This was in response to a similar survey carried out for Mandarin learners and later for Tamil learners as well.

Studies of English-Malay Bilingualism in Singapore

Most of the research on bilingualism in Singapore has focused on English and how this has impacted the learning of Mandarin. Research on the English-Chinese pair has been conducted by Pakir, (1993, 2003, 2004), Gopinathan, (1998, 2003), Borkhorst-Heng, (1999), Wee, (2003), and Kuo, (1979, 1984), among others. These studies generally look at the problems faced by the Chinese community in coping with the need to balance the use of English and Mandarin against the widespread use of dialects among the Chinese community in Singapore.

By contrast, there have been few studies of bilingualism and its effect on Malay language planning in Singapore. The impact of the use of English on Malay was only felt in the 1970s, and only in the 1980s have there been studies looking at this effect. Prior to independence in 1965, Malay used to be the language of wider communication in Singapore. From that date onward, English became more prominent and began to seep into non-formal domains. According to Kuo and Jernudd (1994: 28),

> ...the role of (bazaar) Malay as a lingua franca has also declined, and with the increasing use of English, few non-Malays now acquire proficiency in Malay.

The above statement contrasted with the one made 14 years earlier in Kuo's (1980) earlier study, conducted in 1978, in which he found that the communicative index of Malay was higher than that of English, namely 0.45 as compared to 0.38, respectively. This shows that a higher proportion of the population was using Malay to communicate among themselves compared to English. Thus, in the late 1970s, Malay was still the language of choice for inter-racial communication in Singapore.

However, there has been research on the use and trends in the use of Malay relative to English. This research includes Kaur (1983), who noted the Malay population's concerns over the development of the language. In her study, Kaur highlighted the community's concern that Singapore should not lag behind in the development of Malay as it plays an important role as a second language. However, in his study of language planning and policy in Singapore, Teng (1993) noted that in general, there is a continuing shift toward English among the younger generation of Malays, even when communicating with each other.

A comprehensive data-driven review of English-Malay bilingualism was conducted by Tham (1990). Tham specifically based his study on the 1990 Census of Population, comparing it to the 1980 census. Although Tham set out to analyze the effect of the bilingual policy, which at that time had been in motion for over 30 years, on the linguistic behavior of Singaporeans. Tham showed that the challenge faced by Malay Singaporeans appeared less complex but problematic nevertheless. This is due to the fact that, although Malay is the common language of cultural and religious activities among Malays, the acceptance of English-medium education has increased the need to acquire greater competence in that language, albeit for economic reasons. Tham questioned whether "the perceived value of the English Language by Singapore Malays affected language usage patterns in the household" (Tham, 1990: 3).

The study shows that although age and generational differences are important factors in determining language use in Singaporean households, for Malays, it is a less important factor. Based on the census report, Tham was able to note the generational shift to the use of English among all households, thus indicating the practical usefulness of the language in Singapore. Tham also noted that official support through the bilingual policy has helped to maintain the status of Malay. However, he also noted the increasing use of English within Malay families. As the study focused on the nature and extent of language shift or maintenance, Tham highlighted that over the inter-census period, English overtook Malay as the language most widely spoken in Singapore. Malay dropped from second position in 1980 to fourth in 1990, whereas English remained at number three.

Bibi Jan (1994) commented on the shift in the use of Malay in terms of importance, status, relevance, and values. She noted that students were increasingly using English outside the classroom, especially with their peers, thus limiting their use of Malay. This observation was confirmed by Poedjosoedarmo (1995), who noticed the ever widening gap in the use of Malay between the older generation and younger Malays, with the former constantly lamenting the poor standard of the Malay spoken by the latter.

Kamsiah (2000) explains that the trend toward English use among younger Malays is all encompassing and is a predictor of the future. Kamsiah concluded that the Malay community in Singapore is undergoing language shift from Malay to English, even though the shift is much more apparent in oral communication. Kamsiah further highlighted the fact that if this trend is not addressed, the impact may well spill into written communication as well.

All of the above-mentioned research indicates one common concern, namely the ever-increasing use of English within the Malay community. However, there remains a lack of research pertaining to the Malay language proficiency of the Malay-speaking community compared to their proficiency in English. Thus, the available research is inadequate for a comprehensive review of language proficiency pertaining to English-Malay bilinguals to be conducted.

Available research includes a preliminary report on the teaching of Malay as a second language in Singapore schools by Mardiana (2005), which offers preliminary descriptive data on Malay classroom practices. This report summarizes observations based on 78 Malay language lessons in 21 schools. Lessons were from Primary 5 (P5) and Secondary 3 (S3) Malay classes from the various streams. The study found that the features of pedagogical practices in Malay language classroom in Singapore are generally at a high level of engagement, with a great deal of time being devoted by the curriculum to oral communication skills. However, classroom practices are mostly textbook- and worksheet-based, with a teacher-centered approach and only few higher-order questions being asked and even less cultural transmission taking place.

The study makes two broad recommendations. Firstly, the implementation of an expanded in-service training program for Malay teachers, including the introduction of a wider range of pedagogical models and strategies. Secondly, there should be greater emphasis on teaching language and linguistics at pre-service level as against the current emphasis on literature and culture.

The study also noted the teachers' lack of ability in structuring more collaborative activities in their classrooms. Furthermore, this collaborative work should transcend mere worksheet-based exercises that amount to little more than one-dimensional, single-task peer collaboration. These classrooms should place greater emphasis on sustained collaborations that allow for continuous interactions among students and teachers. Students should also be allowed greater opportunities to practice oral skills and enhance their communicative competence via role plays, debates, and drama. There is also a need for teachers to regularly expose students to quality Malay texts chosen from different genres in order to increase their appreciation level. Lastly, the study advocated an increase in the intellectual expectations of teachers for their students, which would result in higher quality Malay language classes. The study noted that only in this way will these classrooms realize the language's full potential and eradicate the attitude among students that Malay is an easy subject.

A notable but controversial study on Malay Singaporeans, which covered language, culture, and political standing, was undertaken by Zubaidah (2001). This study indicated that the active promotion and the subsequent demotion of Malay-medium education put paid to the educational development of Malays who were proficient in the language. Even though Malay was made the National Language and teachers had to pass at least Standard 1 Malay from 1959 onward, it did little to promote the wider use of the language as the Malay of even Malay school graduates was of low quality due to the lack of resources in terms of qualified teachers and good textbooks. This affected their employment prospects as "English reigned supreme as the language of administration and commerce in the fast industrializing island" (Zubaidah, 2001: 190).

Clearly, a wider range of research is available on English-Chinese bilingualism (e.g., Wong, 1993; Sim & Loh, 1987; Soh, 1992). Equally clearly, implications for bilingualism involving other languages could be drawn from their findings (Loh & Sim, 1993).

Among the limited research available on Malay language proficiency as against English language proficiency is a study of the attitudes and motivations of Malay students in Singapore regarding Malay and English (Kamsiah, 1984). The study reported that the participants have more positive attitudes toward English compared to Malay. English is said to enjoy higher prestige and greater practical consideration in the economic and higher education spheres as well as for purposes of social, commercial, and business networking.

Kamsiah (1987) reported that after testing different ability groups of Malay and non-Malay students on the separate language components – listening comprehension, dictation, sound discrimination, reading comprehension, composition, and verbal ability in both English and Malay – the Malay students were found to be more proficient in their "mother tongue" than in English. At the same time, she noted that considerable progress in English had been achieved. Generally, the study showed a disparity in language achievement for English-Malay bilinguals, using various measures involving language tasks set in English and Malay. In another study of English-Malay bilinguals in Singapore, (Kamsiah, 1994) reported on the effects on the "mother tongue" of increasing language competence in English and especially the threat of erosion of the functional use of Malay. The study involved 580 students, consisting of Malay native speakers from 12 schools. The participants were grouped according to their bilingual proficiency level. This study confirms Kamsiah's earlier findings on the negative effect of attitude and motivation on instruction in Malay compared to English. The result of regression and path analyses on Malay language achievement indicated that general academic achievement and English language proficiency contributed the most to Malay language achievement. It is especially interesting to note the finding that English language proficiency is a positive factor in reaching success in Malay language learning. However, the study suggests further investigation into Malay-English bilingual achievement if we are to explore further trends and relationships between English and other relevant linguistic or socio-affective variables and Malay language proficiency.

In 2007, Kamsiah presented a paper on Malay language research in Singapore from 1959 to 2000. This initial and reflective work consists of a review of all research on Malay conducted in Singapore during the period mentioned. Kamsiah divided the period into two phases: the early phase (1959-1982) and the developmental phase (1982-2000. Kamsiah indicated that during the early phase, most of the research was conducted by faculty members of the University of Malaya's Malay Language Department (which was later to become the University of Singapore and subsequently the National University of Singapore) and the Teachers' Training College. This early research dealt mainly with the historical development of Malay and also generated books and studies of Malay grammar. Even though they were not written in standard academic language, these studies showed the extent of the love for the language as well as its importance during that era. Indeed, an *Ikrar Bulan Bahasa* (Language Month Pledge) was read out during the closing ceremony of the National Language Month on 11 December 1965 at the Singapore National Theater. Its English translation reads as follows:

> We the citizens of Singapore pledge to do our utmost within our field to help the government in promoting the teaching and learning of our National Language in the community. We are confident that the National Language can play its part as our language and help in promoting a unified community of different races, languages, cultures, and religions.

This phase also saw a substantial amount of research on the educational development of Malay students as well as an MA thesis by Zahoor Ahmad (1969) on the policies and politics of Malay-stream education in Singapore. Mostly, however, during this era, there were far more numerous publications of textbooks for schools.

In the developmental phase, Kamsiah noted that with the advent of the Institute of Education (later the National Institute of Education), more academic research on Malay language development and teaching and learning took place. The research conducted during this period focused mostly on the question of language erosion and vitality and the declining standards of Malay among students. With the introduction of standard spoken Malay, or *sebutan baku* in 1993, a few studies on the implementation of this system were produced. However, Kamsiah was the trailblazer, with her numerous study on language attitudes and maintenance.

In general, the research shows some movement away from Malay and a growing emphasis on English. Researchers also noted the changing attitudes of students toward Malay, with a greater inclination toward English, which by that time had become an important language in education.

Studies on the Standardization of Malay in Singapore
In addition to studies of English-Malay bilingualism, there has been a total of four studies of the impact of standardizing spoken Malay on speakers and learners of the language. Standardization of Malay was implemented in 1993 in all primary schools, followed by secondary schools, junior colleges, and higher institutions over the subsequent years.

The program was implemented quite successfully, as indicated by Kasmadi (1993), who was then the Ministry of Education's (MOE) Specialist Inspector tasked to oversee its implementation. According to Kasmadi, students at the lower primary level (Primary 1-3) were better able to adapt to the new spoken standard compared to those at the upper primary level (Primary 4-6). This may have been due to the fact that the upper primary students had been exposed to the local Riau-Johor variety at the lower primary level and needed more time to get used to the new standard.

Paitoon (1996) was the first researcher to present an academic perspective on the use of *sebutan baku* and how it has impacted the teaching and learning of Malay. Although this working paper was based on personal observation rather than research, Paitoon observed that the form of *sebutan baku* in use was not the standard form required by MOE, but a local variant affecting especially final syllables.

Ali (2002) conducted research on *sebutan baku* used by radio and television newscasters in Singapore. Similar to Paitoon's observations, he found that the spoken form is still influenced by the Johor-Riau variant even though efforts to use *sebutan baku* were obvious. However, this could be an interim period during which users are still getting used to the new spoken standard. Ali argues that more time should be given to newscasters to familiarize themselves with the new spoken form.

Pairah (2007) conducted a survey of 300 secondary school students and 76 teachers to ascertain their *sebutan baku* standard and their feelings and thoughts about it. The findings showed that a higher percentage of younger teachers do not use *sebutan baku* while teaching and that most of the students who fail to use it do so because they are more comfortable with the Johor-Riau variety. In spite of this, a high percentage of students and teachers were of the view that *sebutan baku* aids in their teaching and learning of Malay. According to Pairah, 77.6% of the respondents felt that *sebutan baku* is important to their leaning of Malay, while a further 88.3% indicated that *sebutan baku* aids them in their reading and spelling. However, a high percentage of non-Malay students view the use of *sebutan baku* as helping them in learning Malay. The data collected showed that 82.7% of the non-Malay respondents felt that *sebutan baku* aided their reading and spelling, while 74.5% indicated that it helped them learn Malay better. In comparison, 61.3% of the Malay students attributed their acquisition of reading and spelling skills to *sebutan baku*, whiled 50.3% felt that overall, *sebutan baku* helped them learn Malay. Teacher respondents too felt that *sebutan baku* has given an edge to their students and improved their Malay, especially in terms of reading and spelling. This could be attributed to the writing system in *sebutan baku*, where a single letter represents a single sound.

Thus far, studies of the implementation of *sebutan baku* have either come too early to indicate its effectiveness, or, when conducted more recently, they have tended to indicate that the reform was successful and has helped in the teaching and learning of the language, particularly in enhancing reading and spelling skills. Yet, there has been dissatisfaction on the grounds that *sebutan baku* has taken the spirit out of the language and that Singaporeans should revert to using the Johor-Riau spoken variety instead. As indicated by Cooper (1989), standardizing the spoken form is more difficult compared to doing the same thing for the written form. Milroy and Milroy (1985:) state categorically that "no spoken language can ever be fully standardized." They highlighted that while the written form and spelling can be standardized relatively easily, it is not so for spoken language. They also noted that spoken standardization is an "ideology," not a reality but an idea, an imagined state.

Malay as a Language of Commodification in a Globalized World

Lastly, there have also been studies of Malay in terms of its role in a globalized world as an instrument of trade with value as a commodity. In terms of its status, Alsagoff (2008) highlights the historical development of Malay along with its special status as the National Language of Singapore and how language planning since independence has impacted its official and perceived status. Alsagoff (2008: 45) uses the analogy of "commodification of language" to refer to how the government looks at the four languages as commodities – English for its economic worth, and "the three local languages Chinese (Mandarin), Tamil, and Malay as cultural commodities."

According to Alsagoff, the status of Malay spiraled downward from the 1950s, when it was the language of a nation, entrusted "to foster national identity and understanding among the races" and as an expression of a "distinct and unique national identity, to a language of Singapore Malay ethnic identity" (Alsagoff, 2008: 51). This downward spiral was highlighted earlier by Bokhorst-Heng (1998), who pointed out the shift in language ideology that took place when in March 1982, a campaign to promote the use of the language was referred to as a "Malay Language campaign," not as a "National Language campaign," befitting its new status.

Furthermore, Malay was promoted not by the government but via Malay cultural organizations under the umbrella of Majlis Pusat, a cultural organization. As Alsagoff (2008: 51) notes,

> The dissociation of Malay from nation saw the tandem association of Malay with race. Malay began to be promoted, equally with the other two local languages, Mandarin and Tamil, simply as a mother tongue tied to ethnicity.

This downward trend for Malay, that is, from the status of National Language to one of four official languages and now to a community language, is also the result of political as well as social and economic concerns. The emergence of China and India as well as the economic and financial crisis that hit Southeast Asia in 1997 has affected the development of Malay in the region. The wider use of English in both Indonesia and Malaysia also put paid to the economic capital of using Malay, while the rise of China has led to a rise in interest in Mandarin. There has been no such rise in the level of interest in Malay as Indonesia and Malaysia have turned to foreign technology and investments to kick start their economy again, using English as a tool to facilitate trade and the transfer of technology.

Wee (2003) touched on the issue of linguistic instrumentalism, whereby the justification for the use of a language within a community is based on its usefulness in achieving specific utilitarian goals, which may be in the form of access to economic development or social mobility. Wee indicated that a language can be viewed non-instrumentally if it is seen only as a tool in forming an integral part of one's ethnic or cultural identity and its existence is justified only as symbolic value. Thus, Wee argued that there may be factors responsible for this shift toward linguistic instrumentalism for the learning of Mandarin in Singapore, while there can be no parity for Malay and Tamil. As regards Malay, Minister for Home Affairs Wong Kan Seng claimed in 1994 that "the rapid economic growth of South-east Asian countries such as Indonesia, Malaysia, and Brunei should place Malay in a more important position" (The Straits Times, 4 July 1994). However, this argument was not accepted by the public, as evidenced by letters sent to the Straits Times, a major English newspaper in Singapore (Wee, 2003). According to Wee, this could be due to the fact that Singaporeans are less impressed with the economic potential of Indonesia, Malaysia, and Brunei as compared with China.

Thus the question arises of the linguistic instrumentalism of Malay. In the Singapore context, Malay used to be the lingua franca, albeit the Bazaar Malay variety. The language was the language of wider communication before independence up until the late 1960s. With Singapore's economy growing fast in the 1970s, emphasis on English became more central to building a strong and robust economy for the new nation. Although Malay kept its status as the National Language as well as one of the four Official Languages, its use was limited to trading between Chinese hawkers and shop owners with their non-Chinese clients, the domain of religion (namely Islam), and as a school subject as a "mother tongue." Yet even today, the linguistic intrumentalism of Malay has been further eroded in the first two domains mentioned above. Thus Wee's assertion that a language can be viewed non-instrumentally if it is seen only as a tool in forming an integral part of one's ethnic or cultural identity explains the position of Malay as having symbolic value only.

Heller (1999, cited in Wee, 2003) argued that as part of the current process of globalization, three distinct trends have surfaced. The first is the commodification of language, where the language is seen as having value and giving economic benefit to whoever possesses it. This value is inherently economic and not just symbolic or cultural in nature. This is a problem for Malay as there is not much economic value attached to it as compared to Mandarin, and its value is more symbolic, in addition to its role as a cultural repository.

The second trend consists of pressures toward standardization in international communication, a point that will be discussed further in the next chapter. Suffice to say that the issue of standardization has been a thorny issue in Singapore, which needs to be addressed. In the case Malay, the issue of standard Malay pronunciation, or *sebutan baku*, has been discussed since its implementation in 1990. The argument put forward by the Ministry of Education was that this would help in the development of Malay in Singapore and peg the local language to that of the region. However, 15 years after the adoption of the new standard, the regional Malay Language Council of Malaysia, Indonesia and Brunei dropped it, and each member country was allowed to adopt their variant depending on local community use. In the Singapore context, the standard, or baku, form of spoken Malay remains in use based on the fact that it is the international standard and therefore adherence to it is fundamental, the argument being that since Singapore is small, it cannot determine the fate of Malay. Thus, Singapore must maintain the status quo and adopt a standard that can be accepted by all three member countries. Wee (2003) argues that this means a devaluation of the local variety of the vernacular language, in this case the Johor Riau variant.

The third trend affects the valuing of local characteristics in order to legitimate local control over markets and attach value to linguistic forms as commodities in the world markets of culture and tourism. This implies the use of local characteristics to soften the blow of globalization, in this instance, the use of the vernacular riding on English and adding economic value to it. This is the challenge for Malay based on the "cultural ballast" theory, whereby the language is supposed to act as a force against the hegemonization of English and a tool in helping Malays learn about themselves and their culture.

Wee (2003) adds that due to the need to be globally competitive, the vernacular languages have had to be reconstructed on instrumental grounds. Moreover, in the context of Singapore, the challenge is even more interesting since it must take into account an intra-linguistic function (reconciling a language's function as bearer of authenticity along with its economic value) and an inter-linguistic function (the desire to retain parity or equal status among the official "mother tongues"). Wee (2003: 212) summarizes the position as follows;

1. Linguistic instrumentalism is a later addition to a previously existing view that treats the language as a marker of cultural identity and authenticity, resulting in a tension that is not yet reconciled;
2. One consequence is the tendency to devalue or marginalize local vernaculars;
3. Linguistic instrumentalism assumes the continued importance of multi/bilingualism so that the language whose economic value is being championed is acquired in addition to English, never in place of it.

Thus, we will be taking a closer look at Malay to see how, as argued by Wee from a linguistic instrumentalism perspective, its economic value can be championed and acquired in addition to that of English. We will also be looking at the *sebutan baku* issue, or the standardization of spoken Malay that started in the 1980s, and in particular at whether this has instrumental value as compared to the non-standard variation, referred to as Johor-Riau Malay.

Thus, there is a need for academic research that details the concerns, both perceived and real, of how the bilingual language policy, with its emphasis on English, has impacted Malay in terms of its planning and development. This study will therefore address three important questions, as follows:

1. Has the bilingual policy in any way affected the growth of Malay in Singapore, or has the policy thwarted its use in an English-speaking environment?
2. How can the language shift and changing attitudes toward Malay be addressed? What pedagogical approaches should be used to support Malay in an English-knowing bilingual context such as Singapore?
3. Can Malay still play its role as "cultural ballast" for the Malay community in the 21st century, when more Malay Primary 1 students join school with less than basic knowledge of the language?

Conclusion

This chapter has discussed a range of aspects of bilingualism and language planning. Bilingualism, which was defined in general as the learning of two or more languages, is covered by three different theories, which are based on the level of bilingualism achieved by the speaker or the community concerned. However, what is most striking about language planning and the framework for it is this following statement by Kaplan and Baldauf (1997: 3):

> Language issues have some of the characteristics of sex –
> everyone does it, and consequently everyone is an expert.

What Kaplan and Baldauf mean is that language issues should be addressed by language experts, just as adolescents should learn about sex from their teachers or parents and not from other adolescents who themselves know little about the matter. As explained further by Kaplan and Baldauf (1997: 3),

> Every segment of society has language and individuals competently using language for a variety of purposes. However, when users engage in talking about language, which they frequently do, that talk is largely marked by profound ignorance.

Thus language planning and policy in Singapore, and especially that affecting Malay language planning, need to be looked at, analyzed, and evaluated. After 50 years of language planning and bilingual policy, some stock-taking and reflection need to take place. In particular, there is a need to reflect on what has been done, what has been achieved, what has worked, and what could be done better.

The following chapter will present the reports of various language review committees, which are meant to enhance the bilingual policy and impact the Malay language, which forms the basis of this study. This will be followed in Chapters 3 through 5 by an analysis using Cooper's model of status, corpus, and acquisition planning. Chapter 6 will analyze issues concerning new Malay language pedagogy based on the changing demographics of speakers and the changing educational landscape. The final chapter will recommend further directions to be taken in terms of Malay language planning for the 21st century.

2

Bilingualism and Malay Language Planning

This chapter will be divided into two main areas of discussion. Part I will discuss issues concerning government-initiated reports that have played a major part in charting the bilingual policy in Singapore. Each report will then be further subdivided into five areas of discussion. First will be the background to the formation of the review committee being set up. Secondly, the committee's scope of review will be focus upon in order to give a sense of the objectives of the review. Thirdly, the focus will be on the findings of the report, especially those pertaining to the bilingual policy. Fourthly, we will look at the implementation of the findings and, where possible, comment on its general impact on the bilingual policy. Lastly, this section will analyze the impact of the policy implementation based on the reports on the development of Malay as well as its planning.

According to Tan (2007: 75-76), Singapore's language ideology is based on five main attributes. They are: 1) "prima facie parity among the four official languages;" 2) "Malay, as the national language, is a symbolic political gesture recognizing the geopolitical realities in Singapore's locale;" 3) English is the dominant "language of commerce and government;" 4) "English is the surrogate lingua franca of Singaporeans;" and 5) "economic concerns have played a major role in the Government's efforts in boosting the proficiency levels of the English and Chinese languages in recent years."

It is with these five attributes of Singapore's language ideology that we begin our analysis of reviews and reports that have shaped the bilingual system in Singapore, with special emphasis on those impacting the Malay language.

Methodology

Before analyzing the educational reports, we will look at the research methodology used in this study. This research will consist of library research and an analysis of selected document and reports that have been integral to the implementation and development of the Singapore bilingual policy. The framework used will be based on Cooper's (1989) language planning framework model, which is divided into three parts, namely status planning, corpus planning, and acquisition planning. Cooper's model is a widely used accounting scheme for measuring the success of a language planning effort. This being the first comprehensive research on the impact of the bilingual policy on Malay, the use of Cooper's structured model of language planning will give us a clearer picture of the bilingual policy's impact on the language in terms of its status and corpus as well as its acquisition.

Major educational texts dealing with the bilingual language policy in Singapore will be examined in terms of their importance to the bilingual language policy and its impact on Malay. Thus, each report will be analyzed based on five main factors: 1) Background to the formation of the committees that issued the reports; 2) Each committee's scope of review and the objectives of the review; 3) the findings of the reports, especially those pertaining to the bilingual policy; 4) implementation of the findings, and where possible, their general impact on the bilingual policy; and 5) the impact of policy implementation on the planning and development of Malay.

The reports to be analyzed will be:

1. Report by the All-Party Committee of the Singapore Legislative Assembly on Chinese Education, 1956
2. Report by the Ministry of Education, 1978: Assessment of Bilingual Policy
3. Improving Primary School Education Report, 1991
4. Malay Language Steering Review Committee, 1999
5. Mother Tongue Languages Curriculum & Pedagogy Review Committees, 2002-2004

6. Primary and Secondary Education Review and Implementation Committees, 2009-2010

7. Mother Tongue Language Review Committee, 2011

These reports were chosen because they report major reviews conducted during the three main phases in the development of Singapore's education system. These are: the survival-driven phase from 1959 to 1978, the efficiency-driven phase from 1979 to 1996, and the ability-driven phase from 1997 to the present. At every cornerstone of the three phases lies an important document based on a review committee's report, hence the choice of the All-Party Report in 1956 that gave birth to the bilingual policy and that was followed by the Goh Report of 1978, which began the efficiency-driven phase and initiated the New Education System (NES). Then came the 1991 Report, which aimed to review the NES and make it more effective. All the other reports were chosen because they specifically dealt with "mother tongue" issue. Since Malay language planning in Singapore is intertwined with developments within the Malay-speaking region, there is also a need to look at the development of Malay elsewhere and particularly in Malaysia so as to get a sense of how the planning fits into the bigger picture of the Malay Archipelago.

Reviews and Reports Enhancing Bilingualism and Impacting the Malay Language

Language planning is closely intertwined with the social and political forces that are present in a country, and Malay language planning is no exception. Hence, to better understand the planning of the language, it is necessary to look at Malay language planning within its social and political context via the setting up of review committees and their subsequent reports. In education, one of the aims of language planning is to make a particular language the medium of instruction through which the various subjects in the school curriculum are taught while having the language itself taught as a subject in schools and in higher education. This has brought about the practice of various forms of bilingual education in many countries.

This study of Malay in education planning will take as its starting point the Report of the All-Party Committee of the Singapore Legislative Assembly on Chinese Education 1956. This is an important document that not only established the principle of equity but that has always been regarded as the document that initiated language planning and the bilingual policy in modern Singapore. Table 2.1 shows the phases in educational policy since independence in 1965, followed by the reports that were analyzed within that phase and the effect the report had on Malay language planning. As can be seen, the 1956 All-Party report started the bilingual policy, and when Singapore gained independence in 1965, the survival-driven education phase kicked in. During this phase, Singapore as a young nation had to grapple with uncertainties, especially in the economic sense. Thus, the education system was geared toward producing an effective workforce for a newly-industrializing economy. This was also a period during which Malay was taught as a dominant language, especially in Malay-streamed schools. In 1978, a report by the Ministry of Education, popularly known as the Goh Keng Swee report, assessed the bilingual policy that had been in place for 13 years.

As a result of the Goh report, Singapore entered its second phase of educational policy, the efficiency-driven phase. During this phase, the Government acted on the recommendations from the Goh report, which highlighted the wastage caused by high attrition rates in schools and graduating students unable to be effectively bilingual. Thus, streaming was introduced in Primary 3 to ensure that students were sent to educational streams based on their ability. This ability-based streaming became the cornerstone of Singapore's education system and impacted Malay language learning in particular. Specialized courses and programs were rolled out during this phase not only for Malay but also for the other "mother tongues." Malay benefited from the resources provided in terms of teacher training and instructional materials. During the ability-driven education phase, we see reports that were geared specifically toward "mother tongues" and not toward changing the entire educational system. During this phase, emphasis was placed on the curriculum and pedagogical review as well as on specialized higher education programs in the form of an Elective Programme in Malay Language for Secondary Schools (EMAS), Malay Language Elective Programme for junior colleges (MLEP), and degree programs as part of the quest to develop a group of Malay elite. We will now look at these reports in detail.

Table 2 Phases of educational policy and reports, and effect on Malay

Phases of educational policy	Reports	Effect on Malay
Pre-1965	• Report by the All-Party Committee of the Singapore Legislative Assembly on Chinese Education, 1956	Beginning of bilingual policy
Survival-driven education (1965-1978)	• Report by the Ministry of Education, 1978: Assessment of Bilingual Policy	First assessment of bilingual policy since inception
Efficiency-driven education (1979-1996)	• Improving Primary School Education Report, 1991	Streaming at Primary 3 introduced. Top 10% of Malay Primary School Leaving Examination (PSLE) students offered a chance to study Higher Malay at secondary level. Malay Special Programme (MSP) introduced for non-Malay students.
Ability-driven education (1997 to date)	• Malay Language Steering Review Committee, 1999 • Mother Tongue Languages Curriculum & Pedagogy Review Committees, 2002-2004 • Primary and Secondary Education Review and Implementation Committees, 2009-2010 • Mother Tongue Language Review Committee, 2011	Reports emphasizing specific Malay language programs, e.g., Elective Malay for Secondary Schools (EMAS) & Malay Language Elective Program (MLEP) programs, Bachelor of Arts (Education) in Malay Language and Literature at the National Insitute of Education, Nanyang Technological University. Introduction of *Arif Budiman* Vision for Malay language teaching, and learning and differentiated instructions for Malay.

Report of the All-Party Committee of the Singapore Legislative Assembly on Chinese Education 1956

The report of the All-Party Committee of the Singapore Legislative Assembly on Chinese Education 1956, better known as the All-Party Report, played a major part in the development of the bilingual language policy in Singapore. It laid the foundation for the present bilingual education system ever since it was accepted by the first government of the self-governing colony in 1959. To better understand the recommendations of the report, we will need to analyze the social, political, and educational landscape since British Administration after World War Two.

Background to the Report
During British Administration, the government built both English- and Malay-medium schools. While the Malay-medium vernacular schools provided primary level education, there were no Malay-medium secondary schools. The British colonial Government recognized Malays as the indigenous people, and for this reason, the government built schools for the Malays but not for the other ethnic groups.

The aim of the Malay-medium primary schools was mainly to give Malay students basic literacy and numeracy. In 1920, the Chief Secretary to the Government of the Federated Malay States (Maxwell and Kratoska, 1983: 406, cited in Lee, 2007: 121) stated that

> The aim of the Government is not to turn out a few well-educated youths; nor a number of less well-educated boys; rather it is to improve the bulk of the people, to make the son of the fisherman or the peasant a more intelligent fisherman or peasant than his father has been, and a man whose education will enable him to understand how his own lot in life fits in with the scheme of life around him.

Hence, the planning and use of Malay in education was introduced for the sole purpose of maintaining the Malay language, culture, and way of life.

As stated earlier, the British Colonial Government did not build vernacular schools for the Chinese or the Indians. Instead, Chinese and Indian (largely Tamil) schools were established by their respective communities and clan associations as well as wealthy individuals. Being independent, the schools had the freedom to determine both policy and curriculum. From the beginning, the Chinese schools were dependent on China for teachers, curriculum, and textbooks. In the early 20th century, radical, social, and political changes in China affected the Chinese schools in Singapore. These changes politicized the Chinese schools, including their students. They began to organize anti-Japanese activities, which alarmed the Attorney-General. The colonial government subsequently introduced various measures to control the Chinese schools. Among the measures introduced was a requirement to register with the Education Department and making grants-in-aid available with certain conditions that had to be fulfilled by the schools if they were to remain opened.

After World War Two, the hostility between the Chinese schools and the government intensified as the latter supported the English and Malay-medium schools. The Chinese community, especially the Chinese-educated, felt that the Government was practicing discrimination and was not being fair to their community. Their feelings were aroused because the bulk of the taxes the government collected were paid by the Chinese community.

Another factor that made the Chinese community uneasy was a series of political and educational developments throughout Malaya. The Report of the Committee on Education, also known as the Barnes Report 1951, the Razak Report 1956, and the Rahman Talib Report 1961 all recommended the establishment of national schools and the use of two official languages, Malay and English (Wong & Gwee, 1972). The Chinese community felt that their language and culture would be threatened by these developments, and the government acted on these concerns early on.

...the Government realized that there was a hard core of Chinese who would insist on a Chinese education. Wisely the Government decided to tackle the problem as early as possible. (Wong & Gwee, 1972: 27)

The Malay community too had its dissatisfactions, which were caused by the Malay-medium vernacular schools that provided primary level education only. This lack of opportunity for academic progress meant that only a few more able students were able to continue their education in the English schools in Special Malay Classes after their Primary 4 examination. In order to address the Malays' concern, the British colonial government introduced the Re-Orientation Plan in 1951, which instituted changes enhancing the prospects of Malay-medium students. The Plan proposed that:

1. For the first three years, Malay should be used as the medium of instruction and English taught as a subject from the first year;
2. From the fourth to the seventh year, all subjects except Malay language and Malay literature should be taught in English;
3. Students who successfully completed Standard (*Darjah*) VII will qualify for entry to the Special Malay Class in an English-medium school at Standard V level.

However, the plan was not agreeable to the Singapore Malay Teachers' Union (SMTU) because it was feared that it would lead to the destruction of Malay education and culture. The concerns articulated by the SMTU were borne out of a fear that Malay teachers might lose their livelihoods due to the emphasis on the use of English. In response, the Education Department (later renamed the Ministry of Education – MOE) formed the Singapore Malay Education Council Joint Committee (MEC) in April 1954. The committees' task was to look at the issue of Malay education and address the concerns of the SMTU and the Malay community in general. In August 1955, the MEC submitted its educational plan, which recommended, among other things, that secondary Malay-medium education be introduced and that Malay should continue to be used as the medium of instruction, with English taught as one of the subjects in the school curriculum.

Given the fragmented educational landscape and to allay the concerns of the Chinese community, the government formed an All-Party Committee in May 1955 to review Chinese-medium education. By this time, the situation in the Chinese schools was deteriorating at a faster pace than in the Malay schools. The following year the Committee, submitted its Report.

The Committee's Scope of Review

The committee was tasked with looking at the teaching and learning of Chinese in Singapore. Its terms of reference were simple: to investigate the issue and recommend improvements aiming at strengthening "Chinese education in the interest of Chinese culture" (Puru Shotam, 1998: 55). This task was deemed critical by the Chinese community as it feared for the survival of Chinese language and culture, especially given the impending issue of self-government and the subsequent merger with Malaya to form Malaysia.

Findings of the Report

The recommendations of the Report of the All-Party Committee on Chinese Education, which had a bearing on Malay language planning in education and Malay culture, were as follows:

1. Equal treatment for the four language streams of Malay, Chinese, English, and Tamil education;
2. The establishment of common curricula and syllabi for all the schools, the increasing use of a Malaya-centered curriculum, and the free transfer of language teachers across all streams of education;
3. All cultures represented in Singapore should be respected equally and preserved;
4. Language teaching should be greatly improved. The specific ways in which this could be done should be investigated and implemented within the Ministry of Education.

Although it was not in the Committee's Terms of Reference to review Malay education, the report advocated that consideration be given to Malay students to enable them to continue their education beyond primary level. This meant that secondary Malay-medium education would be provided. The report also advocated that the proposed technical education curriculum be taught in Malay.

Implementation of the Report

The committee's recommendation was accepted in full when the People's Action Party (PAP) won the Legislative Assembly elections in 1959. The first-ever Singapore government, led by Lee Kuan Yew, who was a member of the All-Party Committee, accepted and implemented the recommendations, thus supporting the committee's recommendation that schools implement the bilingual policy, that is, all national schools would use English and a choice of "mother tongue:" Mandarin, Malay, or Tamil.

With the government's endorsement, the All-Party Report was not only accepted, but its recommendations were fully implemented. Thus began Singapore's education policy, which was based on three main principles, as outlined below:

1. Acceptance of the 1956 report of the All Party Committee of the Singapore Legislative Assembly on Chinese Education, which provided for:
    a. Equal treatment for the four language streams for Malay, Chinese, English, and Tamil education;
    b. The introduction of bilingual education in primary schools and trilingual education in secondary schools;
    c. The use of Malaya-centered textbooks and syllabi; and
    d. The teaching of civics.
2. The acceptance of Malay as the National Language of the country, thus providing encouragement to non-Malays to learn the language, and, at the same time, the revitalization of Malay education itself;
3. Emphasis on science and mathematics to meet the requirements of an industrializing society and on the study of the four official languages. (Commission of Inquiry into Education, Singapore, Final Report, 1963)

Impact on Malay

The All-Party Report had an impact on Malay both directly and indirectly. Although most of it was positive, there were some unexpected repercussions especially in terms of unsustainable expansion of the language with reference its use as a language of wider communication in education.

Malay as National Language

With regards to positive developments, with self-rule in 1959, Malay was officially accepted as the National Language. This had a favorable impact on the language. It raised its prestige, and this in turn had implications for education, administration, and other aspects of national life. The domain of use of Malay began to expand, as evidenced from the fact that from 1959, the Government made it compulsory for all teachers to pass the Standard 1 National Language Examination for service confirmation. From 1960 onward, three-level examinations in the National Language were conducted, i.e., Standard 1, 2, and 3 for teachers and members of the public.

Revitalization of Malay-medium Education

Malay-medium education was thus revitalized, and secondary Malay-medium classes introduced at Geylang Craft Centre, Monk's Hill, Kallang, and Serangoon. From 1961 onward, secondary Malay-medium schools were built, including Sang Nila Utama Secondary, Tun Seri Lanang Secondary, and Ahmad Ibrahim Secondary. The enrollment of students in Malay-medium schools increased considerably. In 1959, there were 15,784 students in Malay primary schools, a figure that increased to 28,247 by 1965.The same trend took place at secondary level. As the National Language, Malay was made a compulsory subject in schools.

Language Corpus Planning

This positive development for the Malay language created initial technical issues, such as the coining of terminologies. With the establishment of secondary Malay-medium schools, teachers encountered major problems in teaching all subjects (except English) in Malay. This was a problem with corpus planning. There was as yet no institutionalized effort to solve this problem, which was common to all underdeveloped languages. The teachers (especially those who had English-medium education) had to coin their own Malay equivalents for the various scientific and mathematical concepts in English. This was also the case when technical education was extended to the secondary Malay technical stream.

Staffing Issues

Another major problem faced by the secondary Malay-medium schools was that there was a shortage of suitably qualified and trained teachers. Most of the teachers had only a Standard VII primary level qualification, and they were trained at the Sultan Idris Teacher Training College. Their qualifications only allowed them to teach in the primary schools. Suitably qualified teachers had to be recruited and trained quickly to address this problem. The Ministry of Education formed the Malay Education Advisory Committee (MEAC) to look into this matter. In 1960 the MEAC visited Indonesia, and on its return, made a number of recommendations that improved the situation to a certain extent. The Ministry had to introduce Teachers Under Other Scheme (TUOS) to recruit primary school leavers with just Standard (Primary) 7 qualification in addition to recruiting those with the Senior Cambridge School Certificate (equivalent to the Cambridge General Certificate of Education Advanced Level) and the Malaysian Certificate of Education (equivalent to the Cambridge General Certificate Ordinary Level). This move helped alleviate staffing levels but also affected the quality of teaching.

Impact on the Curriculum

Self-government, which Singapore achieved in 1959, brought about a consciousness that education, and particularly the curriculum, could be used as one of the tools of nation-building. Hence curriculum matters began to receive due attention. The Ministry of Education formed the Educational Advisory Council in 1959, with under it a Textbook and Syllabuses Committee. The Committee was assigned the task of drawing up syllabi with a common content in all the four language streams. The proposed syllabi should be suitable for the students' maturity level and intellectual and social development and be able to inculcate a national consciousness in the emerging nation.

In 1960, 19 syllabi used during the pre-1959 period were revised, and by the end of the year, new syllabi for all school subjects were published in the four language media. In 1961, more syllabi were published, and in 1962, ten more, including one for Malay. By 1963, the syllabus for the teaching of Malay as the National Language, as distinct from Malay as a first and second language, was produced.

The Malay language syllabus, which was revised in 1960, was grammatical-structural in nature, and the emphasis was on the teaching of grammar. Although the teaching of writing and reading skills was also strongly emphasized, there was insufficient emphasis on listening and speaking skills. The number of objectives for teaching the various language components and the range of language activities suggested was limited.

Impact on Teacher Training

With the revitalization of Malay-medium education and the establishment of the secondary Malay-medium schools together with increased enrollment in schools, there was an urgent need to increase the Malay language teacher population. The Ministry introduced the Teachers Under Other Scheme (TUOS) to recruit primary school leavers with only a Standard 7 qualification, in addition to recruiting those with the Senior Cambridge School Certificate (GCE A Level equivalent) and Malaysia Certificate of Education (GCE O Level equivalent).

Impact Post-independence

On 9 August 1965, Singapore became an independent, sovereign nation, separated from Malaysia politically. Although Malay was maintained as the National Language, its importance, relevance, and function has declined gradually over the years since that date as a direct consequence of the social, political, and economic developments that have taken place locally and globally.

After independence and until the early 1970s, the main features of development in the education system were the increasing number of integrated schools (schools where English and a vernacular language stream, either Chinese, Malay or Tamil are run concurrently), the increasing emphasis on the importance of the bilingual policy, and the rapid decline of enrollment in the vernacular schools as more parents sent their children to English-medium schools. The closure of the Malay-medium schools effectively ended the use of Malay as the vehicle for transmitting knowledge and skills in the education system. Henceforth, Malay became just a school subject except for the teaching of Moral Education in the primary schools and Malay Literature to pre-university students who wished to take Malay at "A" level and, at a later date, a restricted number of secondary students.

With regard to the teaching of Malay, the significant change in the 1970s was that in 1976, the Ministry of Education accepted the new Malay spelling system, which had been formulated and implemented by Malaysia and Indonesia in 1973. The new spelling system was implemented in the GCE "O" level Examination from 1979 onward. The implementation of the new spelling system is an instance of Malay language policy being determined by an external factor.

In 1987, with the demise of the vernacular schools, the Ministry of Education implemented the National System of Education, with English being the first school language as well as the medium of instruction while the "mother tongues" were designated as second languages. Kaplan and Baldauf (1997: 31) calls this process "exogenous planning." This refers to an instance where a foreign language is used as the main language of communication as against an indigenous language.

Report on the Ministry of Education, 1978: Assessment of the Bilingual Policy

The Report on the Ministry of Education, 1978, widely known as the Goh Report (Goh, 1979), was another important milestone in the development of the bilingual language policy in Singapore. Its importance lies in the fact that "it became known as the report which introduced ability streaming in the education system" and "pinpointed the "unnatural" conflict between the languages taught in school and those that students spoke at home" (Lee, 2011: 144). The review committee, which was formed in April 1978, was led by the then Deputy Prime Minister, Dr Goh Keng Swee. The report set out to assess the bilingual education program, and it offered an explicit and authoritative critique of Singapore's bilingual language policy and of its implementation in schools.

Background to the Report

Starting in 1956, the bilingual education policy had been first recommended and later implemented in all schools in Singapore by 1959. After 20 years of implementation, the concern was whether the bilingual education policy has succeeded in effectively educating bilingual citizens ready for the workforce. The report indicated some of the problems that were causing concern and needed to be addressed in order to meet the challenges ahead.

Firstly, there was the issue of educational wastage due to the automatic promotion system, whereby, irrespective of the student's final grade, he or she was promoted to the next level. Other forms of educational wastage included failure to achieve the expected standards and premature school leaving.

Secondly, there was the problem of low literacy levels. Based on the findings of the Ministry of Education,

> ...at least 33% of the P6 population in the English stream and 25% in the Chinese stream did not meet the minimum literacy levels of P6 standard... Most of the P4 pupils performed satisfactorily in the tests on following instructions, but almost 60% showed poor proficiency in the use of the English Language. (Goh, 1979: 4)

The above findings showed that the education system was only able to produce 75% of the expected literacy level for the English and Chinese streams and a 40% proficiency level in English Language use at P4. These figures show low literacy levels for the two major language streams as well as an alarmingly low proficiency level in English for the P4 cohort.

Thirdly, the bilingual language policy had not been effective in effectively educating bilingual citizens. This was a case of an unnatural school system in which 85% of the students did not speak English or Mandarin at home. These two languages being the languages of delivery in schools, students' performance was affected and led to a very high drop-out rate. This problem was exacerbated by the influx of students from Chinese-stream schools into English-stream schools. The influx was due to parents' pragmatism, fearing that Chinese-stream education did not promise a good job compared to the economic value of being proficient in English. The decision by the government to combine examination papers at the University of Singapore and Nanyang University and setting all examinations in English became the impetus for the government to pay special attention to bilingual education and address the educational wastage that had been taking place.

The Committee's Scope of Review

According to the Chair of the Review Committee, Dr Goh Keng Swee, the committee had no terms of reference at the start but was simply tasked by the Prime Minister, Lee Kuan Yew, with studying problems in the Ministry of Education. Thus, Dr Goh construed the committee's task as requiring it to "identify the more important problems in the Ministry of Education and recommend possible solutions." (Goh, 1979: i) The committee took a general approach to its work, and although it was able to identify most of the weaknesses in the education system, it was less certain about solutions.

Findings of the Report

With regard to bilingualism, the findings were as follows:

1. Low Literacy: At least 25% of the Primary 6 population did not attain minimum literacy levels. Among early school leavers in the armed forces, only 11% of recruits were competent in English;

2. Between 1975 and 1977, 62% of those who took the Primary School Leaving Examination (PSLE) and 66% of those taking the GCE "O" Level Examination failed in either the first or the second language;

3. As regards performance in various types of tests as well as newspaper and book reading, students fared badly;

4. The review team also discovered that the various teaching strategies used were not effective. Although exposure time to languages had increased, this did not contribute to enhancing the students' language proficiency.

(Goh, 1979: 1-2)

The low literacy rate and the failure of the system so far to generate effectively bilingual individuals resulted in the Chair of the Review Committee noting the waste of resources:If we make calculations of how much money we spend to produce this enormous number of illiterates, the sum must come to well over $1,000 million. Most countries produce illiterates without spending any money. (Lee, 2011: 144)

Implementation of the Report

In August 1978, the same team reviewed the whole education system and made recommendations. The Report was officially accepted and it formed the basis of the New Education System (NES) implemented in 1980 in primary schools and the following year in secondary schools. The main aim of the NES was to reduce wastage caused by failure and to enable more students to make it through the education system. The cornerstone of the NES was the introduction of streaming in both primary and secondary schools so that students could progress through the system at a pace suited to their ability. In primary schools, based on the results of the Primary 3 Examination, students would be streamed into the Normal Course, the Extended Course, or the Monolingual Course. At the secondary level, students would be streamed into the Special Course, the Express Course, or the Normal Course based on the results of the Primary School Leaving Examination (PSLE) (Goh, 1979: 6-1)

Impact on Malay

The Goh Report had a positive impact on the teaching and learning of Malay. It provided avenues for students who did well in the subject to pursue it at a higher level, including a wider spectrum of high-ability students who were not necessarily Malay-speaking. In terms of curriculum planning, the report established a more professional approach to helping teachers with teaching resources, and it expanded the teaching pedagogies for teaching Malay.

Wider Array of Malay Language Courses

At the secondary level, Higher Malay as a subject was offered from 1987 to Secondary 1 students who were in the top 10% of the PSLE cohort in 1986. Later, it was offered to the top 20%, and from 2004, to the top 30% of the PSLE cohort. Starting in the same year, the Ministry of Education introduced a new Malay language program called the Malay Language Elective Programme, or MLEP. This is offered to Secondary 1 students in the top 10% of the PSLE cohort who are non-Malay and who have never learned Malay in primary school. At the end of their fourth year of study, they take Malay as a Second Language sub-component of the GCE "O" Level Examination.

Syllabus Revision

The implementation of the NES brought about a radical change to the teaching of Malay (as well as to the other "mother tongues"). An unprecedented move in the education system, the teaching of Malay had to be redesigned to cater to the differing needs and abilities of the students in the various courses in both primary and secondary schools. Previously, there was only one teaching syllabus each for primary and secondary schools together with the prescribed textbooks and workbooks for each level.

The Curriculum Planning Division (CPD) of the Ministry of Education, which was responsible for designing syllabi, had to revise the existing syllabus and draw up the teaching syllabi for the various courses or streams. The revised syllabi, which were implemented in 1983, were an improvement over the existing one. Although the revised syllabi were still grammatical-structural in approach, more emphasis was given to the teaching of the other language skills, including listening and speaking. In order to widen the repertoire of learning objectives and to provide a greater variety of learning activities, the number of objectives and activities was expanded. Clearer guidance was also given to the teaching of proverbs, and lists of proverbs for the various levels were included in the syllabi. The syllabus for the Malay Language Elective was also developed at a later date.

The Setting Up of the Curriculum Development Institute of Singapore

In terms of language acquisition planning, 1980 also saw an important change in the educational landscape with the formation of the Curriculum Development Institute of Singapore (CDIS), a division within the Ministry of Education specializing in curriculum design and development. This was a significant move as the Ministry of Education was taking over the role of the private publishers. The Institute was assigned the task of producing teaching packages, which were to be based on the syllabi prepared by the Curriculum Planning Division. The CDIS formed project teams to prepare teaching packages for the various subjects.

The primary Malay language project team at CDIS produced the first series of *Sari Bahasa* for primary schools. The secondary Malay language project team produced the first series of *Intisari Bahasa*. Beside the textbooks and workbooks, the project teams also produced teachers' guides, charts, flash cards, overhead transparencies, and audiotapes. The result was a greater variety of instructional materials than could be produced by the private publishers. In this respect, the formation of CDIS aided in the development of instructional materials for the teaching and learning of Malay.

Improving Primary School Education Report 1991

Ten years after the implementation of the New Education System (NES), another round of major reviews was conducted to look again at the issue and recommend changes to the education system. In March 1991, the Ministry of Education released the Improving Primary School Education report, which recommended far-reaching changes to primary and secondary education. (MOE, 1991)

Background to the Report

The main reasons for the proposed changes were as follows:

1. Additional time was required for the weaker students to master bilingualism;

2. A high incidence of lateral transfer between streams made it necessary to postpone streaming by one year;

3. Monolingual stream students who continued their education at the Vocational and Industrial Training Board (VITB) were poorly prepared for employment, and many dropped out early.

(MOE, 1991: 8-9)

The Committee's Scope of Review

The committee was tasked with reviewing "our primary school system and consequently our secondary school system, to ensure that they will continue to meet our needs in the 1990s and beyond as we become a developed nation" (MOE, 1991: 1).

The committee looked at the primary schooling system and especially streaming at P3 and the various pathways open to students with varying needs and abilities. The committee then concentrated its resources on the progression to secondary schools and vocational training for academically challenged students. It was the committee's main task to study and recommend pathways for the "less able pupils" (MOE, 1991: 5), who consisted of the bottom 20% of every cohort of students. The committee studied the students' competency level in English and mathematics as well as streaming at P3 and in vocational training.

Findings of the Report

There were notable changes in the education system due to the Ministry's acceptance of the report's recommendations. Among them was streaming being delayed from P3 to P4. This was significant as there had been concerns among educationists that streaming at P3 was asking too much of students who were still in the early stages of education. Other changes included the delineation of the six-year primary education into a two-tier system consisting of a four-year foundation stage (P1-P4) and a two-year orientation stage (P5-P6), with emphasis on English, the "mother tongue" language (MTL), and mathematics. The report recommended an ME3 stream (M referring to "mother tongue", E referring to English, and 3 referring to the level of English to be taught) in which the "mother tongue" would be taught at first language level and English at third language level while mathematics would be taught at the "mother tongue" stage. The report also recommended a reallocation of curriculum time, with more teaching hours being given to English. Lastly, the report recommended renaming the three streams in primary schools as EM1 (English and "mother tongue" at first language level), EM2 (English and "mother tongue" at second language level), and EM3 (English and "mother tongue" at oral proficiency level). (MOE, 1991: 15-19)

Implementation of the Report

The present education system at primary level is based on the recommendations of the Report. However, in June 2004, Acting Minister for Education Tharman Shanmugaratnam announced the merging of EM1 and EM2 into a single stream. The rationale for this change was the fact that both streams are in fact similar except for the Higher Mother Tongue subject component.

The Report received both positive and negative responses from the various communities, particularly the Chinese-educated section of the Chinese community. In June 1991, the Minister for Education announced the formation of the Chinese Language Review Committee headed by a Deputy Prime Minister. In March of the following year, the Committee submitted its report, also known as the Ong Teng Cheong Report.

Impact on Malay

The significance of the report insofar as Malay is concerned was that Malay as a second language was renamed Malay Language and ML1 Higher Malay. The change in nomenclature was appropriate as the second languages were in actual fact the mother tongues of their respective communities. Another significant impact of the report on Malay was the greater emphasis to be given to traditional cultural and social values. This renewed emphasis was partly a reflection of the substantial inroads made by the spread of English and by westernization in general in Singapore society as well as the role played by the "mother tongues" in addressing these trends.

Impact on the Curriculum

Due to the change in the year of streaming, i.e., from Year Three to Year Four of primary education, the introduction of two-tier primary level education, and the new ME3 stream, the teaching syllabi were revised. The revision was also geared toward ensuring the teaching and learning of the language (and of other subjects as well) on the basis of research and development in language teaching and to enhance teaching and learning effectiveness. The syllabi were thus revised and the teaching and learning approach adopted was the integrated communicative approach, using eight broad themes. A list of sub-topics related to each theme was provided in the syllabi. The language teaching and learning activities revolving around each sub-topic were also suggested. All language components, proverbs, and grammatical items were to be integrated into the textbooks. As the teaching approach was new to the teachers, guidelines were provided in the syllabi to assist teachers in constructing integrated lessons. While the previous approach had consisted essentially of learning about the language, the integrated communicative approach consisted of acquiring the language through interesting, meaningful, and challenging content and activities.

CDIS was accordingly assigned the task of producing teaching packages using the new approach. The primary project team produced the second series, KITA, and the secondary project team produced the second series, *Pancaran Bahasa.* Included in the packages were teachers' guidebooks, textbooks, workbooks, and other instructional aids. The revised syllabi, together with the new teaching materials, were implemented in schools starting from 1993 onward.

In 1998 the Ministry of Education instituted changes to the curriculum in order to accommodate some innovations in the education system. In particular, MOE wanted to integrate three important national initiatives, namely National Education (NE), Information & Communication Technology (ICT), and Thinking Skills within the school curriculum. As curriculum time was limited and already packed with various subjects, the only alternative was to reduce the content of the existing syllabi, textbooks, and workbooks and of the prescribed literature texts. With regard to the textbooks and workbooks, the criteria used for the reduction were the length of texts and suitability for the level concerned. Word difficulty levels and use of concepts related to science, technology, and communication were also taken into account. There were to be no unnecessary overlap of content between topics at the same level for various subjects or repetition of enrichment activities. As regards the syllabi, the number of proverbs for each level was reduced as the teaching of Malay as well as Mandarin and Tamil were based on not only language but also literature and culture. Some grammatical items that were considered difficult for a particular level were assigned to the next higher level.

Impact on Standard Spoken Malay

With regards to Standard Spoken Malay, an important change took place in 1993. This was the year of the implementation of the new pronunciation system, or *sebutan baku* (Standard Pronunciation) at all levels in primary schools. In 1994, this was implemented at all levels in secondary schools also. Note that the *sebutan baku* variant is meant to be used in formal situations only, such as teaching and learning in educational institutions, public speeches, broadcasts over the electronic media, and formal communication and discussion in the civil service. It is not aimed at replacing the Johor-Riau pronunciation, with which the speech community is familiar.

Nevertheless, initial reactions to this change were mixed. Some sections of the community, notably older Malay speakers and the literary elite, who view Indonesia as the heart of Malay language and literature, felt that this change was long overdue. At the other end of the spectrum, there were sections of the community who rejected the change as they were very comfortable with the Johor-Riau pronunciation and felt that the change was not required (why fix something if it isn't broken!). Once the change was adopted by the Ministry of Education, it became part of education policy for Malay to have *sebutan baku* as its standard pronunciation.

The change was integrated into examinations in the subsequent year. The decision was made by the Ministry after deliberating on a paper submitted by the Malay Language Council, Singapore in 1990. This change exemplifies the integration of corpus planning in education. Like a change in the spelling system, this change was brought about following a similar move in Malaysia's education system, which adopted the new pronunciation system in 1988. This is another case of a language policy for Malay that originated externally but was later accepted by Singapore.

Malay Language Steering Review Committee, 1999

In early 1999, the Ministry of Education formed the above committee to review Malay language teaching and learning in schools and to make the necessary recommendations. The Committee was chaired by the Minister for Education and co-chaired by the Minister in Charge of Muslim Affairs, the de-facto minister in charge of Malay issues.

Background to the r Review Committee

The formation of this Committee was partly the result of the application of the equity principle based on a review committee for Chinese Language chaired by then Deputy Prime Minister Ong Teng Cheong (MOE, 1992). This was the first official review of Malay language teaching and learning ever undertaken by the Ministry of Education. It was conducted along somewhat similar lines as the review undertaken by the Chinese Language Review Committee in 1991 in order "to look into all aspects of Chinese language learning, from teaching methods and textbooks to curricula and examinations" (Lee, 2011: 176).

The Committee's Scope of Review

The review was comprehensive and covered syllabi, instructional materials, examinations, programs, and teacher training. The Committee formed sub-committees to review the instructional packages and teacher training. A survey was also carried out among selected students who were learning Malay. A sub-committee was formed to obtain feedback from teachers, Malay language experts, community leaders, and parents (including non-Malay parents whose children were learning Malay) through formal discussions. A total of five sessions were conducted and a wide range of topics was discussed, including the proficiency of students, curricula, teacher training, and teaching strategies. The sessions also brought up the different concerns and views of both senior and younger teachers, linguists, parents, and community leaders.

Findings of the Review Committee

The Malay Language Steering Review Committee introduced a radical change to Malay language teaching by setting a new broad objective, which was that every Malay Singaporean should study Malay for as long as possible to as high a level as he or she is capable of. This objective was based on the rationale whereby students have different abilities and customization will therefore allow all to realize their full potential. In line with this objective, the committee chose to maintain a broad base of Malay Singaporeans who have learned Malay and continue to use it beyond formal education. Subsequently, this base would be narrowed down to a Malay elite capable of directly accessing, understanding, and appreciating Malay culture and values.

Similar to other "mother tongue" committees, the Malay Language Steering Review Committee also made recommendations pertaining to instructional materials, syllabi, examination formats, and teacher training. These recommendations were officially accepted and subsequently implemented by MOE. In addition, the Committee also made recommendations for the introduction of the following Malay language programs in schools.

Firstly, the committee recommended the introduction of a Malay Language Basic Programme (ML"B") for students who are exceptionally weak in the language. Students needed to satisfy certain criteria before they could be admitted into the program, including being consistently weak in the subject. Although there would be such a program at the secondary level, no program would be introduced at the pre-university level as the number of students would be very small.

Secondly, the committee recommended the introduction of the Malay Special Programme. This was formerly known as the Malay Language Elective for the top 10% of the PSLE cohort who have never learned Malay in primary schools. These are bright students who may become future leaders. This program was designed to enable them to acquire communicative competence in Malay and understand the language and its cultural heritage in accordance with its regional importance. The level of language proficiency has been modified since it was first introduced in 1986. At the end of Secondary 4, the students' level of proficiency is expected to be equal to that of a Secondary 2 Express Malay language course.

Thirdly, the committee introduced an Elective Programme in Malay Language for Secondary School (EMAS) at the Bukit Panjang Government High School. This school was selected as it had a sizable number of students studying Higher Malay. In addition to Higher Malay, the students were allowed to study Malay Literature. At pre-university level, the committee introduced the Malay Language Elective Programme (MLEP) at Tampines Junior College. Students at these two institutions have a relatively high academic standard, and both are co-educational. These two programs began in 2001. A variety of enrichment programs are also organized for the students, including educational visits, creative writing workshops, and overseas field trips so as to give the students a more holistic Malay language education.

Implementation of the Review Committee's Recommendations

Based on the review committee's recommendations, the syllabi were up for another round of revision, even though it was less than 10 years since the last revision. This was necessitated by the fact that a number of changes had already taken place, particularly with the incorporation of the three national initiatives as well as the need to accommodate the recommendations of the Malay Language Steering Committee. The syllabi were thus revised, but the integrated, communicative, and thematic approach continued being used. The three national initiatives implemented in 1998 and the recommendations of the Malay Language Steering Review Committee continued to be implemented.

The teaching materials for primary and secondary schools were revised and implemented according to levels. The new series for primary schools was called AKAR, while the series for secondary schools was called JENDELA. However, the teaching materials were revised by the Curriculum Planning and Development Division, an amalgamation of CDIS and CPD into a single Division in 1997. In line with the recommendation of the Malay Language Steering Review Committee, greater emphasis was to be given to the teaching and learning of aural and oral skills. In addition to the traditional textbooks and workbooks, a CD-ROM was added as a new teaching aid. At the primary level, flashcards, picture cards, wall charts, and other audio-visual aids were to be produced. In terms of content, NE, ICT, and Thinking Skills were to be better integrated into the new teaching packages. Instructional materials were produced for ML"B" students, and schools began using the revised teaching packages from 2002, starting with P1 and P2, followed by Secondary 1 (NA) & (NT) and thereafter at subsequent levels in the following years.

Impact on Malay

With the slew of new initiatives being recommended, more teachers needed to be recruited and retrained to meet the new challenges. To overcome the shortage, MOE had to recruit Malay language teachers from Brunei and Indonesia on a contract basis. Another measure taken by the Ministry was to introduce a four-year course for GCE "O" level entrants. These two measures were of a stop-gap nature and were meant to ease the problem of not having enough teachers to teach the varied courses introduced.

As a long-term measure, the committee recommended the introduction of undergraduate courses at the National Institute of Education, Nanyang Technological University, in order to enhance and upgrade Malay language and literature teaching. The courses, which began in 2001, were welcomed by Malay language teachers. The Bachelor of Arts in Education (Malay Language and Literature) was not only well-received by the Malay language teaching community but also long overdue. Before the introduction of this course, there was no upgrading course for teachers after they completed their diplomas in education. Although no-pay leave for serving teachers to enroll in such courses was offered in Malaysia, having such a course in Singapore was a welcome relief for many. For once, there were not only qualified Malay language teachers but also graduate Malay language teachers. Before this, most graduate Malay language teachers came from the Malay Language Department in the National University of Singapore, where most modules were either sociology-based or not conducted in Malay.

At the beginning of the 21st century, a variety of Malay language programs were offered in order to meet the differing needs and abilities of students, as were initiatives to produce better qualified and better equipped teachers in order to meet the new challenges. From the educational point of view, this was a positive development and an improvement over the previous practice of having only one monolithic program offered to all students. However, from the point of view of members of the Malay community, there were different views and responses. Some felt that there was no need for a Malay Basic Programme in schools as it was more critical for the Chinese students. At this juncture, Malay students were coping relatively well with their Malay language. However, this range of programs was not fixed once and for all. As time passes and with new developments, modifications will need to be made. For instance, when the "B" program was first implemented, it was for Secondary 3 students upward. However, from 2011 onward, the program was to be implemented from Secondary 1. What further changes will take place in the future and whether the programs are viable remains to be seen.

The Mother Tongue Language Curriculum and the Pedagogy Review Committees

In 2004 and 2005, the Ministry of Education set up three review committees that looked at the three "mother tongues" – Chinese, Malay, and Tamil individually, with the emphasis on reviewing their curriculum and pedagogy. The background for the three committee was identical, namely a generational shift in language use at home. Based on the Chinese Language Curriculum and Pedagogy Review Committee (CLCPRC) report, the percentage of students entering P1 with a predominantly English-speaking home background had risen from 36% in 1994 to 50% in 2004 (MOE, 2004: 22), While the picture was more positive as regards Malay, there was a growing concern over the "increasing numbers of younger students who come from homes where English is also spoken and over a growing minority who come from exclusively English-speaking homes" (MOE, 2005: 16). As regards Tamil, it was noted that 55.7% of Indian students entering P1 in 2004 (MOE, 2005) came from homes that spoke predominantly English. Importantly, this was the first ever review of Malay that solely looked at curriculum and pedagogical matters as the earlier reviews were more general in nature and looked at pathways to learning the language.

Terms of Reference

The terms of reference for the three "mother tongues" were identical in nature. The Chinese Language Review Committee was tasked with:

1. Articulating the objectives and target groups of the different Chinese Language syllabi;

2. Examining the implementation of the various Chinese Language syllabi in schools to determine whether they were aligned with the curriculum objectives as well as achievable with reasonable effort by the various target groups;

3. Reviewing the effectiveness of the structure of the present Chinese Language curriculum and the teaching of the assessment modes for the respective target groups;

4. Recommending appropriate refinements to the structure and the different Chinese Language syllabi to better achieve MOE's MTL policy objectives;

5. Examining the feasibility of facilitating the lateral transfers of students across the different Chinese Language syllabi; and

6. Advising on the effective implementation of the above.

In addition to Point 5, the Malay Language Curriculum and Pedagogy Review Committee (MLCPRC) and the Tamil Language Curriculum and Pedagogy Review Committee (TLCPRC) were provided with identical terms of reference. For Malay and Tamil, there was no lateral transfer of students simply because there was no differentiation in syllabi to begin with. Unlike in Chinese classes, where students are differentiated based on their linguistic ability and follow different syllabi, all Malay and Tamil language students are placed in a class based on their ability and use the same syllabi. Thus, the differentiated Chinese approach offers greater variety compared to the Malay and Tamil varieties.

Findings of the Report

In the event, the findings in the three committee's reports were quite similar to each other. All three committees agreed on recommending a differentiated approach to the teaching of the languages concerned, thus emphasizing greater customization at the primary and secondary levels as well as placing greater emphasis on oral communication and reading skills.

Customization at the primary level

Based on the ability-driven education platform, the committee recommended "a differentiated approach to engage and motivate students" (MOE, 2004: 5). For Chinese, the differentiated approach was meant to take into account the different ability levels of students taking the subject. For all Chinese Language students, the objective was to "enthuse" them. For the majority, it was to ensure "effective oral communication and reading." For those with high linguistic ability, the objective was to achieve a high level of competence in Chinese based on the four language skills. Thus, a modular approach was recommended for the language at primary level, which aimed for greater customization and flexibility in teaching and learning. In a similar vein, the Malay Language committee recommended a somewhat similar differentiated approach. Differentiated Instruction (DI) was to be carried out at P1 and P2 levels, with support given by MOE. For Tamil Language also, the emphasis was on taking into consideration the students' differing abilities.

Greater emphasis on oral communication and reading skills

The committee recommended greater emphasis on oral communication skills as communicative competence was seen as integral to the stated objective of learning Chinese. For students to develop fluency and confidence in oral communication, the committee recommended that the language be taught systematically through a variety of strategies. For students to sustain an interest in the language for future generations, the committee recommended that students' reading ability be developed at an early age. The committee further recommended the use of the "Recognize First, Write Later" pedagogical principle. Although broadly similar, the Malay Language committee recommended the use of a contextual approach along with providing opportunities for students to use the language in authentic settings. Similarly, the Tamil Language committee highlighted and recommended a "Listen First, Speak Later" principle.

Implementation

The implementation of the reports' findings was quite similar in nature. The main similarity was the setting up of a Language Learning and Promotion Committee to oversee the implementation of the suggestions in the respective reports. Thus, a Chinese Language Learning and Promotion Committee (CLLPC) came into being. Likewise, a Malay Language Learning and Promotion Committee (MLLPC) and a Tamil Language Learning and Promotion Committee (TLLPC) were set up and tasked with implementing their respective committee's findings. In addition, the differentiated approach and the emphasis on oral and reading skills were to be introduced progressively, starting with P1 to P4 in 2008. Subsequently, there were to be changes made to the Primary School Leaving Examination (PSLE) examination format from 2010 onward. The same measure applied to Malay and Tamil.

Impact on Malay Language

The recommendations made by the review committees constituted a watershed in the teaching and learning of Malay in Singapore. It will thus have a far-reaching impact as it will change the way Malay is taught in the classroom.

A differentiated approach to teaching Malay

The MLLPC report introduced the concept of differentiated instructions (DI) to Malay language teachers. The DI approach involves differentiating the content, process, or product in the teaching of Malay based on students' interest, readiness level, and profile. Teachers are required to ensure that their lessons are content differentiated, process differentiated, or product differentiated. They are also to determine whether their choice of differentiation is based on the students' interests, readiness level, or profile. By doing so, teachers will ensure that their lessons are engaging to the students and better tailor their lessons to their students' needs, interests, and abilities. This will make Malay language lessons student-centered and much more interesting for the students. The approach taken is to address the feedback received by the review committee, which indicated that 25% of Primary 4 students and 32.8% of Secondary 2 students who dislike learning Malay do so because they found their lessons uninteresting (MOE, 2005: 63).

In order to achieve the objective of an engaging classroom based on the DI approach, teachers were sent for training at the National Institute of Education, where in-service courses on differentiated teaching and learning were conducted. Schools too played their part by organizing communities of learners among teachers in an effort to promote the differentiated approach. MOE also played a part by organizing workshops and seminars as a platform for teachers to share their expertise and learn from each other.

The setting up of MLLPC

The MLLPC was set up in February 2006 under the purview of MOE. Its terms of reference were twofold. Firstly, the committee was to elicit the support of the community in implementing the recommendations of the MLCPRC. Secondly, it was to collaborate with Malay community organizations in organizing activities to support the teaching and learning of Malay. The collaboration was to focus on the promotion of spoken Malay and on generating interest in and appreciation of Malay language, literature, and culture among the young, outsourcing and developing reading materials, promoting reading among students, organizing literary activities, competitions, and camps, organizing seminars and workshops for teachers, and organizing talks and workshops and publishing reference resources for parents to promote the use of Malay at home (MOE Press Release, 13 February 2006). These terms of reference for MLLPC were identical to the terms of reference for CLLPC and TLLPC.

The MLLPC committee consisted of 22 members from various professional, educational, and cultural organizations impacting Malay language and culture and was headed by Senior Parliamentary Secretary (Education and Manpower), Hawazi Daipi. Since its inception, MLLPC has supported 101 Malay Language and Literary activities organized by various community organizations. In an MOE Press Release of March 2011, it was reported that the activities "reach out extensively to different groups of the community, are of commendable quality, and receive positive responses and feedback from participants." In 2011, MOE increased the funding for the MLLPC by an additional $3.6 million" over the next five years to support the Committee's efforts to create environments conducive to the learning and use of the Malay language" (MOE Press Release, 14 March 2011).

In line with the added funding, the MLLPC has streamlined its funding process and identified five iconic activities and four core activities for funding. An iconic activity is one that runs for three years continuously, while core activities refer to an activity organized annually. Both types of activities receive full funding from the committee. Among the iconic activities are a quiz on Malay language and culture for primary school students, which is aired live (finals only) on the only Malay Language free-to-air channel, and the *Arif Budiman* Lecture Series, whose main aim is to provide a platform for members of the community to enhance their knowledge of Malay language and culture, empower them to ensure the sustainability of the language, and provide opportunities for the community to learn from experts in the field of language and cultural development. To date, six *Arif Budiman* lectures have been offered by experts from Malaysia, Indonesia, and most recently China. Another iconic activity is the *Arif Budiman* Award, which is given to Malay language teachers who have performed well in their professional duties. The aim of the award is to recognize the contribution of

Malay language teachers and to identify those who can act as role models in pursuing excellence in their respective fields. Such recognition goes a long way in motivating Malay language teachers in their pursuit of effective teaching.

Report on Primary Education Review Initiative (PERI)

The Primary Education Review and Implementation Committee report was submitted to the Minister for Education in March 2009. The committee, which was set up in 2008, was tasked with studying and recommending ways to enhance primary education for 21st-century challenges. The report was meant to chart the next level of growth for primary education and to identify initiatives and programs required to achieve this.

Background to the Report

The Primary Education Review and Implementation (PERI) Committee was set up in October 2008 to study ways of enhancing primary education, especially in the light of recent changes in the educational landscape. This change started in 1977, with the rolling out of the "Thinking School, Learning Nation" (TSLN) vision that was part of the greater plan to transform Singapore's economy into one that was knowledge-based. Several initiatives were then introduced to realize this vision. Among them were greater diversity in the secondary and pre-university educational landscape. Emphasis was placed on students' differing abilities, and this led to a variety of pathways and choices for them. In order to ensure maximum benefit for students from these changes, MOE embarked on a review at the primary level first as this "provides the foundation upon which a child builds future knowledge and skills" (MOE, 2009: 17).

MOE sees primary education as a critical stage in the building of confidence and the shaping of attitudes toward the learning process. The values and soft skills developed at this critical stage in the educational process will go a long way toward establishing the students' "moral compass." It is with this in mind that the committee was set up with terms of reference that focused primary education stakeholders on the philosophy and desired outcomes of holistic education at the primary level, and secondly, to study and recommend strategies on how this could be implemented. With regards to recommendations, the committee was tasked with studying in detail the rolling out of Single-Session Primary Schools, the feasibility of moving toward an all-graduate teacher recruitment policy by 2015, and the recommendation to rebalance the learning of content knowledge and the development of skills and values so as to prepare the young for the future.

The review and consultation process involved a wide-ranging group of stakeholders from senior management in schools to classroom teachers. Feedback was also obtained via small-group discussions and seminars organized by MOE.

The Committee's Scope of Review

The Terms of Reference or scope of review of the committee were twofold. The committee was charged with looking first at investing in a quality teaching force and second at the need to enhance infrastructure.

Findings of the Report

The committee completed its study in early 2009 and submitted the report to the Minister of Education in March 2009. The committee's recommendation was divided into three aspects of primary education. First was the need to balance knowledge with skills and values, followed by investing in quality teachers, and finally enhancing the present infrastructure to support earlier initiatives.

Balancing Knowledge with Skills and Values

The committee reported that there was a need to strengthen and balance teachers' pedagogical content knowledge with a renewed emphasis on non-academic programs within the curriculum. The committee suggested the implementation of a Programme for Active Learning (PAL) at the lower primary level along with its continuation at the upper primary but with added enhancement in the quality of Art, Music, and Physical Education. The committee further recommended a more holistic assessment at lower primary level and for provisions to be made with respect to "clear guidelines on the learning outcomes for each subject..." and an "increase [in] students' continued mastery of foundational skills" (MOE, 2009: 11).

Investing In a Quality Teaching Force

The committee further recommended provisions for recruiting more teachers and Allied Educators. With regards to a quality teaching force, the committee recommended that future intakes be concentrated on university graduates in order to provide "current non-graduate teachers with avenues for professional development and/or academic upgrading" (MOE, 2009: 12). Teachers were also to be equipped with the necessary knowledge via pre- and in-service training and provided with "rich learning resources and packages" (MOE, 2009: 12).

Enhancing Infrastructure

The committee was of the view that after looking at the "software" involved in the educational process, there was a need to enhance the "hardware" also. Thus, in ensuring that the emphasis was on the student, all schools were to become single-session, with "additional support for a more holistic education" (MOE, 2009: 14). Going further into what the school can offer students, the committee recommended that schools support social services such as after-school care, to be provided within the school, especially for disadvantaged families.

Implementation of the Report

With the acceptance of the committee's report, MOE announced the facilitation of the transition "in all government schools to the single session model by 2016" (MOE, 2009: 13). In maintaining the caliber of new teacher intakes, MOE was to focus on the pool of university graduates or those who qualify for undergraduate education by 2015. Those who do not qualify under the above scheme were to be encouraged to enroll as Allied Educators (Teaching and Learning). The job of these Allied Educators would be to work with teachers to enhance the teaching and learning of the students in both academic and non-academic areas. By doing so, Allied Educators would have the opportunity to become fully-fledged teachers in the future. More resources were also disbursed to schools for the implementing of their own Programme for Active Learning (PAL). These resources in the forms of funds were to be used by schools "to engage trained coaches, instructors, and service providers" to help school administrators and teachers "conduct quality PAL activities as well as to procure equipment for Art, Music, Physical Education, and other PAL activities" (MOE, 2009: 10). Teachers were sent for holistic assessment courses in order "to help build pupils' confidence and desire to learn" (MOE, 2009: 11).

Impact on Malay

In terms of impact on Malay, it was stated under the subject of Mother Tongue Languages (MTL), including Mandarin and Tamil as well as Malay, that "the focus of language teaching and learning should be on oral communication and customization to meet the learning needs of pupils with different abilities" (MOE, 2009: 30). With the added emphasis on PAL, schools were to be provided with resources for conducting speech and drama lessons or music and movement activities as part of their extended Malay Language program.

Mother Tongue Language Review Committee 2011

Less than six years after publishing the MTL Curriculum and Pedagogy Review Committee's report in 2004/5, MOE embarked on another review of the mother tongue teaching and learning. Although this review was not as all-encompassing as the former, it was nevertheless significant, for several reasons. Firstly, the timing of the review, i.e., about five years after the previous one, made it a kind of mid-term review. Secondly, the faster than expected changing demographics of P1 students created the impetus for a mid-term review. Thirdly, there was a need to re-assess some of the recommendations made in 2004/5 and to realign these toward the 21st-century goals set by MOE. The report was released in January 2011 and was entitled Nurturing Active Learners and Proficient Users.

Background to the Report

The MTL Review Committee was set up in 2010 and was led by the Director-General of Education, with two stated trends faced by the mother tongues in mind. First was the changing language environment in Singapore homes, where more of the new cohort of P1 students' parents registered English as their home language, though there remains a group of students who are effectively bilingual. Secondly, there is growing interest around the world for bilingual or multilingual individuals, and there have been corresponding breakthroughs in the teaching and learning of more than one language.

The Committee's Scope of Review

The committee was tasked with reviewing the teaching and testing of mother tongues (MTL) in Singapore schools. In his letter to the Prime Minister reporting on the findings of the committee, Minister for Education Dr Ng Eng Hen indicated that the review was important as "bilingualism is the cornerstone of our education system," and it is therefore imperative that the mother tongues 'stay effective and relevant with the changing language environment in homes and the community' (*Straits Times,* January 20, 2011).

Findings of the Report

The committee met with and engaged a wide range of stakeholders, from teachers to academics and community leaders. In addition, a survey was also carried out involving 22,000 teachers, students, and parents. These stakeholders were generally satisfied with the developments that followed the 2004/5 MTL review. In its study of multilingual societies abroad, the committee found that the "learning of languages is most effective when learners are taught to use the language in an active and interactive manner for a variety of real-life settings" (MOE, 2011: 2). The committee made four key recommendations with a view to developing Active Learners and Proficient Users. The recommendations were as follows:

Recommendation 1: Aligning Teaching and Testing to Achieve Proficiency

The committee recommended that MOE provide proficiency descriptors at key stages of learning as a guide for students to monitor their learning progress. To help students achieve the desired proficiency level, MOE was to increase the emphasis placed on both written and oral skills. In addition to the continued emphasis on oracy skills, MOE was to continue with its focus on differentiated learning, with the added emphasis on the "greater use of authentic materials reflective of everyday situations and contexts" (MOE, 2011: 2). This would be done to equip students with the necessary skills to use their mother tongue in real-life situations. The committee also recommended greater emphasis on the use of ICT resources.

As most students are savvy users of new media, this platform should be fully utilized as a teaching tool in engaging them. The committee further recommended that MOE "align school-based assessment and national examinations to the desired language proficiencies and test language use in authentic contexts" (MOE, 2011: 3). MOE was to introduce the use of e-dictionaries for interactive writing items based on a stimulus so as to provide a real-world feel to each activity. Subsequently, video clips were to be given as stimuli for oral examinations as they provide a more engaging and realistic context by stimulating conversation. Computer-based writing was also to be introduced at secondary and junior college level, followed by the introduction of oral examinations for Higher Mother Tongue Language (HMTL) at "O" level. With these recommended changes, MOE aimed to provide lead time for students and teachers to change to the new curriculum and adopt the new assessment modes in classrooms and in school examinations.

Recommendation 2: Enhancing Different Provisions for Learners of Different Abilities

In making different provisions for learners of different abilities, the committee recommended that MOE provide all the support required and opportunities for students who show interest in and ability for Higher Mother Tongue Language (HMTL) to excel and "attain higher levels of language proficiency and deeper cultural knowledge" (MOE, 2011: 4). To achieve this, MOE was to enhance and expand the MTL special programs, introduce a new "A" level subject in Chinese Linguistics and Translation, and award more scholarships. However, for those facing difficulty coping with their mother tongue, the committee recommended that MOE place greater emphasis on developing their communication skills through more activity-based approaches.

Recommendation 3: Creating an Environment Conducive to MTL Use and Learning

The committee saw the need to involve the community in MTL use and learning so as to provide the authentic environment that is required to make the mother tongue not just a classroom language but a living language. Schools, parents, and the community form a three-way partnership and a potentially conducive environment. Thus, the committee recommended that schools introduce a structured program that would create an environment conducive to students using the mother tongue and appreciating their heritage and culture. This could be done via MTL Fortnights, camps, and structured reading programs, where schools could partner with community groups and other stakeholders. MOE would provide an additional $45 million for schools and the respective MTL Learning Promotion Committees over the next five years to help kick-start this effort and create a conducive environment for the use of the mother tongues.

Recommendation 4: Developing and Deploying More MTL Teachers

The committee realized the importance of having not only qualified teachers but also the right number of teachers to see through the initiatives, especially the range of programs to be offered. The committee recommended that the number of MTL teachers be strengthened by 500 teachers by 2015. MOE should encourage more "A" level students to take their MTL at a higher level and offer more teaching scholarships and awards. The training and development of present MTL teachers should also be strengthened, especially in the field of teaching and assessment, so as to meet the learning needs of students with different MTL abilities. Lastly, oral examinations should be introduced at "O" level Higher MTL in 2016.

Implementation of the Report

As part of the recommendations, a time line for the proposed changes, especially in examination format, were outlined. The use of video stimuli for oral examinations will be implemented in the 2017 PSLE examinations. Depending on the respective programs, implementation will begin in 2014. The introduction of new items testing interaction skills will begin in 2014 and be fully implemented by 2017. These test items will allow the use of dictionaries and e-dictionaries for written interaction tasks. Meanwhile, the use of keyboard input for selected sections of examinations will begin at "A" and "O" levels in 2013 and 2014, respectively, depending on the program. The committee has promised sufficient lead time for students and teachers to prepare themselves for changes in examination formats.

As part of the enhancement and expansion of MTL programs at secondary level, an 11th Special Assistance Plan (SAP) School was set up at Nan Chiau High School and a third Elective Programme for Malay Language for Secondary Schools (EMAS) center at Anderson Secondary School. An SAP school is either an independent or autonomous secondary school in which the top 30% of every PSLE cohort (Primary School Leaving Examination – a placement examination primary students' take before going on to secondary education) can apply to join provided they obtain Distinction grades for English and Mandarin in the PSLE examination. Both programs will begin operation in 2012. Meanwhile, the pre-university or junior college (JC) level saw the introduction of a new subject in Chinese Linguistics and Translation from 2015, additional funding for the Chinese Language Elective Programme (CLEP), and an additional insertion point for the Bicultural Studies Programme at first year of junior college studies from 2012. With regards to the mother tongues, a third Malay Language Elective Programme (MLEP) center was set up at Pioneer JC, and there was an increase in the number of scholarships for MLEP as well as additional funding for their immersion programs. All three new programs and enhancement initiatives will be implemented in 2012. For Tamil, there is to be a National Elective Tamil Language Programme (NETLP) for secondary and JC students aimed at enriching their learning of the language, its literature, and its culture. Scholarships will also be awarded to deserving NETP students at JC level. These initiatives will be fully functional by 2012.

Impact on Malay

This latest review seemingly cements parity across the mother tongues, as was initially outlined in the All-Party Report of 1956. Although the level of parity may have started from different base lines, there is something for everyone. For Chinese, the enhancement and expansion of programs involved a new subject, an 11th center for Special Assistance Plan (SAP) schools, and an additional insertion point for its Bicultural Studies Programme at JC 1. For Malay, an additional center for EMAS and MLEP programs was added, while Tamil received the NETLP program. All three were given additional funding to run these programs, including scholarships for students.

For the mother tongues, the establishing of a third center for EMAS and MLEP will provide an opportunity for a larger number of Malay language students to attain a higher level of proficiency in the language and a deeper appreciation of Malay culture and literature. The increase in the number of scholarships given and additional funding for overseas immersion and programs under MLEP will be an additional incentive for students to apply for the program. These enhancements and expansions augur well for the future of the specialized programs.

Conclusion

The various reports highlighted in this chapter have helped in charting the starting point and subsequent growth of the bilingual language policy and entrenched it as the main pillar of the education system in Singapore. The government has shown its commitment to the policy by spending time and resources on building up the system and addressing its shortcomings. Nevertheless, a clear pattern emerges whereby all the review committees were initiated of a concern by the Chinese leaders over the Chinese language and the impact that the use of English is having on the teaching and learning of Mandarin.

3

Status Planning

Introduction

The two previous chapters outlined the state of bilingual policies and language planning in the international as well as the local context. The discussion is important as it sets the stage for a more in-depth investigation of the effects of the bilingual policy on Malay language planning in Singapore. This chapter will look at status planning as regards Malay in Singapore's bilingual environment. It will chart the development of status planning for Malay from 1956, the start of the bilingual policy, to the present. It will also analyze the development of the language since independence and the impact of the bilingual policy on the status of Malay. Issues touched upon will include the commodification of the language as well as those pertaining to linguistic instrumentalism.

Status Planning

According to Cooper (1998: 99) status planning is the deliberate effort "to influence the allocation of functions among a community's languages." As we will see in the case of Malay in Singapore, this function is often codified in the country's Constitution, or it may be the object of campaigns aiming at popularizing the use of the language or to give it a certain status. These functions are further explained by Stewart (1968, cited in Cooper, 1989: 100-119) in his discussion on national multilingualism as the function of an official language, a provincial or regional official language, a language of wider communication, an international language, the language of the capital, a group language, a language of education, a language as a school subject, a literary language, or a language of religion.

Function of Official Language

The function of official language is mostly "specified constitutionally" (Stewart, 1968: 100). Stewart's definition specifically refers to "those languages which a government has specified as official or declared as appropriate by law." However, Cooper adds another dimension to this list by distinguishing two further types of official language. These are: a language used for day-to-day activities, and a language used mostly for symbolic purposes. Thus, these three types of official languages are referred to by Cooper as: 1) the statutory official language, 2) the working official language, and 3) the symbolic official language. In Singapore, the statutory official languages are Mandarin, Malay, Tamil, and English. This is provided for in the Constitution of the Republic of Singapore, a point that will be discussed later. The working official language in Singapore is English, whereas the symbolic official language, or what we refer to as the National Language, is Malay.

Function of A Provincial or Regional Official Language

This function is not nationwide but limited to a small geographical area (Cooper, 1989: 103). Due to the small size of Singapore (approximately 700 square kilometers) and its status as an island state, there are no provincial or regional official languages.

Function of Language of Wider Communication

Stewart further defines the function of language of wider communication as "a linguistic system predominating as a medium of communication across language boundaries within the nation" (1968, cited in Cooper, 1989: 104). He shows categorically that official or provincial official languages do not come under the language of wider communication label but are in fact separate. Cooper thinks otherwise and concludes that an official or provincial language can also serve the function of language of wider communication. He questions whether there are cases of status planning for languages of wider communication. He believes that there can be if the language is meant for vertical integration, or "a link between ruler and ruled, between center and periphery" (1989: 105).

From the 1950s until the early 1970s, the language of wider communication in Singapore was Malay. The language was the lingua franca in the markets and coffee shops and among neighbors. Even in the work place, knowledge of spoken Malay was a prerequisite for employment, promotion, and job tenure. The media promoted Malay as the language of unity among the people. From the 1970s onward, after Singapore left the Federation of Malaysia in 1965, the government embarked on rapid industrialization and needed skilled workers to ensure Singapore's survival. Thus, English was chosen not only to unify the people but also as a language of trade and commerce, overtaking the status of Malay.

Function of International language

In this respect, Stewart defines such a function as a language that acts as a major medium of communication "which is international in scope" (1968, cited in Cooper, 1989: 106). Stewart also makes reference to languages that function as links between citizens of different countries. Thus, a country may have one language as its working language but may appoint a totally different language for trade and commerce with another country. The main international language at present is English. Previously, when Singapore was part of the Federation of Malaysia, Malay was the lingua franca. Although it functioned more as a regional language, it was used as a link between Singapore and the Malay-speaking world. With independence, Singapore began to turn to English as the language of use at the national level as well as regionally and internationally.

Function of Language of the Capital

This refers to a language that functions as a major medium of communication in and around the capital city of a country. As was indicated earlier, Malay was the language of the capital in Singapore during the time when it was part of the Federation of Malaysia. It was the also medium of communication within the government and amongst its people. The language was thus promoted officially by the government of the day. This began to change upon independence as English overtook Malay in this respect.

Function of Group Language

Stewart refers to this language function as pertaining to "communication among the members of a single cultural or ethnic group, such as tribe, settled group of foreign immigrants, etc." (1968, cited in Cooper, 1989: 107). Each community in Singapore has its own group language. The Chinese had several depending on which part of China they came from, and similarly the Indians even though by and large they came from Tamil Nadu and spoke Tamil. Even though the Malays are made up of populations of Javanese, Boyanese, or Sumatran descent, they speak Malay and embrace the language as their wider group language, or language on intra-ethnic communication. This has remained the case to this day even though English is now widely-used for inter-ethnic communication.

Function of Educational Language

This refers to a language that functions as a medium of instruction in education. In Singapore, this function is now played by English. Since 1985, English has been the only language used for instruction in Singapore's education system. Mother tongue languages such as Mandarin, Malay, and Tamil, are only taught as school subjects. The only other subjects that are taught in the mother tongues are Civics and Moral Education. These consist of a values-laden study of how to be a worthy person and a responsible citizen. Although this is taught using the mother tongue in primary school but is replaced by Social Studies in secondary school and is taught in English.

Function of School Subject

This refers to a language that functions specifically for teaching a particular subject. As we saw, the mother tongue, i.e., Mandarin, Malay, or Tamil is used in Singapore to teach Civics and Moral Education at primary level. However, during the early years of independence until about 1983, there was a Malay education stream, in which particular subjects, including mathematics, science, and economics were taught in Malay. With the phasing out of the Malay schools and the Malay stream due to falling enrollment, the status of Malay as a school subject began to diminish. To date, Malay is only a school subject and is used for teaching Civics and Moral Education at primary level. All other knowledge-based and content-based subjects are now taught in English.

Function of Literary Language

This refers to the use of a language specifically for literary or scholarly purposes. As part of this function, the language is used not only as a language of education. Instead, it is a prestige language used by the elite for writing literary and scholarly works, and it is used as a language of communication in these fields. Singapore used to be the center of Malay literature in the Malay Archipelago. Most printed literary works came out of Singapore, and the literary scene was dynamic. A sign of the importance of Malay as a literary language in Singapore during the 1950s and 1960s was the Third Malay Language and Literary Congress, which brought together renowned writers and language experts from the entire Malay Archipelago and was held in Singapore in 1956. This was an important meeting as it became the trigger for Malay language development later. *Angkatan Sasterawan 50* (Literary Movement 50), better known as Asas 50, was founded in Singapore during the 1950s and is still actively involved in promoting Malay via literary works.

Function of Religious Language

This refers to the use of a language specifically in connection with rituals performed as part of a particular religion. These rituals should be related to three overlapping and related sub-functions of a language functioning as a religious language. Firstly, it is used as a language of exhortation, conversion, and religious instruction. Secondly, it is used to explain the meaning of the sacred texts, thus requiring or promoting sacred-text literacy. Thirdly, it is used in public prayer. Malay is the religious language of Malays. Practically all Malays in Singapore are Muslims, and they learned the religion via Malay, the link language enabling Muslims to learn and understand Islam in the Malay Archipelago. The status of Malay as the religious language of the Malays for the purpose of learning Islam is equivalent to that of English in the learning and understanding of Christianity.

Status Language Planning for Malay

Before 1956, Malay was the lingua franca of Singapore, and it remained so until the early 1970s. Malay has a long history in the region as the language of trade, administration, religion, and wider communication (Ismail, 1981). Its prominence reached its apex when Indonesia chose Malay as its language of national unity during the events referred to as *sumpah pemuda*, or the oath taken by Indonesian youth that was created on October 28, 1928 in the then Dutch East Indies. The young nationalists took this oath to proclaim three ideals for the formation of Indonesia: one motherland, one nation, and one language. That one language was Malay. This occurred even though there were other, more widely used languages in Indonesia, including Javanese, Acehnese, Sunda, Minangkabau, and many others. While Singapore was part of Malaya, Malay was the language of wider communication, especially in its Bazaar Malay form. It received the status of National Language when in June 1959, Singapore gained self-government status and the government rolled out a five-year plan that included the use of Malay as the National Language. It was also subsequently recognized as one of the four official languages, which also included English, Mandarin, and Tamil.

Language Policy in Singapore

After Singapore left the Federation of Malaysia in 1965, there was a shift in Singapore's official language policy from one that was Malay-friendly to one that favored English-knowing bilingualism. According to Pakir (1992), English-knowing bilingualism refers to proficiency in English and one mother tongue that can be chosen from three: Mandarin, Malay, or Tamil. English was chosen in spite of the fact that the population of Singapore consisted of around 77% Chinese, 15% Malays, 7% Indians, and a sprinkling of "Others." English was chosen as it was deemed politically neutral for the three main ethnic groups and thus better able to function as a language of unity. This sense of fair play and fairness for all is another aspect of Singapore's language policy, along with parity theory, that is, equal treatment for the three major ethnic groups.

Malay as National Language

Malay became the National Language of a newly self-governing Singapore in 1959 in spite of the fact that 85% of the population was non-Malays Yet, the People's Action Party (PAP) had since its formation indicated its stand on promoting Malay as a National Language. The first Prime Minister of Singapore, Lee Kuan Yew, indicated this clearly in a parliamentary debate discussing the All-Party Report of 1956, and then went further in promoting Malay as the language of choice for second or third language learning in vernacular schools , stating that

> The Party believes that not only must Malay education in this country be developed beyond primary level as soon as possible, but it should also enjoy undisputed priority over any other language as the compulsory second language to be taught in all schools, be they English, Chinese, or Indian schools... Instead of [offering] a free choice of a second or third language, we wanted to state categorically that Malay should and must be the predominant language in this country. (Singapore Legislative Assembly Debates, Vol. 2, 1956-58, 1st Series: 71)

This shows that the government of the day was committed to a policy of recognizing Malay as the National Language as well as one of the four official languages. According to Tan (2007: 89), the selection of Malay as the National Language was more of "an instrumental political act," bearing in mind Singapore's geographical location at the heart of the Malay-speaking region and especially after its "turbulent separation from Malaysia." In effect, the status of Malay widened further to include the function of language of unity among the many ethnic groups in Singapore, especially since it was the predominant language of the country at that time.

In spite of this widening status, Lee Kuan Yew was aware that changes could not happen overnight and there needed to be proper planning for the promotion of Malay. He reiterated this point clearly when he said:

> I believed in being realistic: Malay would become the most important language once Singapore was part of Malaysia, but the people could not master it overnight. The civil servants who had long used English and the schools which had long used their own respective languages would need time to adapt. (Lee, 2011: 53)

In realizing its language planning goals for Malay, the government aggressively promoted the learning and use of the language in all branches of government and the daily lives of the people. Programs in the National Language were produced for the airwaves, National Language months were organized and promoted, knowledge of the National Language became a prerequisite not only for entry into the civil service but also for promotion, and Malay language classes were organized by the Adult Education Board. In line with this policy, officials in the civil service with knowledge of and competence in the National Language were duly rewarded with bonuses of between $200 and $500 if they obtained Standard II and Standard III Malay, respectively. These initiatives created a "buzz" for the learning of Malay and its use as the National Language of Singapore.

The status of Malay in Singapore received a further boost in 1963, when Singapore became one of the 14 states of newly-independent Malaysia and the implementation and promotion of Malay as the National Language became more intense. Among the additional steps taken to enhance the status of Malay were columns for the learning of Malay in the premier English Language newspaper, the *Straits Times*, additional air time given to programs in Malay on TV and radio, the wider use of Malay as the National Language by the Ministry of Education, and use of the National Language as the main language in public announcements and official state communications (de Souza: 1980).

Even though Singapore left the Federation of Malaysia in August 1965, the status of Malay was enshrined in the Constitution of the Republic of Singapore as the National Language and one of the four official languages of the country. This is indicated in the Singapore Independence Act 1965, which states that

> 7. (1) Malay, Mandarin, Tamil, and English shall be the four official languages in Singapore.
> (2) The national language shall be the Malay language and shall be in the Roman script. (Republic of Singapore Independence Act: Revised Edition 1985)

With this Act, the status of Malay was set in stone and its development for the next ten years reached a pinnacle in modern Singapore. However, enshrinement does not necessarily mean status quo. With independence, the status of Malay declined in terms of its use within government agencies as well as in the media and education. There was a sense that emphasis on the learning of the National Language had plateaued, especially after separation from Malaysia and as a result of the need for Singapore to look beyond the region for investment and economic success.

> It became obvious that Malay – the National Language – was
> not destined to serve as the main medium of instruction in a
> national school system of the future or to assume the functions
> of a chief working language. (de Souza, 1980: 212)

This concern was not unwarranted, as we will see later. For now, however, the status of Malay as the National language and one of the four Official Languages remained intact. As a symbolic language, Malay still plays an important role in official ceremonies as the national anthem, *Majulah Singapura*, is in Malay, and commands given during National Day parades are also in Malay. However, despite these symbolic gestures involving the National Language, there have long been signs of the diminishing importance of the language.

Among early signs was the closure in 1969 of the National Language and Culture Council, whose main task was to promote the use of the National Language. The media also slowly did away with programs in the National Language, taking away the air time previously devoted to promoting Malay. Taken away were also the bonuses previously given to civil servants proficient in the Malay language. In their place was the implementation of a pay incentive scheme for non-graduate teachers who obtained distinctions in English, English Literature, and Mathematics in their GCE "O" Level examinations. Knowledge of the National Language as a prerequisite to job tenure and citizenship status were also done away with, and in their place, knowledge of any one of the official languages sufficed. Public notices and road signs were changed to not only use Malay, but greater emphasis was given to the use of English. Lastly, Malay was taught only to Malay students and not as a compulsory second or third language in other vernacular or English-medium schools.

Thus, even though Malay maintained its status as the National Language and one of the four Official Languages, it lost its status as the language of unity, administration, and wider communication. As was indicated by a language and cultural expert, Ariff Ahmad,

> Due to the fact that "national" is a terminology of politics, the role of the language is determined by the political forces. In short, the development of the language is inherent in the development of the politics surrounding it. (Singapore Malay Teachers' Union 25th Anniversary Book: 1972)

Malay as Official Language

An official language is a language used in an official function or in the administration of a country. Thus, Malay, as one of the four official languages along with English, Mandarin, and Tamil, can be – and should be – used in an official capacity. The most official platform in this context is parliamentary debates. In Singapore, these can be conducted in any of the four official languages. Although the use of the official languages was introduced in 1958, it is still enforced today. As indicated in the Parliament of Singapore website,

> A Member participating in a debate may use any or all of the four official languages in his speech. To facilitate understanding by all Members, simultaneous interpretation is provided in the Chamber. (PMO, downloaded 2012)

The official language is also used at all entry and exit points in Singapore. At the Changi International Airport, signs are in the four official languages even though English is the language of choice in most instances. Announcements within the public transport system are in the four official languages. In the Mass Rapid Transit system (MRT), announcements on arrivals and departures as well as general information are read out in the four official languages, beginning with English and followed by Mandarin, then Malay, and lastly Tamil. The four official languages are also used in general announcements, public notices, and traffic advisories. These are either in English only, English and Mandarin, or all four official languages (English, Mandarin, Malay, and Tamil).

Malay as a Language of Cultural Transmission ("Cultural Ballast")

The learning of Malay (and also that of Mandarin and Tamil) is meant to act as "cultural ballast" given the ever-widening use of English within schools and society at large. Thus, the status of Malay as a language of cultural transmission was reinforced by then Prime Minister Lee Kuan Yew, in his reply to Minister for Education Goh Keng Swee and in his report on the state of the bilingual system of education in 1978. According to Lee (MOE, 1979: iii),

> A language can be taught in the schools. But unless what is taught in school is reinforced by daily use, it cannot become a natural part of their lives.

Subsequently, Lee reiterated the point that there should be a balance between the use of English and the mother tongues.

> The best of the East and of the West must be blended to advantage in the Singaporean. Confucian ethics, Malay traditions, and the Hindu ethos must be combined with skeptical Western methods of scientific inquiry, the open discursive method in the search for the truth. (MOE, 1979: iv)

Lastly, Lee clearly indicated the importance of teaching the mother tongue.

> The principal value of teaching the second language is the importance of moral values and understanding of cultural traditions.

Thus, the mother tongue plays the role of cultural ballast relative to the ever-widening use of English within the community, given that "language and culture are organic and evolve constantly in accordance with changing times. Their true value lies in helping a person meet changing circumstances." (Lee, 2011: 75).

Malay as Language of Religion (Link Language)

Malay is considered the de facto official language of Islam in the Malay Archipelago beside Arabic, which is the original language of scripture. Its status as a link language to the learning of Islam in the region is well documented.

The use of Malay as a link language for Islam has its roots in the Malacca Sultanate in the 15th century, when Islam came to the shores of the Malay Archipelago via Indian traders bringing spices and silk along with their beliefs. Alisjahbana (1977) argues that the ease with which Malay became used as the link language for the learning of Islam was due to the language's simplicity in terms of form and function. Al-Attas (1972) also noted the choice of Malay as the language chosen by early missionaries due to its status as a lingua franca in the region and to the fact that it was "not an aesthetic religious language like Javanese." Asmah (2005) echoes the same sentiment by showing that Malay had by then achieved H-language status as it was the language of governance and diplomacy as well as the lingua franca of the region and was also the link language for the spread not only of Islam but also of Hinduism and Buddhism.

Another factor that reinforced the status of Malay as a link language with Islam was the substitution of the old Malay script, which was of Indian derivation, for a Jawi script based on "all the 29 letters of the Arabic alphabet together with five newly invented non-Arabic letters to suit the tongue of the Malays" (Sa'eda: 2010: 39). This happened when Islam came to the Malay states in particular during the Malacca Sultanate during the early 15th century. Sa'eda stresses that, thanks to this new script, Malay flourished and evolved from its traditional oral roots to a literary status.

Language of Exhortation, Conversion, and Religious Instruction

As a language of exhortation, conversion, and religious instruction, Malay is the link language in terms of religious instruction for Islam in Singapore and across the Malay Archipelago. The bond between language and religion is so strong that when non-Malays convert to Islam, they were often referred to in the old days as *masuk Melayu, or* entering and being a Malay, and nowadays simply as a *saudara baru*, or a new family member. Although more through persuasion than exhortation, Malay thrived as a link language that helped the spread of Islam. In Singapore, all dealings concerning the religion are conducted in Malay. There are a total of 69 mosques in Singapore, catering mainly to the Malay-speaking community. Although there are a few mosques that cater to the Indian-Muslim community and that use only Tamil in their religious instruction, the majority use Malay during religious instruction. Even though the Muslim Converts Association of Singapore, or Darul Arqam, an organization that is only 32 years old, is the only Muslim organization that runs religious classes in English, Malay is is used predominantly in the religious schools, or *madrasah*. Sa'eda (2010) conducted a historical survey of 19 *madrasah* in the late 1950s and observed that 65.5% offered Malay under the heading of Writing and Grammar. Thus, Malay has gained in prominence as a language of knowledge.

Learning of Scripture and Religious Instruction

The learning of scripture and religious classes are mostly held in Malay. Most Malay-owned bookstores stock a substantial amount of Islamic books in Malay, published either locally or imported from Indonesia or Malaysia. Before the turn of the 21st century, it was difficult to purchase a book on aspects of Islam in English. Well-known bookstores such as the Malaya Publishing House, or MPH, did not cater for interested readers who might be looking for Islamic books. Only with the coming of mega-bookstores such as Borders and Kinokuniya did we see the appearance of English language books dealing with issues on Islam, though not necessarily with those related to learning Islamic rituals such as prayers.

Language of Public Prayer

Although prayers are conducted in Arabic, Friday sermons are normally delivered or read out in Malay. However, the use of Malay is not restricted to the Friday sermons but also covers all other forms of public prayer that do not involve the use of Arabic. Although there has lately been encroachment by English in this domain, especially after the 9/11 bombings, there has been a marked increase in the number of sermons delivered in English at mosques during Friday prayers. The website of the Islamic Religious Council of Singapore shows that in 2011, out of a total of 69 mosques over a period of 52 Fridays in that year, 394 sermons were delivered in English as against 3,588 in Malay, with the rest consisting of 52 in Tamil. In terms of percentages, 11% of all Friday sermons in 2011 were delivered in English as compared to 87.6% in Malay. However, in 2010, only 107 Friday sermons, or a total of only 3%, had been delivered in English. This 8% spike shows the encroachment of English into the Malay domain, which could potentially affect the status of Malay as the link language for Islamic religious practices. Nevertheless, sermons for major Islamic celebrations such as *Eid* are still delivered in Malay.

This increasing use of English in the religious domain is seen as a positive factor by the Minister-in-Charge of Muslim Affairs, Dr Yaacob Ibrahim. In a speech given at the Islamic Religious Council of Singapore's Work Plan Seminar in 2009, he reiterated the importance of diversity in Islam in the following terms,

> Islam embraces diversity. And the Singapore Muslim community is indeed a diverse one in its roots. Although mainly Malay, we also have a good number hailing from South Asia and the Hadramaut region in the Arabian Peninsula. Over the many decades, they have contributed much and blended with the locals to become what we locally term as the Malay/Muslim community. The community must now similarly be open to new arrivals who may not speak Malay or be familiar with the local culture. (Islamic Religious Council of Singapore, 2009) www. muis.gov.sg/cmc/news/speeches)

The use of English in Islam was studied by Vaish (2008). She indicated that Malays predominantly use Malay in the domain of religion. In her survey conducted, 79.5% of respondents indicated that they use Malay in the domain of religion, while only 3.7% said that they use English. Thus, Vaish indicated that Malay remains the dominant language in the domain of religion within the Malay community.

However, there has been a rise in the use of English and the repositioning of Malay within the *madrasah* system of education. Sa'eda (2010) suggested that there is a face-off between the two languages, with Malay coming out the worse for it. In responding to globalization and a knowledge-based economy, Malay has had to give way to English even in Islamic education. As Sa'eda explained,

> English is widely accepted as a universal language, deemed better able to equip students with communicative skills for future economic and technological advancement. (Sa'eda, 2010: 48)

A similar step was also taken by the Islamic Religious Council of Singapore (MUIS), which runs three of the six full-time *madrasah*, after analyzing the 2000 population census, which shows that 7.9% of the Malay/Muslim community stated English as their home language. In fact, this wider usage of English among the Malay community at home has been on the rise based on the 1990 and 2000 censuses. Thus, MUIS believes that switching to English, especially in an English-knowing bilingual framework, will enhance *madrasah* students' mastery of English and improve their performance in academic subjects and examination. This may be so for national schools, but if the sole purpose of madrasahs is to develop students into religious leaders, the emphasis should not just be on English and academic subjects but on their core business i.e. subjects on Islam which predominantly need to be taught in Arabic.

Status of Malay

Currently, Malay is the National Language of Singapore and one of the four official languages, the other three being English, Mandarin, and Tamil. English is also the designated language of administration and commerce. The status of

Malay is first mentioned in the Singapore Constitution, Part XIII of the General Provisions, which states that:

> The Government shall exercise its functions in such manner as to recognize the special position of the Malays, who are the indigenous people of Singapore, and accordingly it shall be the responsibility of the Government to protect, safeguard, support, foster, and promote their political, educational, religious, economic, social, and cultural interests and the Malay language. (Article 152 (2) Minorities and Special Position of Malays, Constitution of the Republic of Singapore)

The above Article categorically states the duty of the government concerning the special position of the Malays and its duty not only to protect the Malays' political, educational, religious, economic, social, and cultural interests but also the Malay language. This clearly defines the official status of Malay in Singapore not only as one of the four official languages but as the National Language of the Republic.

Impact of Bilingualism on Status Planning

There is a mix of impacts on the status planning of Malay due to the bilingual policy. Firstly, there is the positive impact of Malay as the language of cultural transmission. Within the bilingual policy and the English-knowing bilingual framework, the status of Malay as a language of cultural transmission and enhancement as well as a repository of values is cast in stone. The language becomes much more important as a result of having a clear goal and function, and its status as a language carrying values gives it credibility as well a high status. A second positive impact is its status as a literary language. As language and literature go hand in hand, Malay acts as a tool in cultural education. Lastly, its function as an official language is enshrined in the Constitution and thus remains firm, thus forming an important component of Singapore's language policy.

In terms of negative impact, the status of Malay as a group language and language of wider communication has diminished. Even though the use of the language is strong within the Malay community in certain domains, especially that of religion, English has started to creep in and will gain a stronger foothold as time goes by. As a language of wider communication, Malay has been overtaken by English and is only spoken by the older generation, or those who grew up in the 1950s and 1960s within the Federation of Malaysia. Further impact is also being felt in terms of Malay as an educational language and a school subject. It is now only taught as a subject as part of teaching the language itself along with values via Civics and Moral Education at primary level. A greater impact has been the receding status of Malay as the link language for the teaching and learning of Islam as well as its practice, a domain that is slowly being encroached upon by English.

Malay used to be promoted via the National Language Month, which was organized by a government agency under the purview of the Ministry of Culture called the National Language and Cultural Institute (Dewan Bahasa Kebangsaan dan Kebudayaan). The Institute, which was set up via the Dewan Bahasa Kebangsaan dan Kebudayaan Ordinance 1960, is aimed at promoting the National Language and promoting the Malayan culture (Straits Times, 8 April 1960, page 7). With an annual budget of $200,000 it was tasked with "enrich[ing] and develop[ing] the Malay language into an adequate and comprehensive medium of expression as well as to spread the national language among non-Malays." The other objectives outlined under the bill were to:

- Conduct research into the national language and literature;
- Simplify Malay so as to give as many people as possible a working knowledge of the language in the shortest possible time as well as to provide suitable reading material to achieve this aim;
- Standardize the spelling and pronunciation of the national language as regards both spoken and written Malay;
- Guide and nurture the evolution of a Malayan culture;

- Encourage and develop literary talent in the national as well as other languages but with the aim of fostering the growth of a Malayan culture and consciousness;

- Publish or help in the publication of Malay, Chinese, Tamil. and English books as well as pamphlets;

- Translate local and foreign books that would nourish and raise the standards of Malayan culture;

- Encourage the study of and research into various aspects of local cultures;

- Publish textbooks with a Malayan emphasis in cooperation with the Ministry of Education;

- Publish a journal dealing with linguistic and cultural matters; and

- Encourage, and where necessary, provide facilities for the active development of Malayan fine arts.

This long list of objectives and the $200,000 budget gives sense of the importance of Malay in 1960 as compared to the present.

Presently, the Malay Language Month is celebrated annually for a month but not at a national scale as the target is only the Malay-speaking community. It is organized by a government agency under the purview of the Ministry of Information, Communications and the Arts (MICA), with a budget of only $60,000. This is a clear indication of the reduced status of Malay from being a truly national language that is a language of unity, culture, and knowledge to one that is a symbolic national language owing to its past and now more of a heritage language.

Given that bilingualism is the cornerstone of Singapore's language policy and ideology, Tan (2007: 78) lists four key principles supporting it. These are: 1) The "state-ascribed mother tongue policy," whereby English is the language of knowledge and commerce; 2) The "state-ascribed mother tongue," namely Mandarin, Malay, and Tamil acting as "cultural transmission vehicle providing each race with the critical cultural ballast;" 3) "The creation of a core of cultural elites for each race with urgency being accorded to the Chinese language;" and 4) "A pragmatic approach to the learning of mother tongues and the fundamental of economic relevance in language planning." It is precisely this policy that has affected the status of Malay. There are positive and negative effects. Positive because Malay is able to 'ride on' the 'cultural transmission' vehicle even though it's a minority language and receives funding for its development. Negative because it gets overshadowed by the "urgency being accorded to the Chinese language". Chinese language gets first priority in terms of needs e.g. SAP schools, review committees etc. Malay and Tamil will follow suit only after the Chinese language problem has been addressed. Thus, the Malay language planning has never been based on the real needs of the Malay language itself.

These findings echo those of Pakir (2004b), which show that the bilingual policy has led (perhaps inevitably) to an increase in the use of both English and Mandarin across all domains. This downward spiral in terms of status was also highlighted by Alsagoff (2008) when she indicated that Malay started off as a language that "foster[ed] national identity and understanding among the races" but ended up as "a language of Singapore Malay ethnic identity." Bokhorst-Heng (1988) also highlights the same point when she notes that the shift began in 1982, when the Malay Language Month became a campaign for Malay as a language for Malays and not as a language for the general population.

Conclusion

As we can see, the status of Malay has been maintained in terms of its official status as the National language and as one of the four Official Languages. Nevertheless, Malay has become more of a symbolic language rather than one that spreads its domain of use. This occurred as a result of the emphasis on English as the language of wider communication in government as well as in education.

In fact, its domain has shrunk, especially in the field of religion. Thus, there needs to be overt status planning for Malay so as not to erode further its position within as well as without the community. One area where this can be done will be a reconstruction of the status of Malay on grounds of linguistic instrumentalism.

Being a pragmatic society, Singaporeans at large can reinvigorate the status of the language and go beyond it being simply a cultural repository but turn it into a commodity that will bring benefits to the community and contribute to the economy, just as occurred to Mandarin as a result of the rise of China.

4

Corpus Planning

Following on from the previous discussion of issues related to status planning, this chapter will analyze corpus planning for Malay from a historical perspective. Since the historical development of Malay in Singapore is intrinsically linked to that of Malaysia, there is a need to review developments in that country so as to make sense of the issues involved. This chapter will first explain the concept of corpus planning based on Cooper's (1989) model. It will then present a historical journey through the development of corpus planning for Malay along with issues surrounding the standardization of the language itself and its implementation in Singapore.

Corpus Planning

Corpus planning focuses on change through deliberate planning to the actual corpus, or form, of a language. Cooper (1989) applies to corpus planning the concept of "form follows function," which is derived from the field of architecture. According to Cooper, form follows function in corpus planning in two ways: firstly, via design based on a given function, overt or covert, which can be served by a modification or treatment of the corpus. The given functions can refer to communicative functions of the language. The example given in Cooper is drawn from the late nineteenth and early twentieth century Palestinian Jews, who started to use Hebrew as a medium of instruction in settlement schools. Language planners had to find or create terms so that teachers and students could use them to discuss issues in the classroom. Thus form followed function, that is, terminologies were created to meet the needs of a given function, namely to provide a tool for communication.

History has shown that not all corpus planning arose out of the need for new communicative function but more for symbolic purposes. An example given by Cooper is that of the United States in the 1960s. At the time, activists promoted the use of the word "negro" when referring to someone of African descent and "gay" when referring to someone of homosexual orientation. The use of non-androcentric generics of this type and of easily understood words were meant to – and eventually did – enhance the power of gays, blacks, women, and consumers as well as that of the leaders who propagated these terms. Here, their given function was not as a tool for communication in nature but as a symbolic gesture of freedom of expression.

Categories of Corpus Planning

Cooper outlines three traditional primary categories in corpus planning, namely graphization, standardization, and modernization. Additionally, there are two further categories: codification and elaboration. However, these are subsumed by Cooper under the rubrics of standardization and modernization, respectively. Cooper further suggested a fourth major category, namely renovation.

Graphization

Graphization is the process of reducing the form of the language to writing. In terms of the development of the Malay language in Singapore before 1956, the writing form used was the Jawi script. Post-1956, at the Asas 50 Malay language conference, conference participants agreed to propagate and popularize the use of Malay in the romanized form instead of the Jawi script. The Jawi script is a form of writing that is more akin to the Arabic script but with some additional letters to represent sounds that are inherent to Malay. This monumental change in approach resulted in the Malay language being used even more widely and effectively becoming the lingua franca, which aided the development of Malay itself among non-native Malay speakers (Sa'eda, 2010).

Standardization

The main reason for the existence of languages is their role as means of communication. It is this need that also determined the reason for the standardization of languages. According to Rubin (1977), all human interaction requires a degree of standardization. If each participant in an interaction process uses different norms, then there will be a communication breakdown. Cooper (1989:132) adds that

> When communication is largely confined to the local community, in which most people know one another and interact mainly with one another, regional and national variants pose few problems. When networks expand beyond the local community, local variants may impede communication.

There lies the need for the standardization of language. There are essentially two ways in which language standardization takes place: as a result of unplanned evolution, or through a process of overt planning.

Ferguson (1962: 10), explains the criteria that need to be met for a properly standardized language. According to him,

> [the] ideal standardization refers to a language which has a single, widely accepted norm which is felt to be appropriate, with only minor modifications or variations for all purposes for which the language is used. Differences between regional variants, social levels, speaking, and writing, and so on are quite small.

Thus, even in standardization, there is room for minor changes or modifications as absolute uniformity is ultimately impossible.

According to Cooper (1989), the standardization of written varieties has typically been more successful than the standardization of spoken varieties. He outlines three main reasons for this. Firstly, the need for a single standard written variety is greater than that for a single standard spoken variety. This greater need then creates a push for standardization since the benefits are clearer. A formalized and standardized written form outwardly helps in the teaching and learning process as well as in use of the language in printed form. Secondly, a written standard is easier to impart via schooling as a standard literary variety, which students acquire from the start of their studies, than to impose uniformity a variety the students do not already speak when they enter school. Therefore, students do not have baggage attributed to the written form since they will learn it in the formal surrounding of the classroom only. Thirdly, writers can usually exercise more control over their writing than speakers can exert over their speech. It is always possible to erase or edit writing before publishing it. However, what is to be said cannot be edited and what has been said cannot be retracted. This element of spontaneity in spoken language makes standardization difficult.

A good example is English, where an essentially standardized written form exists with only minor differences in spelling and vocabulary across the Anglophone world, whereas numerous regional and national varieties of spoken English co-exist.

Codification

Codification refers to written rules pertaining to the language, and the root word "code" implies a set of written rules explaining the formation of words and sentences along with their structures. Codification is an integral cog in the standardization process. Rubin (1977, cited in Cooper, 1989: 144) divides the standardization process into six parts. The first three are the isolation of a norm, followed by the evaluation of this norm, whether it is "correct" or "preferred," and lastly, the prescription of the norm for specified contexts or functions. According to Rubin, the first three steps always occur together, and if the prescription goes unnoticed, standardization will ultimately fail. In order for standardization to take effect, the prescribed norm must be accepted by the community, be used by its members, and remain in effect until a replacement of the norm takes place.

Modernization

Modernization refers to the process of a language becoming "an appropriate medium of communication for modern topics and forms of discourse" (Cooper:

1989, 149). In other words, it is a process that permits a language to fulfill new communicative functions. The functions mentioned can either be new to the community or have formerly been fulfilled by another language. There is then rapid expansion as well as the enhancement and application of this new knowledge to the economy and the well-being of the people in modern societies. Thus, there is a need for language modernization to meet demands within this new framework. This is also sometimes referred to as elaboration, where the new knowledge and technology requires the crafting of new terminologies by industrialists and technologists, who demand new genres and forms of discourse.

As a result of globalization and the information age, there is a greater need to produce terminologies that can be used and accepted within modern modes of discourse. Thus, coining new terms becomes imperative in the modernization of a language. In this respect, Cooper (1989) highlights the fact that language planners face two alternatives. Firstly, terms can be built from indigenous sources. This can be done either by giving a new meaning to an existing word, by creating a term based on an indigenous root, or by translating from a foreign term. However, the easiest approach is to borrow a word from a foreign language.

In spite of this seemingly straightforward method of creating a term either based on indigenous sources or directly borrowed from a foreign word, creators face a conflict of goals. This was pointed out earlier by Jernudd (1977, cited in Cooper, 1989: 151) in cases where it is necessary to balance the goals of wanting the terms to be readily understood within the target speech community and to facilitate communication beyond the borders of the country. Although the two ends are incompatible, there are good reasons for a language planner to consider both in the process of creating terminology.

Renovation

Renovation is an effort to change an already developed code, whether in the name of efficiency, aesthetics, or national or political ideology. According to Cooper (1989: 154),

Replacement or reform of an existing writing system is not graphization but regraphization. Purification of an already standard language is not standardization but restandardization.

A language that has been thus renovated fulfills no new communicative functions. A renovated language that carries old communicative functions carries with it the non-linguistic goals that ultimately motivated the linguistic renovation. These non-linguistic goals may include the legitimatization of new elites and effectively discredit old ones, the mobilization of political support, or the raising of consciousness. By contrast, modernization serves a different function since it permits language codes to serve new communicative functions. The difference is that renovation only permits the language codes to serve old functions in new ways. Therefore, effective corpus planning is a process that requires a delicate balancing act. It balances the old and the new as well as traditionalism and rationality.

Corpus Planning for Malay

Before the advent of Islam in the Malay Archipelago, Malay already had a writing tradition in the form of the Lampung or Rencong scripts. According to Rogayah (2010), the writing system was quite developed and used syllabic symbols and symbolic lines to show differences in sound. With the coming of Islam, the Malays started to use a writing system more akin to that of Arabic. This system, which was also known as the Jawi system, faced a daunting challenge when the British came to Malaya and introduced the Roman alphabet through the colonial administration. In addition, printing and publication facilities that were more roman-alphabet-friendly dealt a severe blow to the development of the Jawi system of writing. The decision in 1956 during the Third Malay Language and Literary Congress to adopt the romanized writing system dealt a fatal and final blow to the development of the Jawi script. The script is still used today but only as a cultural repository, to remind Malays of a bygone era.

Corpus planning for Malay has evolved from a process that is arbitrary to one that is planned. According to Ghazali (1974), there were two ways in which Malay developed: via an arbitrary process of coining, shortening, and joining words, and later through a planned process of corpus planning that was meant to modernize and unite the use of the language within the Malay Archipelago. This section of the chapter will outline corpus planning for Malay in the region, including Singapore.

Corpus Planning in the Region

In terms of the history of Malay corpus planning in the region, there have been instances of cooperation, especially between the two "superpowers" of the language: Indonesia and Malaysia. Even though Indonesia refers to the language as Bahasa Indonesia and Malaysia has switched between Bahasa Melayu and Bahasa Malaysia over the years, they are largely one and the same. This linguistic cooperation began as early as 1959, when both countries signed the Treaty of Friendship between the Federation of Malaya and the Republic of Indonesia. Article 6 of the accord categorically stated both countries' intent to work together toward the development of Malay:

> The two High Contracting Parties, conscious of the fact that the Malay and Indonesian languages have a common origin, shall strive through cooperation, collaboration, and consultation to achieve the greatest possible uniformity in their use and development. (Asmah, 2004: 4)

Thus the agreement was for both countries to cooperate, collaborate, and consult over the development of their languages so as to achieve uniformity in their use and development. This was an important development as it opened the possibility of further development of the language in the Malay-speaking region of Southeast Asia known as Nusantara which includes Indonesia, Malaysia, Brunei and Singapore. One of the outcomes of this agreement was a discussion of a standard spelling system called the Melindo spelling. Even though the system did not materialize as expected, it was an important start for the two superpowers to meet and agree to work together in developing the language regionally.

In 1972, a more concrete agreement was signed by the two countries. This agreement was important as it was considered a prototype of a firmer agreement signed in 1985, which included Brunei Darussalam, one of the four countries in the region that have Malay as their national and/or administrative language. The 1972 agreement was referred to as *Majlis Bahasa Indonesia-Malaysia*, or Language Council of Indonesia-Malaysia (MBIM). The 1985 agreement was referred to as *Majlis Bahasa Brunei Darussalam-Indonesia-Malaysia*, or the Language Council of Brunei Darussalam-Indonesia-Malaysia (MABBIM). An important aspect of this naming process is the non-appearance of the word "Malay." Asmah (2004: 2) highlights this and explains the rationale as follows:

> "The responsibility and activity of the organization is the development of the Malay/Malaysia/Indonesia language, i.e., the national language and language of wider communication in the three countries.

Therefore, she adds,

> It is not important to include the word Malay in naming the organization as it is not important what the language is called. What is important is that the language be the basis of social life in the three countries mentioned, hence Bahasa Melayu in Brunei, Bahasa Indonesia in Indonesia, and Bahasa Malaysia in Malaysia.

History of Corpus Planning for Malay

Long before the formation of MABBIM, Malay language planning for both status and corpus had been conducted via the Malay Language and Literary Congress since 1952. This congress, which was initially attended by organizations in Malaya and later Indonesia, served as a platform for discussing and proposing planning for the use of Malay in the public domain and in administration. Language-in-education planning was also touched upon during the congress, which was well attended by academics, educationists, practitioners of Malay language, and literary figures.

Malay Language and Literary Congress I (1952)

The main motivating force for the congress was the Malay literary organization Angkatan Sasterawan 50, better known as Asas 50. This organization was formed on August 6, 1950 and became the de-facto language planning body for Malay before *Bahasa* and *Pustaka*, or the Institute of Language and Literature, was formed and MABBIM even existed. As Asas 50 is based in Singapore, it was therefore apt that the first Malay Language and Literary Congress in 1952 be held there. The congress was attended by 72 representatives from the organizing committee and 20 language and literary societies and government agencies from Malaya.

The discussion for the first congress centered around three main themes. Firstly, there was a need to unite all literary societies in Malaya, Singapore, and North Borneo. Secondly, the organization was to act as the decision maker in the development of Malay language and literature. Lastly, discussions centered on the need to fight for the rights of writers and other users of Malay (Abdullah, 2007). The congress was a success as far as Asas 50 was concerned as it served as a platform for the literary society to act as the de-facto language planning institution in Malaya and Singapore as well as in Borneo at that time. It also acted as confirmation of Asas 50 as a body fighting for the rights of Malay writers.

Malay Language and Literary Congress II (1954)

The second congress was held two years later in Negeri Sembilan, Malaya. The congress was attended by 68 representatives, including the organizing committee and 24 organizations and government agencies, of which five had observer status only. The issues discussed during the congress had expanded from the previous meeting. This time around, the issues brought up were more specific and required greater cooperation with another "superpower" in the Malay-speaking region, namely Indonesia. The issues discussed included promoting the use of the romanized script for Malay writing and greater cooperation between writers in Malaya and Indonesia. The congress also proposed the unification of the Malay and Indonesian languages as well as a uniform spelling system. Lastly, the congress discussed the need to publish a Malay dictionary (Abdullah, 2007).

Malay Language and Literary Congress III (1956)

The third congress was the most important of all in terms of Malay corpus planning and standardization of the language. It was held in at the then University of Malaya in Singapore. Among the issues discussed was the use of Malay in education, popularizing the use of the romanized writing and spelling system, the need for unity in matters of Malay language, the fact that Bahasa Indonesia was synonymous to Malay, the need to have an authoritative body for Malay in Malaya similar to *Balai Pustaka* in Indonesia, the development of a Malay library, the development of a working relationship with Indonesia on matters pertaining to language, terminologies, publications, and the wider development of Malay in all areas and fields.

Significance of the Third Congress for the future of Malay Language Planning in Singapore

As was mentioned earlier, the proposal and resolutions passed by the Third Congress had a direct impact on the development of Malay, especially in terms of both status and corpus planning in the future. Among the significant resolutions passed based on the proposals presented were the setting up of the Malay Language and Literary body *Dewan Bahasa* and *Pustaka* (DBP), a proposal for the status of Malay and its domain of use, a proposal to form a committee to look at terminologies for use in the arts, and most importantly the issue of standardizing spelling and speech forms (Abdullah, 2007).

Dewan Bahasa and *Pustaka* (DBP)

The setting up of DBP was meant as a move to centralize and control the development of Malay, particularly in Malaya and Singapore. The proposal set out two main objectives for the setting up of DBP. These were, firstly, for the organization to be the center for the development of Malay language and literature in order to benefit the Malayan peoples' cultural development and understanding among them. Secondly, the DBP's role was to investigate, explore, collect, and refine traditional Malay literature (Abdullah, 2007). Given these two objectives, it seems that as early as 1956, the learning and use of Malay was linked to culture and how it might be possible to maintain and, if possible, to enhance it. This is equivalent to modern Singapore's bilingual policy, in which the learning of any one of the three mother tongues acts as "cultural ballast" to the ever-increasing use of English in our daily lives.

Proposal for the status of Malay and its domain of use

The main proposal was for Malay, which was already the National Language, to be made the Official Language of Malaya and Singapore. In this respect, there were also proposals for Malay to be made the language of administration, commerce, education, and the learning of Islam. Thus, the congress proposed the wider use of the language. In addition, non-native speakers and foreigners were to be given the opportunity to learn the language in a structured manner so that they could be assimilated into the larger Malayan community. This overt language planning proposal gave Malay a higher status not only as a National and Official Language but also as a language of wider communication in schools, markets, offices, and the judiciary (Abdullah, 2007).

Standardizing Spelling and Speech Forms

This was the most important proposal of all as it had a far reaching effect on the development of Malay not only in Malaya and Singapore but also the region as a whole. One of the most important proposals was for the standardization of the spelling of Malay. The proposal for policies regarding the spelling of Malay in the romanized form was as follows:

1. Spellings in Malay and Indonesia should be equated or combined;
2. Spelling rules must be simple and use the phonological system where emphasis is on patterns of sounds with the knowledge of how the patterns of sound is made as against the phonetic system where emphasis is on the production of speech sounds without prior knowledge of the language

needed, and each phoneme should be represented by just one letter of the alphabet;

3. The spelling system should be consistent and based on one method; and

4. Foreign loan words should follow the rules of the Malay phonological system. (Abdullah, 2007: 45)

Among other things, the congress proposed then addition of two phonemes to the Malay language from the 18 original consonant phonemes and six vowel phonemes, namely the two consonants /sh/ and /z/. The congress also proposed that there be three Malay diphthongs, namely /ay/, /aw/, and /oy/.

Another important proposal that impacted Malay as it had been spoken in the region affected overall pronunciation. The congress deliberated and came to the conclusion that the Johor-Riau spoken variety was not to be considered the standard for the modern age. Based on a paper presented during the congress, the committee on spelling and language sounds accepted that the sound of the vowel /a/ in the last syllable of any word should be /a/ and not /e/. This was a defining moment for the development of Malay in Singapore and the region as the standard spoken Malay shifted from the Johor-Riau variety to one that was more northern and, some may say, even Indonesian.

Thus, it seems apt that Malay was impacted twice by decisions made in 1956. Firstly, the All-Party Report set in motion the bilingual policy in Singapore, and secondly, the standard spoken variety changed from Johor-Riau to one that was different from the Singapore norm. However, nothing much happened from 1956 onward as the next congress was only held 28 years later in 1984, with a different worldview by that time, Malaysia and Singapore having become separate entities. By then, the main mover was the DBP, a government agency within the Ministry of Education in Malaysia, with powers given to it under the DBP Statute of 1959, whereas Asas 50 remained a non-governmental organization in Singapore.

Malay Language and Literary Congress IV (1984)

The fourth congress was held at the DBP in Kuala Lumpur, Malaysia December 7-10, 1984 and marked only the second time in its history that it would be reviewing the role and functions of the DBP and its effectiveness in promoting and enhancing Malay language development. The congress was well attended and represented 14 government and non-government agencies from Malaysia (Abdullah, 2007). The congress had turned into a Malaysia-centric meeting of Malay language and literary organizations within Malaysia, with the aim of taking a fresh look at their role in Malay language development in the country as well as within the region. There were also representations from Malay-speaking countries around the region, including Brunei Darussalam, Indonesia, Singapore, and Thailand as well as a number of European countries.

Among the issues discussed was the development of Malay in the Malay Archipelago and the need to set up a Regional Malay Language Centre modeled on the Regional English Language Centre (RELC) in Singapore (Abdullah, 2007), which was set up by the Southeast Asia Ministers of Education Organization (SEAMEO). SEAMEO was founded in 1968 by the education ministers of participating countries to increase proficiency in the use of English within the region as the language was considered essential for economic, social, scientific, and technological advancement. The proposal, which was made by four language experts from Malaysia, stated the role of the Malay Language Centre as one where research and teaching in the language as a vehicle for knowledge could be planned and where an open and wider understanding of the role of the language in the Malay Archipelago could be built, unconstrained by geopolitical limitations. There was also a proposal to build a normative form for Malay development and to coordinate Malay language curriculum development within the region.

However, this Malaysia-centric outlook and the subsequent discussion failed to take into account the language planning ideology in other Malay-speaking countries in the region. Yet, participants to the congress were aware of the limitations they were facing in unifying Malay in the region. They listed eight reasons for these limitations. These were:

1. The haphazard development of the language;

2. The influence of vernacular languages and dialects;

3. Prejudices and emotions;

4. Attitudes toward former colonial languages;

5. Implementation that ran contrary to philosophy, ambition, and policy;

6. Developments in the field of descriptive linguistics;

7. Failure by one country to understand the problems or limitations in another country; and

8. Failure to realize the importance and benefits of a union. (Abdullah, 2007: 390)

After deliberating on these problems, the congress made recommendations to address the situation. Firstly, it recommended that a coordinated Malay language curriculum be established in all schools within the region and an exchange of reading materials among Malay-speaking countries be implemented so as to widen understanding and cement the union in the region. Secondly, they propagated the teaching of standard (*baku*) Malay at all levels of schooling in order to address the haphazard development of the language and to counter influences from vernacular languages as well as dialects. Thirdly, they agreed to promote Malay as the language of the Archipelago. To achieve this, it was proposed that language and cultural bodies in Malaysia involve Brunei, Southern Thailand, and Singapore as well as Indonesia in their activities. Fourthly, in strengthening the union and enhancing the language, there should a greater effort to exchange ideas and publications at the academic level within the region. Fifthly, as a name change would give greater vision to the current council, this body should be renamed *Majlis Bahasa Melayu Nusantara* (MBMN), or Malay Language Council of the Archipelago to depict its new status as the language planning body for the Malay Archipelago and not just of the three countries originally named. Sixthly, the newly named council should redouble its efforts to standardize Malay in terms of grammar, speech forms, and the spelling system, and the policy on word creation should be strictly adhered to. As a result, the language would be able to realize its full potential within the region. Lastly, the committee was to make recommendations to SEAMEO to set up a Malay Language Centre modeled on RELC for the English Language and to include Malay-speaking countries such as Indonesia, Malaysia, Brunei, and Singapore (Abdullah, 2007).

Though these wide ranging recommendations were made with great conviction, their effectiveness could be seen only 16 years later when the Fifth Congress was held in the same venue in 1998. Yet, none of the earlier recommendations or proposals were reviewed or reported in terms of their development.

Malay Language and Literary Congress V (1998)

The Fifth Congress was held on 2-3 May, 1998 at the DBP, Kuala Lumpur, Malaysia. Nationalistic fervor seemed to run freely during the congress, as is evident in the *sumpah bahasa*, or Language Oath that was part of the proceeding's recommendations. Among other things, the pledge promoted the use of Malay as a rallying cry for political, cultural, economic, national, and educational unification. There was also a pledge to make Malay a vehicle for knowledge and intellectual freedom and for freeing the minds of the people and ensure the continuity of Malay ethnicity (Abdullah, 2007). Gone were the calls to unify the language within the region and to exchange information to enhance Malay language development. Malaysia-centricism in Malay language status and corpus planning via the congress had turned into a nationalistic cry for the development of Bahasa Malaysia.

Malay Language and Literary Congress VI (2002)

The Sixth Congress was held at the Tun Abdul Razak Hall in Tanjung Malim, Perak, Malaysia on September 5, 2002. The congress remained Malaysia-centric but was faced with developments within the country that impacted the status of Malay. Participants were faced with the changing policy of the Malaysian government and its decision to use English in the teaching and learning of mathematics and science. Even though the participants agreed with the rationale for the change in policy, they were worried that the change would thwart the growth of Malay especially in the fields of knowledge and technology. Thus, three resolutions were passed. These were as follows:

1. The government was to maintain the use of Malay as the medium of instruction for the teaching of mathematics and science in the national education system;

2. The Ministry of Education of Malaysia was to set up a committee to look into ways of enhancing English language proficiency without affecting the status and function of Malay; and

3. Congress organizers were to meet the Prime Minister of Malaysia, Dr Mahathir Mohamad, to hand over the resolutions of the congress. (Abdullah, 2007: 800)

This development shows that the status and importance of Malay as a language of knowledge and science were being threatened and would have an impact on both the status of Malay in Malaysia and continued corpus planning for the language.

The Role of MABBIM in Corpus Planning

MBIM/MABBIM acts as the sole Malay Language planning body in the Malay Archipelago, which includes Indonesia, Malaysia, Brunei, and Singapore, the four countries in the region that have Malay as their National Language. Through the years, MBIM/MABBIM has played a significant role in corpus planning for Malay.

Language planning and language development as initiated by MBIM/MABBIM concern status planning and, most importantly, corpus planning. MABBIM's greatest contribution is the development of a structured process in the cycle of corpus planning and the making of Malay into a dynamic and relevant language through the 21st century. Among the structured process that was put in place by MABBIM through the years is the identification of problems, the determination of policy, and the creation, formulation, coordination, standardization, implementation, and assessment of its corpus planning process.

Corpus Planning – Spelling System

Pre-1972, there were various forms of spelling used, especially in Malaysia and Indonesia. Among these was the *Ejaan Za'ba* (Za'ba spelling) system, also known as the *Ejaan Sekolah* (school spelling) system. These spelling systems were practiced widely in educational institutions, especially in schools. They were developed by Za'ba, or Zainal Abidin, who was a prominent Malay language expert of his time, who developed the system for use in schools to facilitate the teaching and learning of the language. Subsequently, there was the *Ejaan Fajar Asia* (Fajar Asia spelling) system. This was propagated by a book publishing company, Fajar Asia, as a form of standardization to be used in the books published by the company. Thirdly, there was the *Ejaan Melindo* (Melindo spelling) system, a system to be developed by a working committee consisting of Indonesian and Malaysian experts in 1959, two years after Malaysia gained independence from Great Britain. As a result of this meeting, a joint statement was issued by both parties in 1961, introducing the *Melindo* spelling system. Among the notable features of this system was the acknowledgment of the differences in the spelling system between Indonesia and Malaysia. The most distinctive feature was the understanding that the *Melindo* spelling system is based on three principles: the link between one phoneme and one phonetic sign only, the use of phoneme-based word structure, and limited exceptions to these rules. Unfortunately, this system was never implemented or made known public due to the impracticality of its principles, especially that of the one phoneme-one sign principle (Asmah, 2004).

Lastly, prior to 1972, the University of Malaya had come up with a spelling system that came to be known as the University of Malaya spelling system. In response to the various systems and the failed attempt at standardization of spelling via the Melindo system, the University of Malaya decided to implement its own system, which was to be used by the university. However, this system did not last long either as its usage was limited to courses conducted within the university and to publishers producing academic textbooks in Malay. This varied, confusing, and often disjointed system came to an end in 1972 when a unified spelling system was introduced.

The new system was launched by the prime ministers of both Indonesia and Malaysia in recognition of the importance of a simplified spelling system as the main infrastructure in the building and development of the national language as a language of knowledge. The new system was called the *Ejaan Bersama* (Unified Spelling) system. It can be seen as the first constructive achievement of the MBIM in terms of corpus planning for Malay in the region.

Singapore's acceptance of the new system meant that Malay Language development in Singapore would always be pegged to the region's and to the determination by member states of MABBIM, namely Indonesia, Malaysia, and Brunei. Having only observer status, Singapore has no say in the proceedings, even though from time to time, the country is allowed to express viewpoints, though these carry no weight in the determinations of the council.

Codification of Malay

Codification of Malay under the auspices of MABBIM can best be seen in the published General Guidelines for the Establishment of Malay Terminologies, or *Pedoman Umum Pembentukan Istilah Bahasa Melayu*. These general guidelines were developed by MABBIM and accepted for use in member countries. It is the most comprehensive effort at corpus planning for Malay ever undertaken. Even today, it is used for reference whenever the terminology committee meets to discuss the need for new terminology, and it is now into its third edition since 1975.

The General Guidelines outline the steps to be taken in establishing new terminology for use in various fields.

The first step in establishing a new word is to choose from words within Malay itself, either from the general domain or from any dialect group. Once there is a match to the concept, the word must be a perfect match as it cannot have a negative connotation attached to it, whether in terms of meaning or pronunciation, and it must be concise and brief. If there are no matches, the subsequent step is to look from within the Malay cluster of languages itself. Once there is a match, there should be reconciliation in terms of its spelling to fit into the Malay spelling system. If after these two steps, no matches can be found, then the guide allows for a loan word from English or outside of English, if need be. However, this last step requires an absorption and adjustment process to streamline the spelling into the Malay system. In addition, the translated word must be accurate and brief.

Standardization of Malay

The term corpus planning, which was devised by Kloss (1969), refers to changes that are deliberately planned to the actual corpus, or form, of a language. This planning of the corpus of a language includes, among others things, the codification of morphology and spelling, the development of specialized vocabulary, the creation of a new alphabet, the imposition of terms propagating particular attitudes to certain groups of people, and standardization.

The standardization of any language encompasses not only its spoken form but also its spelling and writing system, its written grammar, terminologies, vocabulary in terms of meanings of words and word forms, language registers, and lastly, the spoken form. Historically, the standard form of Malay (*Bahasa Melayu baku*) is the Riau-Johor variety. According to Asraf (1984), this is due to the fact that the earliest Malay texts originated from the region, so this became the standard from. Among the texts that originated from the Riau-Johor region was the *Sejarah Melayu*, or the Malay Annals, written by Tun Seri Lanang. The sentence pattern in this widely read text was subsequently adopted as the standard variety. Even standard spoken Malay was the Riau-Johor variety as the development of Malay had originated in the region.

However, some linguists and language experts felt that there was a problem with the Johor-Riau spoken variety. The vowel "a" at the end of an open syllable does not always represent the sound /a/. There are occasions when it is pronounced /e/, as in "paper." An example is the word "ada" (have)," which is pronounced as /ade/ and not /ada/. It was felt that there should be a standardization of sounds based on the one-letter one-sound system. In the northern Malay states as well as in Indonesia, the vowel "a" is pronounced /a/ at all times. Thus, it was felt that there was a need to standardize this feature if the development of Malay was to be common to all of the Malay Archipelago.

Thus in 1956, the Third Malay Language and Literary Congress passed a resolution calling for a change in the standard variety. In the spirit of standardizing the spoken variety through a system of one letter to one sound, the Johor-Riau spoken variety was to cease being the standard. The new standard was to be based on phonemic sounds and not phonetic signs. The sound emphasized was the use of /a/ at the end of a word. It should be pronounced as "a" and not "e". However, little was done to ensure that the resolution was adhered to. The Johor-Riau spoken variety maintained its status as the standard variety as this was how the language was taught in schools. This was to change in 1984, when the Malaysian Information Minister announced that the new spoken standard would be implemented with immediate effect.

A strong proponent of the spoken *baku* Malay is Asraf, who in 1984 during the Fourth Malay Language & Literary Congress, presented a paper entitled "The Malay Language Spoken Baku based on the Phonemic Principle." Asraf questioned the need to maintain the Johor-Riau spoken variety as the official standard for Malay due to its many weaknesses. Among these was the seemingly haphazard manner in which the spoken variety had developed. Asraf highlighted the use of the vowel "a" at the end of a final syllable, which can be pronounced either as /a/ as in "drama" or as /e/, as in "bawa," which is pronounced /bawe/. Asraf gave several more examples of this discrepancy between the spelling and the spoken form and proposed that this problem be resolved through the adoption of the one-letter one-sound principle. This phonemic approach, Asraf claimed, was a more scientific approach. Unfortunately, he did not elaborate on the research done in this respect but merely listed the sequence of events from 1956 (the time of the Third Malay Language and Literary Congress) to date along with the developments in reaching a new standard, which is referred to as *sebutan baku.*

However, Farid (1980) debunked the notion that the Johor-Riau variety is not based on systematic knowledge and is less scientific than the new variety. According to Farid, in the Johor-Riau variety, the vowel "a" is reduced to /e/ in word-final position but retains its basic shape in affixed forms. This fundamental difference in pronunciation had been the reason for the switch to the new variety. However, Farid insists that this is a rule of this variety and should be referred to as "vowel reduction."

Need for Standardization

Ismail (1992: 17) gave various reasons for the need to have a uniform standard especially for spoken Malay. He listed three main reasons. These were:

1. To have a single variant of standard spoken Malay that can be used in formal situations or during official events;
2. To improve the efficiency of standard spoken Malay among all of its users; and
3. To strengthen the system and the internal structure of Malay so as to ensure consistency and uniformity in the spoken system, in line with the consistency and uniformity of grammar, vocabulary, and the spelling system.

In the planning for the standardization of the spoken form, DBP produced general guidelines for standard spoken Malay, or *Pedoman Sebutan Baku Bahasa Melayu*. This set of guidelines, which was first published in 1994, is the same set as the one used later by Singapore in its *sebutan baku* program. The general guidelines stipulated in the guidelines state that:

> ...the pronunciation of words must be based on the spelling system, whereby every word is articulated based on the Malay sound system. In reference to the romanized spelling form, this means that, in general, every vocal letter is represented by a vocal sound (phoneme), and every consonant letter is represented by a consonant sound (phoneme). (DBP: 1994, xii)

However, there are a few consonants that represent more than one sound or phoneme. This includes the letter "k," which represents four different sounds or phonemes. These are:

1. The /k/ sound at the beginning of a syllable, as in the word "kaki," which is pronounced [ka.ki];
2. Glottal stops /?/ at the end of a word, as in the word "kapak," which is pronounced [kapa?];
3. The nasal sound /?/, as in the word "takzim," which is pronounced [ta?zim],; and
4. The sound /q/, which is equivalent to the letter "qaf" in Jawi, as in the word "kadi", which is pronounced [qa.di].

The uniformization of the standard spoken form was applied to all three categories of general words in Malay. These are original Malay words, loan words form English and other European languages, and loan words from Arabic. The guidelines then went on to outline the features of the pronunciation for each category. This document is important because it outlines clearly the steps to be taken when approaching matters concerning the standardization of the spoken form while avoiding any misconceptions or mistakes.

Issues with the Standardization of Spoken Malay

Since the implementation of the *sebutan baku* in Malaysia and subsequently in Singapore, two opposing views emerged. One camp involves the proponents of the *sebutan baku*, while the other groups consist of opponents. Since Ismail (1992) gave reasons for the implementation of standard spoken Malay, the opposing camp has offered its own reasons. Among these were the issue of language variation, the monocentric versus pluricentric argument, the issue of Malay intonation, the "ideal" state of the language, and the argument concerning "normalcy" in speaking as Malays in general do not articulate every sound clearly, especially those with a glottal stop, for example /k/, /p/, or /t/ at the end of a word.

Language Variation

The most ardent voice against *sebutan baku* has been Asmah Haji Omar, an Emeritus Professor from the University of Malaya, who has documented the arguments she has been propagating since its implementation as a policy in Malaysia and purportedly adopted by MABBIM in 1972. Asmah (2004: 136) differentiates between the term *keseragaman*, or uniformity, which to her refers to *baku*, and the term "standard language." According to her, *keseragaman* (or *pembakuan*) is rigid and does not allow for any differences or room for variation. However, in standard language, there is in fact room for variation, or differences at the individual or the group level and according to geographical location, and these differences are accepted as a set of norms.

Asmah (2004: 137) argues that a uniform language can never be achieved. Since *baku* is a form of uniformity in the corpus planning of the language, it can never be successful. The reason, according to her, is that every language has its own individual or group quirks. Whatever these quirks are, research on language variation can then be used as an indicator in the teaching of the language for communication and in determining its norms. The result of the research will help language users and learners determine whether a certain type of language use is right or wrong. She points out that what is deemed wrong may not be wrong at all but a form of language variation. Acceptance of language variation will give more space for the language to "breathe" and make it more dynamic, whereas a uniform standard may go against the natural language system (Asmah, 2004: 138).

Monocentric versus Pluricentric Approaches

There is a notion that standard language is monocentric in nature. Monocentricism refers to a situation where there is only one main center from where the language is disseminated. Asmah (2004: 140) quotes extensively from Clyne (1992) in arguing her case against monocentricism for Malay. She makes it very clear that Malay is not a monocentric language. She explains that in standard spoken Malay, there are two types of language variation: firstly, the "*e pepet*" variant, and secondly, the "a" variant. Even though these are termed as such, their differences are not only limited to the sounds /a/ and /e/ at the end of words as both variants have their own main distribution area. The "*e pepet*" variant has its center in the southern part of the Malay Archipelago, mainly the southern part of Peninsular Malaysia and the east coast, whereas the "a" variant is centered around the northern part of the peninsula and parts of Borneo now known as Sabah and Sarawak. Asmah (2004: 140) adds that if variation in intonation is taken into account, a third center can be identified in Sabah and Sarawak alone.

Intonation in Malay

Based on the *baku* guidelines being propagated today, Asmah indicates that the intonation these recommend is contrary to the way Malay is spoken. According to Asmah, the intonation indicated in the guidelines is equivalent to that of someone giving commands during a march, where the emphasis is on the last syllable of the word. In reality, Asmah argues, the emphasis is placed on the parts of a sentence that are important, thus giving meaning to it (Asmah, 1980: 295).

Ideal State of a Language

According to Asmah, there is no ideal state of a language and no rigid rules whereby a language used in spoken form must be based on the written form. This argument is based on two factors:

1. Written language is rigid and non-contextual. It needs to be spoken to give it life, and we speak it within context and in different ways at different times.

2. There is no writing system in the world that is able to capture the sounds of a language absolutely correctly. The choice of symbols and their function does not always give a clear picture of the pronunciations involved. Therefore, the guidelines insisting that the pronunciation must be absolutely identical to the spelling is far from reality (Asmah, 2004: 123).

Spoken Normalcy

Asmah (2004: 125) argues that *sebutan baku* refers to a spoken form that is not normal. According to the spoken guidelines, the principle is *sebut ikut eja*, or "speak it as it is spelled." This assumes that we learn a language through knowing the writing system first before learning how to pronounce words. Asmah referred to this logic as "reductionist" because it lessens possibilities. An example is the /k/ plosive versus the non-/k/ plosive. In Malay, the letter k at the end of a word is silent. But with the *sebut ikut eja* principle, it will go against the normal way the word is spoken in Malay.

In addition to these reasons, several others were collected by Asmah as part of her life-long quest to express her viewpoint on this matter. Among these were when the rationalizations of the guidelines do not seem to correlate with *huraian*, or the laws governing how the language is spoken. The argument whereby the use of *sebutan baku* gives social prestige to the user holds no water for Asmah (2004: 129), who quotes Milroy (1994) as saying that "standardization is not necessarily about prestige; it comes about for functional reasons." She subsequently argued that standardization is not meant to create uniformity in the use of a language but that its main aim is the promotion of communicative competence at a certain level of efficiency.

Sebutan Baku and its Implementation in Singapore

The word *baku* is a Javanese term meaning "true and correct." *Sebutan Baku*, or standard spoken Malay, was introduced in Malaysia in 1984. It was introduced gradually in Singapore in 1993 by the Ministry of Education, to be used in the teaching and learning of Malay, beginning with primary schools and followed by secondary schools and junior colleges and centralized institutes (an institution that conducts three-year pre-university courses).

The Malay Language Council of Singapore (MBMS), an agency under the purview of the Ministry of Information, Communications and the Arts (MICA) and who represents Singapore as an observer at the regional meetings of Malay language bodies, agreed that Standard Malay, or *Bahasa Melayu Baku*, was to be used within the domains of:

1. Formal teaching and learning in educational institutions by education officials, lecturers, teachers, and students;
2. Public speeches in the form of lectures, debates, forums, and announcements;
3. Official communications and discussions in the public sector, including official meetings, interviews, and speeches during official functions; and
4. Broadcasting of programs through the electronic media (radio, television, and film) by newsreaders, presenters, and analysts.

This is in line with the practice of Malaysia's *Dewan Bahasa & Pustaka* (DBP), the language and literary body tasked with promoting the use of Malay in the public domain. MBMS concurred with DBP that standard spoken Malay must be based on the spelling, i.e. the pronunciation must be based on character symbols and number of syllables as well as their function in the sentence. Emphasis should be placed on the following characteristics:

1. The pronunciation of letters should be based on the sounds of Malay;
2. The pronunciation of words should be based on the spelling and word forms; and
3. The intonation should be based on sentence types and forms in Malay.

Standardization of Malay in Singapore

In implementing the policy on standard Malay (*Bahasa Melayu Baku*), the Ministry of Education of Singapore launched the Standard Spoken Malay Programme in 1993, exactly five years after Malaysia launched its own program. The rationale behind the program was as follows:

1. To function as a continuation of the policy of using the standard form of Malay in terms of spelling, terminologies, grammar, and vocabulary;

2.   To help students learn Malay especially as regards spelling and reading. It was hoped that the close correlation between writing and speaking would assist in the learning process; and

3.   To keep up with the progress of Malay in the region.

The Standard Spoken Malay Programme was introduced in primary schools in 1993 and in secondary schools, junior colleges, and centralized institutes the following year. It became fully functional at all educational levels in Singapore from 1998 onward.

Corpus Planning for Malay in Singapore's Bilingual Framework

Based on the historical perspective outlined above, three major points arise. The first is the question of whether corpus planning for Malay in Singapore based on the bilingual framework aims at the modernization of the language or merely constitutes an act of renovation. Secondly, as indicated by Cooper (1989) and reiterated by Asmah (2004), there is room for minor variation within the process of standardization. Lastly, it is easier to standardize writing than to standardize speaking because the latter is at best more of an ideological construct.

Modernization or Renovation

As was explained by Cooper (1989), the difference between modernization and renovation in corpus planning is that the former permits the language code to serve new communicative functions whereas the latter only permits the language code to serve old functions in new ways. Thus, based on Coopers' corpus planning categories, it can be argued that Singapore's bilingual framework as well as Malay language corpus planning are geared more toward the category of renovating the corpus than modernizing it. This is due to the fact that the standardization and codification carried out so far do not correspond with any change in the functional use of the language. Instead, both were carried out more for non-linguistic than for linguistic reasons, especially when we consider the main reason stated for the move toward standardizing the spoken form, namely greater ease in teaching, as the final step of the language standardization process, and as a form of promotion of regional unity.

Standardization is not Uniformity

There should also be a clearer understanding of the difference between standardization and uniformity. As was explained by Ferguson (1962), even in standardization, perfect uniformity is ultimately impossible. Asmah (2004) reiterated the same point and argued for an understanding of this difference. In the Singapore context, the introduction of standard pronunciation in the form of sebutan baku, has resulted in the uniform usage of only one spoken variety in the teaching and learning of the language and its use in formal situations. The Johor-Riau variety has been deemed unfit for use in education and formal situations even though its use in the family and community domain is widespread. Therefore, in Malay language planning, especially planning of the spoken standard, although the need for standardization is important, there should not be excessive rigidity and acceptance of variety will result in a more dynamic language development.

Standardizing the Spoken Form as an Ideological Construct

Cooper (1989) highlights three reasons why it is easier to standardize the written form than the spoken form. Firstly, the need for a written standard is greater than for a spoken standard. Secondly, it is easier to impart standard writing via schools than for the spoken standard. Lastly, spoken language is spontaneous and not as easily controllable as writing. In addition to these three factors, Milroy and Milroy (1985) argue that standardizing the spoken form is virtually impossible and that this is more of an ideological construct. Thus, this may be the reason for the difficulties encountered in promoting the use of *sebutan baku*. Although the implementation process is clear enough, after more than 20 years, issues of normalcy and context is still being discussed and debated.

Conclusion

According to Cooper form should follow function "in the sense that the desired communicative function precedes the designed or selected structure" (1989: 123). In corpus planning for Malay language, especially concerning the issue of standard spoken Malay, or *sebutan baku*, form does not follow function. If the rationale for having a standard spoken form for the Malay-speaking region is meant to result in better understanding among speakers, this has not happened, as was indicated by Asmah (2004). Thus the quest for an ideal form of Malay not only has not materialized but has pulled the Malay-speaking region apart. In the case of Singapore, there need to be a re-examination of the rationale for the use of *sebutan baku* so as to win the hearts and minds of Malay speakers as the variety is not the standard variety they are used to.

5

Acquisition Planning

This chapter will outline developments in terms of acquisition planning for Malay within the Singapore bilingual framework and analyze its effects based on the implementation of the curriculum. The earlier part of this chapter will explain Cooper's acquisition planning framework, and this will be followed by a review of the framework as it applies to Malay language acquisition planning within the bilingual framework of Singapore. Lastly, this chapter will comment on the effect of the bilingual framework on acquisition planning for Malay.

Acquisition Planning – Definition

Cooper (1998: 157) defined acquisition planning as "organized s to promote the learning of a language," or a method for organizing the learning and acquisition of a language. Within this understanding, he explained further that there are two bases for acquisition planning: one based on an overt language planning goal, the other based on the method employed to attain the goal. In terms of the overt goals, Cooper divided these further into three distinguishable factors: 1) the acquisition of the language as a second or foreign language; 2) the reacquisition of the language by populations for whom it was once either a vernacular or a language of specialized function; and 3) language maintenance, which implies language acquisition by the next generation.

Cooper explained further that in terms of method employed to attain acquisition goals, we may distinguish between three types: 1) those designed primarily to create or to improve the opportunity to learn; 2) those designed primarily to create or improve incentives to learn; and 3) the form of attainment that is designed to create or improve both opportunities and incentives to learn simultaneously.

Cooper further explains that opportunities to learn can be further subdivided into direct and indirect methods. Direct methods include classroom instruction, the provision of materials for self-instruction in the target language, and the production of print and digital media in simplified versions of the target language. Indirect methods include efforts to shape the learners' mother tongue so that it will be made more similar to other languages, some of which may be more widely known, as in changing the written form of Malay from the Jawi script to the present roman script, which made it easier for many to learn to read and write. This leads to a preliminary framework, into which acquisition planning can be classified based on the basis of two variables: overt goal (acquisition, reacquisition, maintenance), and method employed to attain the goal (opportunities to learn, incentives to learn, both opportunities and incentives to learn). This explanation can be seen in Table 5.1:

Table 3   Cooper's Acquisition Planning Model

Goal/Method Employed	Types/Methods of Attainment	Example for Malay
1. Overt Language Planning Goal	a. Acquisition of language as a second or foreign language	e.g., acquisition of Malay as third language or studied under the Malay (Special) Programme
	b. Reacquisition of the language	e.g., re-use or re-acquisition of the use of Malay within a particular domain
	c. Language maintenance	e.g., addressing potential decline in the language via language-in-education planning
2. Method Employed to Attain the Goal	a. Creating or improving opportunities to learn the language	• Direct method – e.g., classroom instruction, instructional materials design, authentic materials in simplified design • Indirect method – e.g., shaping learners' mother tongue to make it easier to learn
	b. Creating or improving incentives to learn the language	e.g., pegging entry requirement to higher education to the attainment of Malay
	c. Creating or improve opportunities and incentives to learn the language	e.g., immersion or bilingual educational programs

Even though acquisition planning includes more than just planning for language instruction, it accounts for the lion's share of acquisition planning. Further, acquisition planning is a feature of the instructional enterprise at every level of an educational organization, from the higher echelons of the Ministry of Education to the basic classroom teacher.

Prator, one of the few scholars who regard language teaching as an object of language planning, states the point clearly when he said (1968, cited in Cooper, 1989: 160),

> Language policy is the body of decisions made by interested authorities concerning the desirable form and use of languages by a speech group. It also involves consequent decisions made by educators, media directors, etc., regarding the possible implementation of prior basic decisions.

Based on this definition, the decision to emphasize in the language classroom specific skills or linguistic forms – even the choice of a textbook – can become part of language policy. This should thus be one of the primary concerns of language teachers.

Prator also argued that the entire process of formulating and implementing language policy is best regarded as a spiral process. He explained that the process begins at the highest level of authority, ideally descending in widening circles through the ranks of practitioners, who can either support or resist putting the policy into effect.

Markee (1988), who also considers language teaching to be a form of language planning, presents a detailed consideration of the status planning and corpus planning decisions involved in teaching English for specialized purposes. He argues that when planners try to promote second or foreign language acquisition, they often turn to the school system. Schools are more likely to succeed in this goal if they use the target language as a medium of instruction than if they merely teach the language as a target of instruction, with both exposure to the language and incentives to learn it being greater in the former case. But no matter how accomplished the schools are in imparting language acquisition, they are unlikely to lead to use of the language outside the classroom unless there are practical reasons for such use. Thus, there is a need not only to emphasize the learning of

Malay in the classroom but also to see how its learning and use can be enhanced outside of the classroom.

However, Dorian (1987) argues that even if acquisition is not translated into use, there may be considerable value in maintenance efforts. She mentions three of these values. Firstly, support for a threatened language by the community and the school can mitigate negative attitudes toward the language and its speakers that typically accompany language decline and that may have been internalized by speakers as well as potential speakers of the language. Secondly, promotional efforts for the language usually help transmit the ethnic history and traditional ways of life that are typically threatened along with the language. Thirdly, citing Spolsky (1978), Dorian argues that there are economic benefits that accrue to local communities engaged in revitalization or maintenance efforts in the form of jobs for teachers, teaching aides, teacher trainers, curriculum and materials developers, and so forth.

Process of Acquisition Planning for Malay

We will now look at the process of acquisition planning for Malay based on the overt language planning goal and the method employed in attaining that goal. Based on Cooper's model as presented in Table 5.1, acquisition planning can be distinguished on two bases: overt language planning goal, and method employed to attain the goal (Cooper, 1989: 159).

Overt Language Planning Goal

According to Cooper (1989: 159), overt language planning goal refers to language planning goal that is outwardly specified. In addition to an overall overt language planning goal, Cooper distinguishes three different overt goals: 1), acquiring the language as a second or foreign language, 2) reacquiring of the language, and 3) maintaining the language. As we can see from Table 5.1, the overt language planning goal for Malay leans more toward language maintenance via language-in-education planning, with the minor goal of acquiring it as a second or foreign language.

Language Maintenance

Language maintenance refers to efforts made to prevent the further erosion of that language. In the case of Malay, language maintenance is carried out in large part via language-in-education initiatives. Initiatives include the Malay Language Curriculum and Pedagogy Review Committee (MLCPRC) report (2005) and the recent Malay Language Review Committee's recommendation (2011), which is targeted at enhancing the learning of Malay and ensuring that the learning is fun and begins with the basic skills of listening and speaking at lower primary level. This is followed by reading and writing skills as they progress. In addition, assessment modes are also widened to take this new teaching initiative into account. Based on the report's recommendations, it is hoped that students will find the learning of Malay to be both fun and functional and provide the impetus for them to want to learn, understand, and use the language.

Malay Language Curriculum and Pedagogy Review Committee

This committee was set up in December 2004 by MOE "for the purpose of conducting a review of the Malay Language (ML) curriculum and pedagogy" (MOE, 2005: 1). This review committee was of special significance because for the first time, a review was conducted specifically to look into curriculum and pedagogical matters and not to offer new policy initiatives. The comprehensive review took nearly one year to complete and involved views sought from "stakeholders in education – professionals, educationists, students, and parents, Malay organizations, and the media through focus group discussions and school visits" (MOE, 2005: 1).

Committee members included academics, educationists, and industry leaders who are practitioners of Malay. The committee was also aided in its deliberations by the findings of "a comprehensive survey involving about 7,500 students, teachers, and parents as well as by findings from research on classroom teaching by the Centre for Research in Pedagogy and Practice, National Institute of Education"

(MOE, 2005: 14). A study trip to Malaysia was also conducted to "provide further insights and help establish useful networking for future curriculum development and teacher training" (MOE, 2005: 1).

The committee was further aided by four Resource Panels that concentrated on three main priority areas: 1) the structure and content of syllabus documents and instructional materials; 2) pedagogy and assessment for Malay; and 3) the role played by the Malay community in supporting Malay teaching and learning.

The committee's terms of reference were as follows:

1. To articulate the objectives of the Malay curriculum used at primary, secondary, and pre-university levels;

2. To examine if the implementation of the various Malay syllabi in schools was aligned with the curriculum objectives that were realizable with reasonable effort by the various target groups;

3. To review the effectiveness of the structure of the present Malay curriculum, the different Malay syllabi, the instructional materials, and the examination modes for their respective target groups;

4. To recommend appropriate refinements to the structure of the Malay curriculum to better achieve MOE's mother tongue policy objectives while recognizing the different linguistic abilities and language backgrounds of Malay language students. In particular, the committee was tasked to study:

    a. The most appropriate way of structuring the curriculum to cater to the different linguistic abilities and language backgrounds of students;

    b. The most appropriate balance among the different language skills (listening, speaking, reading, and writing) across different courses;

    c. The most appropriate balance between language competence and cultural content; and

    d. How the teaching and assessment of the Malay curriculum could be improved to maximize learning by and interest among students across the spectrum of ability;

5. To advise on the effective implementation of the above.

The terms of reference referred to the committee's role in identifying any weaknesses in the acquisition of Malay based on the changing demographics and profile of learners. The committee's task was to propose recommendations on syllabus design and instructional materials for Malay language-in-education planning. Based on these terms of reference, the committee's report outlined the main objectives of Malay language teaching and learning. These were divided into four distinct but linked parts: 1) establishing a common cultural and linguistic vision for Malay; 2) stressing the passion for excellence in the learning of Malay; 3) ensuring the standard of spoken Malay; and 4) specifying a pedagogy for differentiated learning.

Common Cultural and Linguistic Vision for Malay

The committee proposed a vision for the teaching and learning of Malay, namely *Arif Budiman,* or a knowledgeable person who contributes to society. This vision was aligned to MOE's mission and desired outcomes of education. The aim of having the vision was "for all Malay learners to be able to better understand themselves, their aspirations, and their own potential to contribute to community and nation" (MOE, 2005: 19). Moreover, this vision was integrated into three further objectives: passion for excellence, speaking Malay well, and differentiated learning.

Passion for Excellence

As regards passion for excellence, the committee indicated that under the framework of *Arif Budiman*, a student of Malay should strive for excellence in his or her knowledge of Malay language and culture to the highest level he or she can achieve. In particular, the committee would like to see this passion for excellence manifested

> ...in Higher Malay Language (HML) and JC classrooms and in special programmes such as the Elective Programmes in Malay Language for Secondary School (EMAS) and the Malay Language Elective Programme (MLEP). (MOE, 2005: 48)

Speaking Malay Well

The committee was concerned with the "decline in the standard of spoken Malay" (2005: 3). Thus, the committee proposed a stronger approach in developing strong and effective oral skills among students. The committee stated that to realize the *Arif Budiman* vision, "students should be given opportunities to speak Malay confidently and well in a variety of authentic situations" (MOE, 2005: 3).

Pedagogy for Differentiated Learning

Based on the changing demographics of Malay language students and their diverse home language backgrounds and abilities, the committee recommended a differentiated learning approach in the teaching and learning of the language. This can only be achieved if teachers "believe in the uniqueness of each student and are equipped "to identify and nurture their unique talents" (MOE, 2005: 4).

The key recommendations of the committee were spelled out as differentiated instruction, increased importance of oral skills, syllabi and instructional materials, assessment and examinations, special programs for Malay in schools, pedagogy and teacher training, and creating a community cultural milieu for the use of Malay.

Differentiated Instruction

Differentiated Instruction (DI) it is to be carried out especially in the foundation years, i.e., Primary 1 and 2. Malay language students with varied home language backgrounds and abilities will receive scaffolding based on their readiness level, interests, and learning style. Those from English-speaking backgrounds with be helped via bridging materials. Guidelines will be put into place and teachers will be trained in how to use these materials so as to fully utilize the resources that will be provided for maximum impact.

Increased Importance of Oral Skills

The committee felt that with the changing demographics of students learning Malay at P1, there should be greater emphasis on developing listening and speaking skills at the foundation level (P1 and P2) before moving on to the two higher level language skills, namely reading and writing. The approach recommended was a contextual one, whereby students were to be provided with the "opportunity to speak confidently in Malay in a variety of authentic situations" (MOE, 2005: 3). Based on the concept of communicative language teaching, students were to be taught and exposed to various forms of language use in varied authentic situations in and outside of their home environment.

To support this important recommendation, the committee also proposed changes to assessment modes. These recommendations were grouped into syllabus and instructional materials.

Syllabus and Instructional Materials (IMs)

The revisions to the syllabus and to IMs were further subdivided into four main groups: clearly articulated learning outcomes, engaging instructional materials, reading, and information technology.

Clearly Articulated Learning Outcomes

Under this sub-group, learning outcomes were to be based on three levels of achievement called *tahap*, or levels. MOE was to provide descriptors for the three levels: basic, intermediate, and advanced. Based on these descriptors, teachers would be able to differentiate their students depending on their readiness level, interests, and learning styles. The committee also recommended that these descriptors be made available in instructional materials "so that students can self-evaluate their own learning" (MOE, 2005: 5). The rationale for using *tahap*, as indicated by the committee report, was

> ...to help teachers and students to focus on outcomes and thereby broaden the range of language tasks rather than holding on to familiar language tasks in an unreflective way. (MOE, 2005: 5)

Engaging Instructional Materials

The committee recommended that materials be "more interesting and engaging" (MOE, 2005: 5). Instructional packages should form the impetus for greater interaction between teacher and students, leading to higher-level discussions and to "lessons which encourage open-ended response from students to facilitate learning" (MOE, 2005: 5).

Reading

The committee recommended that extensive reading programs be made an integral part of Malay language programs in schools. Members of the committee felt that reading is the best way for students to "raise their command of the language and develop powers of imagination and intellect" (MOE, 2005: 5).

Information Technology

The committee proposed an IT-friendly outlook in the syllabus and in the development of IT-based instructional materials. Teachers should also deem this important and should apply the use of IT in their teaching, thus at the same time encouraging their students to be IT-savvy and "to apply their knowledge of IT in learning Malay" (MOE, 2005: 5).

The committee chose to include the interests of secondary school students as the initial survey conducted by MOE revealed that secondary level Malay language students found their Malay class boring and not engaging. Thus, the committee felt that it was important to capture their interest, "especially those taking HML" (MOE, 2005: 5).

Assessment and Examinations

The committee made recommendations on assessment and examinations as assessment modes and examination types determine stakeholders' "priorities in and approaches to learning" (MOE, 2005: 5). The recommendations for assessment and examinations were sub-divided into five categories.

Firstly, the committee recommended the implementation of school-based oral assessment. With the emphasis on oral skills at the foundation level, the committee recommended that oral examinations be fine-tuned and "cover a broader spectrum of tasks including presentation skills and group discussions" (MOE, 2005: 5). This was to be implemented at school level and worth up to 10% of the overall result in National Examinations at PSLE and "O" levels. It was the committee's hope that in the near future, school-based oral assessment would consist of tasks that highlight students speaking skills. These tasks would be book-related, including story-telling and book discussions.

Secondly, the committee, in line with an earlier recommendation, highlighted the importance of good oral skills for higher education and working life. Therefore, it recommended that oral assessment be a "part of the HML 'O' Level using a school-based approach focusing on the students' ability to carry out intellectual discourse'" (MOE, 2005: 6).

Thirdly, the committee recommended giving greater weight to oral language skills at lower primary level. Based on the recommendation that increased importance be placed on oral skills, there should also be "a graduated shift from a greater focus on oral communication at the Lower Primary level to more emphasis on reading and writing skills at higher levels alongside a continued concern for good listening and speaking skills" (MOE. 2005: 6).

Fourthly, the committee recommended an increase in contextualized and higher-order thinking items in examinations. Such items were present in the 2006 examinations, and this was wholeheartedly endorsed by the committee, with a recommendation for its greater presence in the 2010 examinations.

Fifthly, the committee further recommended that schools look beyond pen and paper where assessment is concerned. Schools should look at alternative modes of assessment, which should include "portfolios, project work, and assessment based on authentic situations" (MOE, 2005: 6).

Special Programs for Malay in Schools

The committee stated that special Malay language programs in schools should be expanded in order to widen the catchment of Malay language learners that can then be enticed to learn the language at a higher level. The committee proposed that the

New Elective Programmes in Malay for Secondary School (EMAS) be expanded from just one school in the West as at present "to a school in the East followed by one in the North or South zones' (MOE, 2005: 6). The committee also recommended that the Malay Language Elective Programme (MLEP) be expanded from one Junior College (JC) to one more JC, to be identified. The MLEP should also "aim to offer an H3 (a higher level of the subject offered) subject in Malay Language and Literature, to be developed in partnership with a suitable university programme" (MOE, 2005: 6). The committee would also like to see "new and creative approaches" to getting more "top Malay students to continue to study Malay at higher levels and to embody the vision of *Arif Budiman*" (MOE, 2005: 7).

In addition to increasing the number of Malay Language Special Programmes Schools, the committee proposed that these Malay Language Centres of Excellence "should also strive to offer teacher training and student activities in specialty areas such as Malay history, performing arts, film/media, and literature" (MOE, 2005: 33). The committee further recommended a combined humanities subject that would include Social Studies and Malay Literature. The committee indicated that "the full 'O' Level subject could also be made available to those who have the aptitude and interest" (MOE, 2005: 35).

Two other recommendations made by the committee included a proposal to introduce an elective module for Malay Studies for Polytechnic students who are interested in Malay and to "encourage them to pursue a deeper understanding and appreciation of Malay language and culture" (MOE, 2005: 35). The module will act as added impetus for Polytechnic students who have the aptitude and knowledge to consider teaching Malay as a career option. Lastly, although expanding the teaching of Malay to non-native users was not within the terms of reference of the committee, it recommended that a Malay Special Programme (MSP) be expanded "to cater to the increasing demand among non-Malays to learn Malay as a third language. The committee fully endorsed initiatives by MOE aiming at improving the present program, which included an increase in the number of centers as well as "a shift in emphasis toward oral proficiency in the teaching and learning of MSP" (MOE, 2005: 36).

Pedagogy and Teacher Training

The backbone of any language program consists of the teachers. Thus, the committee felt that the quality and quantity of teacher training should be enhanced, especially with more Malay teachers entering the profession with degrees in Malay Studies. However, the committee "would like to see ML teachers actively deepening their knowledge of Malay literature, history, and culture so that they can serve as role models for their students" (MOE, 2005: 7).

In addition, the committee highlighted a study conducted by NIE's Centre for Research in Pedagogy & Practice and outlining the characteristics of Malay teachers that came to light in the course of observing Malay lessons at Primary 5 and Secondary 3 levels. Among the characteristics highlighted were the teachers' student-centered classroom strategies and curriculum-focused lessons. The committee recommended that teachers "shift the focus from basic knowledge to more advanced concepts and provide explicit instruction in the use of Malay in different contexts" (MOE, 2005: 8). The committee also recommended that teachers should "expect sustained written and oral text production from students rather than accepting short responses…, to guide students in performing more effective group work and also to assign more individual tasks to students" (MOE, 2005: 8).

In order to bring improvements to the weaknesses mentioned above, the committee made two further recommendations: 1) the introduction of pre-service linguistics and literature training for Post-Graduate Diploma in Education (PGDE) students at the National Institute of Education, or a Summer School before their enrollment in the PGDE program, and 2) the setting up of a range of in-service courses under the framework of the Professional Development Continuum Model agreed upon between MOE and NIE for in-service teacher training and for upgrading courses. The committee proposed the setting up of an Advanced Diploma in Education (ADE) program to help non-graduate teachers upgrade themselves. The committee also proposed exploring the idea of bringing in "external lecturers to conduct short-term courses and modules for degree and post-graduate programmes" (MOE, 2005: 8).

The committee clearly indicated the types of pre-service and in-service courses that would be required to bring Malay teachers to a higher level of teaching and learning. Among them are "courses on knowledge of the syllabus, explicit instruction in language use, differentiated instruction, assessment, pedagogy for weaving culture and values into language learning, and IT-based learning" (MOE, 2005; 8). There was also a recommendation for teachers to engage in research and post-graduate studies.

Lastly, the committee proposed a 'teacher-train-teacher" model whereby teachers step up and develop their own instructional materials and help in the development of more instructional leadership among themselves. The culture of sharing resources and offering workshops to their peers was to be encouraged and promoted.

Creating a Community Cultural Milieu for the Use of Malay

In addition to classroom instruction, instructional materials, and teacher training, the committee would like to see more involvement from community organizations and the media as these play a major role in maintaining a high standard of spoken Malay. Thus, the committee proposed some steps toward promoting this involvement.

Firstly, there is a need for involvement that enhances the understanding of the Malay cultural heritage. Activities such as seminars, camps, competitions, and study trips should be organized. The work of teachers and students in the cultural domain should be supported and promoted in order to encourage a greater appreciation of the Malay language and its literature.

Secondly, Malay Language Month should be organized on a larger scale. The committee highlighted the "focus on the use of Standard Malay for cultural and intellectual conversations related to reading and literature" (MOE, 2005; 9).

Thirdly, the committee proposed the development of resources for parents to use at home with their children learning the language. Such materials could be based on historical places or events and include innovative competitions to raise interest in learning the language in a family environment.

Fourthly, the committee proposed a renewed emphasis on *baku* via activities coordinated by the Malay Language Council of Singapore and Malay organizations involved in Malay Language, literature, and culture. A further proposal to research the use of *baku* was also made.

Fifthly, the committee recommended the formation of an inspiring Malay teacher award and other awards meant to recognize individual teachers or teams of teachers "for their contributions in teaching, leadership, resource development, and research" (MOE, 2005; 9).

Language Maintenance based on Desired Outcomes of Education

In terms of language maintenance as a goal of language planning for the acquisition of Malay, we will now look at the language-in-education planning and the desired outcomes of education as stipulated by the Ministry of Education. The goal of teaching Malay is based on the desired outcomes of education as stipulated by MOE and linked to its philosophy of education, which is that every child has an intrinsic worth, is able to learn and achieve, learns well in an orderly and disciplined manner, and whose learning should be at a developmentally appropriate level. Thus the statement "Ten years to grow a tree; a hundred years to cultivate the person" (www.moe.edu.sg) refers to the ten years of basic education provided for all Singaporeans as well as the concept of lifelong learning. This philosophy is manifested in the desired outcomes of education, which are divided into outcomes for primary, secondary, and post-secondary education.

Desired Outcomes of Education (DOE) (Primary)

At the primary level, the key outcomes that are expected at the end of six years of primary education are as follows;

1. Be able to distinguish right from wrong;
2. Know their strengths and areas for growth;

3. Be able to cooperate, share, and care for others;

4. Have a lively curiosity about things;

5. Be able to think for and express themselves confidently;

6. Take pride in their work;

7. Have healthy habits and an awareness of the arts; and

8. Know and love Singapore.

With reference to the DOEs mentioned above, we will see that Outcome 5, "Be able to think for and express themselves confidently," makes direct reference to the instructional objective for Malay language learning at the primary level "Think critically and creatively to explore, create, solve, agree by consensus, and decide on a particular matter using language critically and creatively" (MOE, 2008: 10). This direct reference is also related to the *Arif Budiman* vision, which refers to being a knowledgeable person who contributes to society.

Desired Outcomes of Education (DOE) (Secondary)

At the secondary level, the key outcomes that are expected are as follows;

1. Have moral integrity;

2. Believe in their abilities and be able to adapt to change;

3. Be able to work in teams and show empathy for others;

4. Be creative and have an inquiring mind;

5. Be able to appreciate diverse views and communicate effectively;

6. Take responsibility for their own learning;

7. Enjoy physical activities and appreciate the arts; and

8. Believe in Singapore and understand what matters to Singapore.

Among these DOEs, Points 2, 3, and 4 have direct relevance to the instructional objectives of speaking clearly and coherently, thinking critically and creatively, and using different skills to further understand and appreciate the Malay language and culture in a national context (MOE, 2011: 10).

Desired Outcomes of Education (DOE) (Post-Secondary Education)

At the post-secondary education level, the key outcomes that are expected are as follows;

1. Have moral courage to stand up for what is right;
2. Be resilient in the face of adversity;
3. Be able to collaborate across cultures and be socially responsible;
4. Be innovative and enterprising;
5. Be able to think critically and communicate persuasively;
6. Be purposeful in pursuit of excellence;
7. Pursue a healthy lifestyle and have an appreciation for aesthetics; and
8. Be proud to be a Singaporean and understand Singapore in relation to the world.

These DOEs have direct relevance to the instructional objectives set out in the learning of Malay at pre-university level, especially as regards collaborating across cultures and being socially responsible, which are cornerstones of the *Arif Budiman* vision. Moreover, being innovative and enterprising and able to think critically and communicate persuasively are also evident in the instructional objectives of thinking critically in Malay and in instilling a positive attitude.

These goals are mentioned overtly in the 2008 Malay Language Primary Syllabus. In this document, MOE (2008: 7) outlined the goal of learning Malay:

> The goal of Malay language learning is to develop every child into being an individual of *Arif Budiman* – a knowledgeable person who contributes to society.

Arif refers to a person who is knowledgeable, whereas *budiman* is a reference to an esteemed person in society, who is well-respected due to his or her demeanor and contributions to society in general. This vision articulates the role of Malay language teaching, which is to equip students with the required knowledge, skills, and attitude to be a knowledgeable person who will subsequently contribute to society. This vision is also supposed to provide a platform for the teachers and students to build language competence as well as for cultural appreciation. The *Arif Budiman* was first coined by the Malay Language Curriculum and Pedagogy Review Committee, which was set up to review the teaching and learning of the language and to ensure its relevance in a globalized world.

Compared to the other Mother Tongue review committees, only the Malay language review committee came out with a clear vision of what should be achieved at the end of a Malay language student's educational journey. This clear vision was further subdivided into primary, secondary and junior college levels. At primary level, in terms of *Arif Budiman*, students are expected to learn as much as possible about Malay language and culture. The journey is introductory in nature and learning is fun. At secondary level, students are expected to become *Arif Budiman* by appreciating the language and culture via various learning activities, while at junior college level, students achieve the *Arif Budiman* vision by sharing their knowledge of the language and culture locally as well as globally.

Malay Language Curriculum Objectives (Primary)

The Malay language learning objective as stipulated in the primary curriculum of 2008 MOE, 2008: 10) is to allow students to have knowledge and understanding of the Malay language and culture as part of Singapore's multi-cultural society. It is also hoped that the students will be available to communicate using standard Malay based on their needs and in their social interactions with society at large.

The instructional objectives for the learning of Malay at primary level are as follows:

1. To hear and understand speech in a formal and informal setting and be able to respond accordingly;
2. To speak clearly and coherently in the standard spoken form with proper intonation on matters pertaining to each speaker and his or her environment;

3. To read various print, electronic media, and digital materials using appropriate reading techniques to gather information, ideas, and knowledge and to respond accordingly;

4. To write various text types based on various prompts for a variety of reasons, people, and situations;

5. To think critically and creatively to explore, create, solve, reach consensus, and decide on a particular matter using language critically and creatively;

6. To know and understand Malay culture and its values as well as those of other countries; and

7. To instill interest in reading and leveraging this in building a culture of lifelong learning.

The learning and instructional objectives thus set out are in line with the *Arif Budiman* vision for primary Malay language education, which is for students to know and understand Malay language and culture as part of the wider Singapore community. This vision is expanded upon when students enter secondary education, where they are required to further understand and appreciate the Malay language and culture in the framework for national development.

Malay Language Curriculum Objectives (Secondary)

The main objective of secondary Malay language education is an extension from the primary objective and is to equip students with language competence so as to help them further understand and appreciate Malay language and culture within the framework of national development.

The instructional objectives for the learning of Malay at secondary level (MOE:2011: 10) are as follows:

1. To hear, understand, and assess speech in formal and informal settings, including those using the mass media, and to respond accordingly;

2. To speak clearly and coherently in standard spoken Malay and to give ideas and viewpoints critically for a variety of reasons, people, and situations;

3. To read, understand, and appreciate various print or non-print materials, including digital materials, either literary or academic in nature, and to gather and process information and be able to apply it effectively;

4. To write various creative and non-creative texts clearly and effectively for various reasons, people, and situations;

5. To use different skills required to plan, generate ideas, investigate, explore, evaluate, make judgments, solve problems, an reach agreement on specific matters using language effectively;

6. To appreciate the language, culture, and values of the Malay community and the nation as well as to know and understand the culture and values of the other communities in the context of national development;

7. To use standard spoken Malay effectively, including grammar, spelling and writing, vocabulary, terminology, language register, and pronunciation in activities pertaining to the four language skills, namely listening, speaking, reading, and writing; and

8. To maintain students' interest in reading and making it a practice as part of building a culture of lifelong learners.

Thus, we can see that the instructional objectives are of a high order. The use of verbs such as "understand" and "appreciate" as against simply "read" is clearly indicative of the increase in difficulty level and is in line with the secondary level *Arif Budiman* vision, which is to explore and appreciate the language and its culture. This is further expanded upon in the syllabus for the pre-university level based on the *Arif Budiman* vision.

Malay Language Curriculum Objectives (Pre-University)

The *Arif Budiman* vision for pre-university level is for the students to build upon Malay language and culture in a creative manner and to show a willingness to face challenges in an ever-changing world. The instructional objectives for the learning of Malay at pre-university level are as follows:

1. To use language to establish identity;
2. To use language as a communication tool, taking into account objectives, people, and the social and community context;
3. To be able to think critically and creatively using Malay;
4. To acquire, evaluate, use, and disseminate information, ideas, and feelings using Malay;
5. To instill positive attitudes toward concepts, ideas, or viewpoints;
6. To immerse themselves in community, national, and universal values;
7. To appreciate and acknowledge elements of Malay culture specifically and other cultures in general;
8. To appreciate language as a medium of understanding culture and knowledge in preparation for studying in a higher institution.

The objectives mentioned above are in line with the *Arif Budiman* vision at pre-university level. Given 12 to 13 years spent learning Malay in a school environment and with clearly outlined instructional objectives, an *Arif Budiman*, a knowledgeable person who contributes to society, will have been born.

Malay Language Programme (Primary School)

Malay language planning is an overt language planning goal with a vision statement, namely *Arif Budiman*. The method employed to attain the acquisition goals is designed to create or improve both opportunities and incentives simultaneously. To analyze the creation and improvement of opportunities, it is necessary to refer to Malay language programs such as ML "B," EMAS, MLEP, subject banding, higher Malay, and foundation Malay. The teaching and learning of the language are based on students' readiness level and interest. Students can learn the language up to the level they are personally able to reach. Thus, opportunities are created and improvements made in terms of teaching and learning as students are able to learn the language based on their ability and readiness level. In terms of incentives, students are able to pace themselves in learning Malay, and if they do well, this will help them with their yearly promotion. Scholarships are given to students who are interested in pursuing Malay at the higher level. Incentives are also given to those taking higher Malay at secondary level since they are not required to take the subject again in JC.

Acquisition of the language as a second or foreign language

Cooper (1989: 158) uses the example of the use of spoken Mandarin by the Taiwanese after China recovered Taiwan from the Japanese in 1945 to show how schools were used as a natural medium for language acquisition. The Chinese banned the use of Japanese, which had been the language of wider communication in Taiwan for the previous 50 years. They then introduced a National Language policy whereby Mandarin was promoted while Japanese was banned, especially in the mass media. In the context of Malay in Singapore, its acquisition as a second language or foreign language was enhanced when in 1987 the Ministry of Education introduced a new Malay language program called the Malay Language Elective Programme, or MLEP. This program offered Secondary 1 students in the top 10% of the PSLE cohort who are non-Malays and are not taking the language as their second language or mother tongue in primary school the opportunity to learn Malay. At the end of their fourth year of study, these students take the Malay as a Second Language Paper in the GCE "O" Level Examination. This scheme was further enhanced in 2005 when MOE began encouraging "more schools to provide school-based Malay (Special Programme) [MSP] and conversational Malay enrichment programmes to their students" (MOE Press Release, 2005: 1). An MSP is an optional General Certificate in Education "Ordinary" Level in a third language subject offered to Secondary 1 students who either are among the top 10% of the PSLE cohort for the previous year or are within the 11-30% band in PSLE with an A* grade in MTL or who obtained a Distinction grade in Higher MTL and at least an A in English Language.

Reacquisition of the language by populations for whom it was once either a vernacular or a language of specialized function

Cooper (1989: 159) highlighted the renativization of Hebrew and Irish as well as the revitalization of Maori as examples of reacquisition of the language by populations for whom it was once either a vernacular or a language of specialized function. Renativization refers to a situation where a language is re-introduced into the community to make it popular again. It also refers to a situation where a language is facing a challenging future in terms of use and teaching and learning. Thus, a movement, program, or campaign is put into place to revitalize it. In the case of the acquisition of Malay, there is not so much renativization of the language as moves to revitalize the language through the language-in-education planning.

Method Employed to Attain Language Planning Goals

In terms of the method employed to attain language planning goals, Cooper (1989) divides these into three categories: 1) methods designed primarily to create or improve opportunities for the learning of a particular language; 2) methods designed to create or improve the incentives to learn the language; and 3) methods designed to create or improve both opportunities as well as incentives to learn the language.

Creating or improving opportunities to learn

Cooper (1989) further sub-divides this approach into two distinct methods: the direct method and the indirect method.

Direct method

In the direct method, Cooper include factors such as

> ...classroom instruction, the provision of materials for self-instruction in the target language, and the production of literature, newspapers, and radio and television programs in simplified versions of the target language. (Cooper, 1989: 159)

In the Singapore context, where the direct method consists of creating or improving opportunities to learn, there is a long list of initiatives that can be evaluated. Among these are the principles mentioned in the Malay language syllabus pertaining to classroom instruction and the development of instructional materials, the communicative approach in teaching, constructivist learning theory, and the differentiated instruction (DI) model.

Principles for classroom instruction and the development of instructional materials

Based on the new Malay language syllabus for the primary level (2008), classroom instruction and the development of instructional materials should be based on a number of principles.

Firstly, it should be student-centered. The teaching method, techniques, and instructional materials should be selected and designed taking into account the students' needs, ability, and learning style. Teachers should be encouraged to vary their teaching strategies to ensure the effective engagement of students at all times.

Secondly, teachers should promote a variety of knowledge types, culture, and Malay values. The use of materials from a variety of knowledge bases will result in more authentic situations and make learning more meaningful. The learning of culture, traditions, and Malay community values should be intertwined and framed within the context of a multi-cultural society. This will help the student link contemporary Malay culture to their own worldview.

Thirdly, classroom instruction should be process-oriented rather than emphasizing products. Process-oriented teaching and learning will ensure the attainment of communicative competence by the students. Process-oriented learning focuses on language and problem-solving strategies that are task-based in nature.

Fourthly, classroom instruction should integrate all the four skills required in learning a language: listening, speaking, reading, and writing. By integrating all four skills in a lesson, students will learn effectively and gain not just language competence but also communicative competence.

Fifthly, classroom instruction and instructional materials developed and used should be contextual in nature. Lessons should be linked to students' daily lives and related to their family and the community. Basic language skills, grammar, vocabulary, and proverbs should be taught within the context of purpose, audience, situation, and culture. Contextual learning will help the students make meaning out in the real world from what is learned in the classroom.

Sixthly, and frequently mentioned, is differentiated teaching. Differentiated teaching refers to a method of classroom instruction that takes into account students' ability, interest, and needs in the classroom. There are three aspects through which a teacher can differentiate in the classroom or when preparing a lesson: 1) differentiating the content taught, which includes differentiating concepts, principles, and skills; 2) differentiating the process in terms of teaching strategies chosen or skills emphasized; and 3) differentiating the product, whereby the end result or the assessment mode is differentiated. Differentiated teaching is dependent on students' needs, ability level, interest, and learning style.

Seventhly, language skills are taught in a structured, hierarchical manner, that is, from listening to speaking, to reading, and lastly to writing. Thus, the higher up in the hierarchy, the greater will be the knowledge and skills learned.

Eighthly, students should be given the opportunity to learn via the communicative approach and to make their learning more active. Through the communicative approach, students will be able to present their ideas and feelings directly. This will develop not only their critical and creative thinking skills but also enhance their communicative competence.

Ninthly, formative assessment, or the concept of assessment for learning, should be propagated as it enhances student learning. Teachers should be encouraged to assess students continuously and interactively.

At the primary level, classroom instruction and instructional material development should be based on both the communicative and the constructivist approaches.

The Communicative Approach

According to Richards and Rodgers (2007: 155), communicative language teaching (CLT) is more of an approach toward language teaching than a method. Thus, they define CLT as an approach (and not a method) that aims to: (a) make communicative competence the goal of language teaching, and (b) develop procedures for the teaching of the four language skills that acknowledge the interdependence of language and communication.

This definition clearly underlines the importance of learning language to attain communicative competence and not just as linguistic competence. In terms of language learning, this definition also indicates the symbiotic relationship among the four language skills and ensures that all learning takes place in context and knowledge learned is functional.

Howatt (1984: 279) agrees with the communicative competence paradigm and adds to it by further differentiating between a "strong" and a "weak" version of CLT, as follows;

> There is, in a sense, a "strong" version of the communicative approach and a "weak" version. The "weak" version, which has become more or less standard practice in the last ten years, stresses the importance of providing learners with opportunities to use their English for communicative purposes and, characteristically, attempts to integrate such activities into a wider program of language teaching. ...The "strong" version of communicative teaching, on the other hand, advances the claim that language is acquired through communication, so that it is not merely a question of activating an existing but inert knowledge of the language but of stimulating the development of the language system itself. If the former could be described as "learning to use" English, the latter entails "using English to learn it."

Therefore, in the context of Malay, the "weak" version of CLT will entail learning to use the language in terms of meta-linguistic knowledge, while the "strong" version will be attained or used only after the learner has acquired knowledge of the language. That knowledge can then be used to further enhance the learner's learning.

Hymes (1972: 281) argued that the goal of language teaching is to develop "communicative competence." He elaborated that when a person acquires this type of competence, he or she attains both knowledge and an ability for language use with reference to:

1. Whether (and to what degree) something is formally possible;
2. Whether (and to what degree) something is feasible in virtue of the means of implementation available;
3. Whether (and to what degree) something is appropriate (adequate, happy, successful) in relation to a context in which it is used and evaluated; and
4. Whether (and to what degree) something is in fact done and actually performed and what it's doing entails. (Hymes 1972: 281)

In order to understand the approach and its stated aims further, we need to look at what communicative competence entails. According to Canale and Swain (1980), there are four dimensions to communicative competence: grammatical competence, sociolinguistic competence, discourse competence, and strategic competence.

Grammatical competence is what Chomsky (1965) refers to as linguistic competence and Hymes terms the "formally possible" (1972: 281). It is a very important component of the learning of a language and is the domain of grammatical and lexical capacity.

Sociolinguistic competence refers to the contextual learning of the language in a society. This societal contextual domain includes the communicative purpose for the interaction, role relationships, and shared information known to the participants. Learning within context and based on functionality is the cornerstone of sociolinguistic competence.

Discourse competence is a persons' ability to interpret elements of individual messages in terms of their interconnectivity with the surroundings and how the meaning of what is said or written is presented and understood within the context of the discourse or the text. This is an important type of competence because it helps speakers understand a discourse or text within its stated domain or field of knowledge.

Strategic competence refers to strategies communicators use to initiate, terminate, maintain, repair, or redirect communication. These are skills to be learned and are sometimes referred to as coping strategies that allow speakers to process information and categorize it and also to initiate or produce information in a form suitable for consumption and understanding.

Thus, the characteristics of the communicative view of language as outlined by Richards and Rodgers (2007: 172) are:

1. Language is a system for the expression of meaning;
2. The primary function of language is to allow interaction and communication;
3. The structure of a language reflects its functional and communicative uses; and
4. The primary units of language are not merely its grammatical and structural features but categories of functional and communicative meaning as exemplified in discourse.

The Constructivist Approach

Oxford (1997: 36) defines constructivism as "the philosophical belief that people construct their own understanding of reality." Students constructing their own meaning is the hallmark of constructivism in education. Cunningham (2006) further outlines seven basic principles of constructivist education. Only through these seven basic principles, Cunningham argues, can a teacher play a crucial role in students' learning and development.

First is the establishment of a cooperative, socio-moral atmosphere for teaching and learning. This is a condition that includes the continuous practice of mutual respect in teaching and learning. There should be, in every classroom, a socio-moral atmosphere that is viewed along a continuum from coercive to cooperative. This state of cooperation should occur among students and teachers as well. This is the most important principle in constructivist education, and all other principles rest on it.

Secondly, curriculum design should be oriented toward meeting the interests of students and providing "meaningful opportunities for construction of knowledge" (2007: 5). A constructivist teacher is able to recognize and stimulate students' interest. This is done through observation of students' spontaneous activities, soliciting ideas about what they want to learn, proposing activities that are enticing, and providing ample opportunities for students to make their own choices in the learning process.

Thirdly, teaching should be designed in terms of the kind of knowledge to be achieved based on three types of knowledge: physical knowledge, logico-mathematical knowledge, and conventional or social knowledge. In constructivism, different strategies for teaching should be applied to each of these types of knowledge.

Fourthly, teachers are required to choose content that is challenging to students. As constructivism is about individuals' construction of their own understanding of reality, a constructivist teacher should promote the creation of a culture of inquiry. Therefore, a constructivist curriculum should focus on the "big ideas" that will allow an in-depth study of concepts, provide activities and materials appropriate to a wide range of developmental levels, and ensure that activities are analyzed in terms of their relevance to the learners.

Fifthly, the promotion of students' reasoning can be achieved via scaffolding tools such as questioning techniques and other forms of interventions that will trigger students' critical thinking. Students' reasoning skills can be enhanced by the constant sharing of ideas and by encouraging students to provide explanations for their ideas.

Sixthly, teachers are to provide adequate time for students' investigation and in-depth engagement. Students will not be able to construct complex relations in their exploration of concepts and ideas if the investigation and engagement time is limited to fifteen or thirty minutes per day. There should thus be time set aside over weeks and even months for the students to fully develop their ideas and construct their own meaning and understanding of the reality in their life.

Lastly, there should be a link between the ongoing documentation of knowledge and the assessment of curriculum activities. Assessment should be made an integral part of teaching and not be separated or left at the end of the knowledge acquisition process. It should be intertwined at every level of knowledge construction to make it more meaningful and provide opportunities for teachers to reflect and intervene during the learning process.

Differentiated Instruction

Differentiated Instruction (DI) was first introduced into Malay language teaching and learning by the Malay Language Curriculum and Pedagogy Review Committee Report (2005). The review committee's terms of reference were:

1. To articulate the objectives of the Malay curriculum used for the different courses at primary, secondary, and pre-university levels;
2. To examine if the implementation of the various Malay syllabi in schools is aligned with the curriculum objectives that are realizable with reasonable effort by the various target groups;
3. To review the effectiveness of the structure of the present Malay curriculum, the different Malay syllabi, the instructional materials, and the examination modes for their respective target groups;
4. To recommend appropriate refinements to the structure of the Malay curriculum to better achieve MOE's mother tongue policy objectives while

recognizing the different linguistic abilities and language backgrounds of Malay language students; and

5. To advise on the effective implementation of the above.

Based on these terms of reference, the committee presented its broad recommendations. One of these, which aimed to develop a dynamic and challenging curriculum, syllabi, and instructional materials, was the pedagogy for differentiated learning. The recommendation was as follows (2005: 48):

> The cultural and linguistic development of the next generation of Malay Singaporeans will require teachers to develop a broader range of teaching skills and a deeper knowledge of language and literature. An ability-driven approach will require differentiated instruction to suit students with differing levels of aptitude and interest in Malay.

The Malay language syllabus for the primary and secondary levels thus suggests the use of Differentiated Teaching in the teaching and learning of Malay. MOE believes that through the use of this method, students will benefit and maximize their potential.

The framework for DI in the Malay syllabus is shown in Diagram 5.1 below.

Diagram 5.1- Differentiated Instruction Model

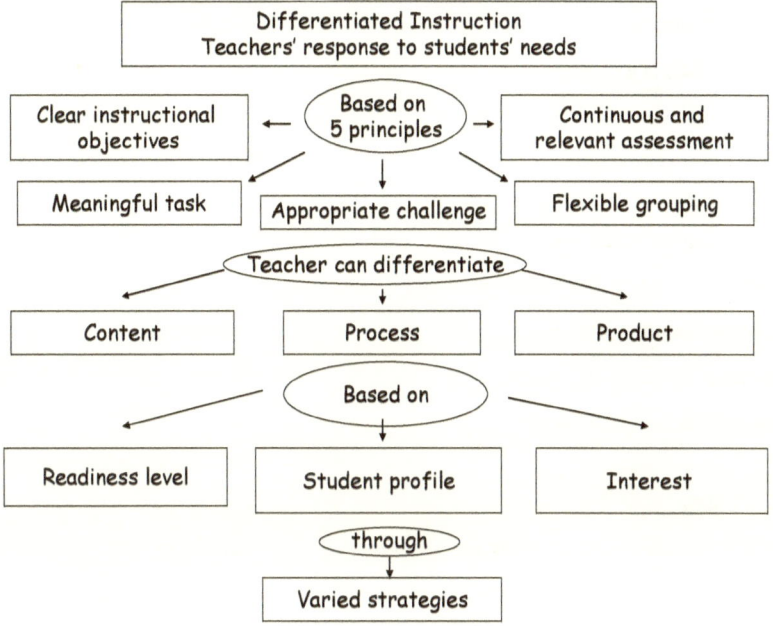

The syllabus further outlines steps to be taken to ensure students' active participation and therefore achieve the DOEs as well as the instructional objectives outlined. The steps, which fit within the framework of Differentiated Instruction, are as follows:

1. Content, aims, and instructional objectives should be made clear;
2. The lessons, activities, and end products should not only be understood by the student but also relevant to him or her;
3. Materials used and assignments given should be interesting, relevant, authentic, and meaningful as well as bring a degree of satisfaction to the student;
4. A conducive learning environment should be provided;
5. Student-centered learning and the use of flexible grouping should be encouraged;

6. Skill difficulty levels and concepts taught should be challenging enough for the students to realize their potential;

7. Continuous and appropriate assessment should be carried out to so that the performance and potential of students can be monitored and improved upon; and

8. Language enrichment activities should be planned to support learning.

Differentiation based on the syllabus

Both the primary (2008) and secondary (2011) Malay syllabi set out to differentiate either the content, process, or product of the lesson, and the choice of differentiation should be based on the students' readiness level, their interests, and their learning profiles. These are follows:

1. Content

    The teacher can choose to differentiate the content or the instructional materials, i.e. what is to be learned by the students and how they can obtain the information. This can be done by varying the reading texts to be used based on students' readiness level, interests, or learning profiles. Teachers are also encouraged to conduct small group meetings or discussions to explain the content to struggling students. The brighter students should be faced with more challenging texts so as to realize their full potential.

2. Process

    Teachers can differentiate the process of teaching by using a variety of activities in the classroom. These activities will turn the students into active learners and help them understand the content and skills taught. The teacher can also differentiate the time spent on specific activities based on differing student abilities. Struggling students will be given more time whereas the more successful ones will require less time. Struggling students should be allowed to complete their assignments or tasks in groups or be given extra scaffolding while the more successful students should be allowed to work independently.

3. Product

    Teachers should set a variety of assignments and tasks based on students' ability and interests. This will give opportunities to students to work individually or in groups, think and re-think, and use and expand what is taught based on their own level of ability throughout the learning process. By differentiating tasks or assignments, students will be encouraged to concentrate on the best ways of producing the target result within the criteria given. Teachers can also differentiate the product by differentiating the assessment mode so as to engage students with differing abilities. Through differentiated assessment modes, weaker students will be given the opportunity to improve while the more successful students will be energized to realize their full potential.

This differentiation can be implemented by using authentic materials as well as by focusing on the functional use of the language being taught. Authentic materials should refer to texts available in the community, such as newspapers, magazines, and online materials while functional use refers to activities that will be of benefit to the students in their daily life.

Indirect method

Cooper (1989: 159) refers to the indirect method as a method whereby "efforts to shape the learners' mother tongue so that it will be similar to the target language" are carried out. In the context of Malay, this was done initially in 1954 when the Second Malay Language and Literary Congress passed a resolution replacing the Jawi script with the Roman script as the official Malay script so as to aid the spread of the language (Abdullah, 2007). This was then followed by the standardization of spoken Malay, which was implemented in 1993 to aid the teaching and learning of the language.

Replacement of the Jawi script with the Roman script

During the First Malay Language and Literary Congress which was held in Singapore in 1952, delegates proposed s change of the official script for Malay from the Jawi script to the Roman script. Heated argument ensued as some delegates felt that the Jawi script should remain as it is the "national Malay writing script" (Abdullah: 2007: 12). Nevertheless, others felt that both have a role to play and they proposed that the Roman script be chosen as the literary script while the Jawi script be used in the writing of Islamic books. Subsequently, a committee was formed to look into the matter and their findings were reported at the 2nd Malay Language and Literary Congress in 1954 held in Seremban, Malaysia. They decided to adopt the Roman script as the official Malay script and use the Jawi script for the teaching and learning of Islam (Abdullah, 2007: 23). This was a momentous decision as it widened the literary catchment to a wider audience, thus increasing opportunities for learning the language.

Promotion of Standard Spoken Malay

Another indirect method used in creating and improving the learning of the language was the introduction of standard spoken Malay, or *sebutan baku*. This was introduced in Singapore in 1992 and implemented in schools in 1993. The Malay Language Council of Singapore, which broached the idea of implementing it in Singapore, had to bring in experts from Malaysia to first explain the reasoning behind the need for this new standard. Secondly, courses were organized for teachers to understand and apply the use of the new standard. Thirdly, there was a move to bring in models of standard spoken Malay. Initially, model speakers from Malaysia were invited to give talks and training sessions for teachers and the media. During the 2010 Malay Language Month, for the first time, Malay language ambassadors from various industries were chosen to lead by example as confident users and speakers of standard spoken Malay.

Promoting the use of the language via Malay Language Month and the Malay Language Learning and Promotion Committee

In shaping learners' attitude toward the language, the Malay Language Council of Singapore (MLCS) used Malay Language Month as a driving force to drive home the message to the community about *sebutan baku* and the benefits that come from using it. Malay Language Month is a yearly program in the Malay language calendar through which grassroots organizations within the community get together to organize events that are language-, literature-, and culture-based. The government sponsors these one-month activities to the tune of $60,000 each year. With the setting up of the Malay Language and Learning Promotion Committee (MLLPC), more activities may be organized. In 2011, the funding given to MLCS to organize its activities was increased to $3.6 million to be used "over the next 5 years to support the Committee's efforts to create environments conducive for the learning and use of the Malay language" (MOE Press Release, 2011: 1).

Creating or improving the incentive to learn

Various incentives are provided by MOE for students to learn the language. These may come in the form of either specialized programs to suit their needs, including Higher Malay programs, Basic Malay programs, or Malay Special programs. Besides these program-based incentives, MOE also provides points-based incentive to students who opt to take Higher Malay. These students receive bonus points for entry into pre-university or junior colleges and may even be exempted from taking the subject if they obtain a Distinction grade. This will act as an incentive for students to do well in their Malay Language examinations.

Creating or improving both opportunities and incentives

With the expansion of the Special Malay Language programs in schools, there has been an improvement in terms of both opportunities and incentives to learn the language. The Elective Programme in Malay Language for Secondary Schools (EMAS) and the Malay Language Elective Programme (MLEP), which were introduced in 2001, were expanded in terms of the number of schools offering them, following the MLCPRC report in 2005. In 2011, three secondary schools offered the EMAS program and three pre-university schools or junior colleges offered the MLEP program. Through these programs, students are able to "attain a high level of proficiency in Malay and a deeper appreciation of Malay culture and literature. Students on these programs are also taken on study trips and immersion programs in Malaysia, Indonesia, and Brunei. As an added incentive, the MOE offers the Lee Kuan Yew Book Prize to the top pre-university level student who obtains a Distinction for both English and Mother Tongue in the General Certificate In Education "Advanced" Level examination.

Conclusion

As a form of acquisition planning, the bilingual policy has had a positive impact on Malay language planning in Singapore. Based on Cooper's (1989) framework of acquisition planning, which can be divided into overt planning and methods for achieving the planning goals, the Malay language has received strong support from the government in terms of creating and improving the opportunities and incentives to learn as well as maintaining the language and enabling it to prosper. The language maintenance goal coupled with opportunities and incentives to learn the language has enabled Malay to remain strong within the bilingual education system.

6

New Malay Language Pedagogy

After analyzing Malay language planning based on Cooper's (1989) framework of status, corpus, and acquisition planning, this chapter will analyze the demographic changes in Malay language users based on the Census of Population 2010 (Census, 2010) as against those conducted in 1980, 1990, and 2000. The demographic changes will give us an insight into the language shift that has been occurring from within the Malay community for the past 30 years and craft a pedagogical response that will help students learn better. Based on these changes, and a comprehensive survey conducted by the Ministry of Education (MOE) in 2004 on the use of Malay among students taking the subject as their mother tongue, this chapter will then offer insights as well as suggestions regarding what a new Malay language pedagogy should focus on. These suggestions will be based on the latest review of the mother tongue entitled Nurturing Active Learners and Proficient Users in 2010 (MOE, 2011). The review committee, which was set up five years after the Malay Language Curriculum & Pedagogy Review Committee report in 2005, shows that there is a need to address the changing language environment in Singapore. According to Prime Minister Lee Hsien Loong, in his acceptance of the committee's report,

> Over the last decades, the language environment in Singapore
> has steadily shifted. We are using English more widely in our
> daily lives. In schools, English is the medium of instruction, with
> MTLs forming an integral part of the curriculum. In homes,
> more parents are talking to their children in English, though

a significant proportion still use Malay, Tamil, Mandarin, or dialects. As a result, students enter school with varied language backgrounds and abilities. (MOE, 2011: iii)

Thus, with the changing demographics and the language shift described above, there is a need "to cater to a wider range of students with different starting points" (MOE, 2011: iii).

This chapter will also review some of the initiatives mentioned in the previous chapter, namely the *Arif Budiman* vision and its impact on Malay language development, issues concerning communicative competence and authentic materials, and approaches to the implementation of the above.

Language shift

There are two main reports indicating language shift within the Malay community. The first report based on the 2010 Census of Population and produced by the Department of Statistics, Ministry of Trade and Industry, a 10-yearly assessment of Singapore's development and changes to its population and households. "It provides benchmark data for all demographic, economic and social statistics" (MTI, 2010; i). The second report is a survey commissioned by the Ministry of Education on Malay language use and attitudes towards the language by students and parents. This survey was commissioned by the MOE for the Malay Language Curriculum & Pedagogy Review (MLCPRC) Report. (MOE, 2005a)

Population Census 2010

The 2010 population census shows the shift in language use from Malay to English among the Malay community. The 2010 census shows that the percentage of Malays aged five and above speaking Malay at home is currently 82.7%. This is a fall of nearly 10% from the 2000 census, which recorded 91.6% of Malays aged five and above speaking Malay at home. There has also been a corresponding increase in the percentage of Malays speaking English at home, from 7.9% in the 2000 census to 17% in the 2010 census, or a nearly 10% increase over ten years earlier.

Table 4   Dominant Home Language of Resident Malay Population Aged Five and Over (in %)

Language used at home	1980	1990	2000	2010
English	1.5	6.1	7.9	17.0
Malay	97.7	93.7	91.6	82.7
Others	0.7	0.1	0.5	0.3

Source: MOE, 2004: 60; Census of Population, 2010: 26

As can be seen from the table above, the largest ten-year decrease in the use of Malay as the dominant home language was from 2000 (91.6%) to 2010 (82.7%), or an 8.9% decrease. By comparison, the decrease was 4% from 1980 (97.7%) to 1990 (93.7%) and 2.1% from 1990 (93.7%) to 2000 (91.6%).

In addition, this decrease in the use of Malay as the dominant home language among the Malay community has been accompanied by a corresponding increase in the use of English as the dominant home language. As we can see from the table above, there was a 15.5% increase in the number of Malay household recording English as their dominant home language between 1980 (1.5%) and 2010 (17%). On a ten-year scale, the increase was greater from 2000 (7.9%) to 2010 (17%), or an increase of 9.1 percentage points. Between 1980 (1.5%) and 1990 (6.1%), the increase was 4.6% but only 1.8% between 1990 (6.1%) and 2000 (7.9%). Overall, this increase shows that the English-knowing bilingualism phenomenon has infiltrated Malay households and will most likely have an effect on the development and maintenance of the language.

An interesting point to note is that of the 78,090 Malays aged 5 years and above who frequently use English at home, 40,920 (or more than 50%) of them reside in Housing & Development Board (HDB) five-room or executive flats and in condominiums and private residences such as terraced houses or bungalows. This shows that there is a link between English language use among Malay families and their residential type. In the Singapore context, a larger house or a private landed or terraced property denotes a professional and/or successful individual or family. This shows that the higher the socioeconomic status, the less Malay is likely to be used.

However, the 2010 census also shows that 47% of Malay graduates frequently use English at home as compared with only 4.4% of those with less than secondary education. Therefore, there is also a link between the use of English versus Malay and level of education.

Changing Demographics of Malay Speakers

Based on the 2004 MLCPRC report (MOE, 2004), a greater number of Malay students entering Primary 1 do not speak the language at home or as their main language at home or among friends. Thus, there is a need to re-examine and re-invent the way Malay is taught not only to non-Malay students but also to Malay students themselves. The MLCPRC report indicates that although Malay remains the dominant home language in Malay homes, a greater number of Malay parents are using English at home with their children.

Table 5 Language Used by Malay Parents with their Children

% of parents who speak to their child in	Level			
	P4	P6	S2	S4
English	9.9	10.6	10.8	10.1
English & Malay	56.9	49.2	46.3	46.9
Malay	28.7	36.8	40.1	39.4

Source: MOE, 2004: 60

The table above shows the percentage of Malay parents who either speak only English, only Malay, or both English and Malay to their children. If we take a closer look, we can see that the percentage of Malay parents speaking only Malay to their children is relatively higher at S2 (40.1%) and S4 (39.4%) levels than at P4 (28.7%) and P6 (36.8%) levels. This difference of between 11.4% and 2.6%, respectively, indicates that the younger generation of parents use Malay when speaking to their children at home less than did their older counterparts. This shift is likely to be reflected in school as these students move up to S2 and S4 levels.

Table 6   Student Use of Malay with Relatives and Friends

% of students who use Malay to converse with	Level			
	P4	P6	S2	S4
Grandparents/older relatives/uncles/aunts	82.2	85.3	87.5	86.8
Father	76.0	79.2	81.4	78.9
Mother	75.6	78.9	84.8	83.4
Brother/sister	71.3	75.7	82.7	81.4
Cousins	72.3	74.4	76.4	71.1
Friends/classmates	51.1	57.5	74.4	71.8

Source: MOE, 2004: 61

The table above further shows that there has been a decrease in the use of Malay by students, especially those in lower school levels. Based on a survey conducted by MOE in 2004, 82.2% of P4 students indicated that they use Malay when speaking to relatives, as compared to 86.8% of S4 students. This is a decrease of 4.6%. Moreover, there has been a similar decrease in the use of Malay when these students speak to their father (P4 – 76%, S4 – 78.9%) and mother (P4 – 75.6%, S4 – 83.4%), or a fall of 2.9% and 7.8%, respectively. The largest decrease is in the use of Malay with friends and classmates, where only 51.1% of P4 students use Malay as compared to 71.8% of S4 students, or a decrease of 20.7%. This decrease points to a decline in the use of Malay among the younger generation of students when they interact with their family members and their friends.

Thus there needs to be a concerted effort to expand the domain of use of Malay among students so that they can practice what is taught in their classrooms. With an expanded domain, there will be greater exposure to and greater use of the language, and students' communicative skills will improve. By contrast, the currently limited domain will affect practice and usage in an authentic environment.

Nurturing Active Learners and Proficient Users

The 2010 Mother Tongue Languages (MTL) Review Committee had as its terms of reference a slew of deliverables required to see through the teaching of MTL to a new group of learners for the 21st century. Among the terms outlined for the committee were the following:

1. Articulate the philosophy and aims underlying the teaching of MTLs to different groups of learners;
2. Identify the implications of longer-term trends and developments in the language environment in Singapore for the teaching and learning of MTLs;
3. Survey best practices in the teaching, learning, and assessment of MTLs;
4. Recommend the appropriate approach to customize MTL learning for learners of different MTL abilities; and
5. Review the use of ICT in the teaching, learning, and assessment of MTLs.

In addition to the five terms listed above, the committee was also tasked with recommending appropriate enhancements or additions to the teaching and learning of MTLs. Specifically, the committee was tasked with looking into the following:

1. Defining learning outcomes for the different groups of MTL learners;
2. Recommend effective pedagogies to engage the interest and maximize the learning of students across the spectrum of MTL ability;
3. Recommend appropriate assessment modes and formats for the various target groups, including the greater use of computer-aided assessment; and
4. Recommend measures to support our most capable MTL learners in achieving a higher level of proficiency.

With these tasks thus laid out, the committee went about its work by consulting the different stakeholders and also made study trips to Australia, China, India, Malaysia, and the United States to observe the latest developments in teaching, learning, and language testing.

Recommendations of the Review Committee

Based on the terms of reference mentioned above, the committee made four recommendations aimed at enhancing MTL teaching and learning in Singapore. These recommendations were:

1. Aligning teaching and testing in order to achieve proficiency;
2. Enhancing different provisions for learners of different abilities;
3. Creating an environment more conducive to MTL use and learning; and
4. Deploying and developing more MTL teachers.

These recommendations will be discussed further below, and this will be followed by a discussion of how these recommendations may be implemented based on evidence-based research.

Aligning Teaching and Testing to Achieve Proficiency

The recommendation for the alignment of teaching and testing to achieve proficiency is further sub-divided into five aspects: 1) recognition of the different starting points for each student; 2) the use of proficiency descriptors to motivate progress; 3) the strengthening of interactive skills; 4) greater use of Information and Communication Technology (ICT); and 5) proficiency tests via continuous assessment and examinations.

Recognizing different starting points

In aligning the teaching and testing of MTLs to achieve proficiency, the committee recommended that the customized teaching approaches recommended in the 2004-5 MTL reviews be expanded and built upon. This customized teaching approach refers to the Differentiated Instruction Model (Tomlinson, 2001), which differentiates between students' readiness level, interests, and learner profiles. Factors thus differentiated are the content taught, the teaching and learning process, and the end product of the lessons.

According to Tomlinson (2001), the Differentiated Instruction Model is one that is proactive and qualitative in nature rather than quantitative. It is also rooted in assessment and student-centeredness. In terms of activities, it promotes a blend of whole-class, group, and individual instruction. It is also referred to as organic, that is, original and authentic.

In addition to the Differentiated Instruction (DI) model, new emphasis is to be given to oracy skills, building their foundations before tackling reading and writing. The report recommends more "systematic teaching of oral vocabulary and sentence structures to develop students' foundational language skills" (MOE, 2011: 6). These oracy skills can be attained via exposure to the language found in the public domain and the use of high-frequency words and sight words (see below for a definition) to give the students a headstart in learning the language.

High-frequency words are words that regularly appear in printed materials. According to Hillerich (1974: 353),

> Just three words: 'I', 'and', and 'the' account for ten percent of
> all words printed in English.

In the English language, these words tend to be abstract words that students are not able to picture or for which phonic clues are of no use. However, by learning to recognize high-frequency words by sight, students will develop fluency in reading. In the learning of English, there is the use of Dolch sight words (www.dolchsightwords.com) and BBC high frequency words (www.bbc.co.uk/schools). However, it is not clear that this can be replicated in the learning of Malay. So far, there has been only one classroom study in the use of high-frequency words by struggling readers. Subhan and Sukaimi (2009) looked at the use of high-frequency words to teach reading for struggling readers in a lower primary classroom in Singapore. The researchers investigated the impact of using these in the teaching of reading to struggling readers as an alternative to the widespread use of phonetics in Malay language teaching. The findings of this study showed that the students' confidence level in reading was boosted, thus making reading less daunting for them.

Meanwhile, sight words refer to words that are recognizable by a reader automatically. The idea of learning via sight word recognition is a concept that was first introduced by Vukelich (2012: 162). The idea is that students first learn to recognize letters before they are ready to learn to recognize whole words and that they will learn significant words earlier than others. According to Temple, Ogle, Crawford, and Freppon (2005), primary students encounter on average 100 high-frequency words before they move on to a higher grade. Sight word recognition is known to be a useful strategy in enhancing reading fluency and reading comprehension.

Thus far, Malay has been taught using the syllable differentiation method whenever a new word is introduced. The word is normally spelled out by being broken up into its syllables and articulated syllable by syllable. This method has served the learning of the language well. However, given the changing demographics and the increase in the percentage of Malay households indicating English as the dominant home language, there should be a reexamination of this issue. The use of high frequency words and sight words may in fact be a better alternative especially with the changing demographics where a greater number of Malay households and families do not speak the language at home. The usage of sight words and high frequency words may be a good way to introduce the language to students especially when they have limited vocabulary.

As regards Malay, there has only been one action research study of the use of high-frequency words in the teaching and learning of the language. The study, conducted by Subhan and Sukaimi (2009), indicated an increase in the ability of students to recognize words and demonstrate reading progress, both factors being linked to the use of high-frequency words. Moreover, one of the objectives of this study was to develop a list of high-frequency words that can be used in the teaching of Malay in order to enhance the teaching and learning of the language among non-native speakers. Given the changing demographics in Singapore, the use of high-frequency words and sight words has the potential to enhance the learning of Malay among Malay students whose dominant language is English.

More studies of this type need to be conducted so as to ensure that new and effective methods can be tried and tested in the Malay language classroom. If more such studies were to be conducted, there could be enough evidence to shift the teaching of Malay from one that is phonetically based to a more visual method of teaching. A list of Malay high-frequency words could also be developed and used at different levels to aid in the teaching of reading and in expanding the vocabulary of students. With the students' confidence boosted, their oracy skills should normally increase. Then, after oracy and reading come writing skills, which will have to be taught in a much more systematic manner in mother tongue classes. These lessons should build on the students' strong oracy foundation and reading programs.

One such program, which is run by schools and supported by MOE, is the Extended Reading Programme (ERP), which aims to widen the students' vocabulary. The ERP has been given a new lease of life within Malay language teaching and learning with the introduction of an island-wide reading program for all schools. This program has been boosted by an injection of resources provided to both primary and secondary schools in the form of funds allocated to the purchase of books and to conducting activities aiming to enhance the reading experience of students. Teachers who attend courses on teaching and promoting reading are awarded the title of Reading Champions, to indicate and recognize their expertise in this skill.

Another approach that could be considered is the bilingual teaching strategy, whereby a language is taught via the students' prior knowledge of the L1. Goh (2002) conducted a pilot project on the bilingual approach as it was being implemented in four schools involving 80 Primary 1 students. The key features of the pilot project were:

1) Chinese as the main medium of instruction and English as a supplementary tool:
    a. To be used as a transitional measure at a learner's early stage of learning Chinese;

    b.   Chinese as the main medium of instruction with English as a supplementary tool;

    c.   Ratio of English use to Chinese: about 30% to 70%; and

    d.   The frequency of English use decreases as the level of Chinese shows gradual improvement.

2) Equal emphasis of the four skills.

    a.   The bilingual approach to include listening, speaking, reading, and writing skills;

3) Actively activate the meta-cognition of learners by:

    a.   Raising of metalinguistic awareness of both languages;

    b.   Enabling students to distinguish similarities and differences between Chinese and English;

    c.   Making the dominant language a resource rather than an obstacle; and

    d.   Viewing the dominant language, which in this instance refers to the predominant home language, as a resource and not as an obstacle that needs to be overcome. (Goh, 2007: 124)

The pilot project was deemed successful enough for the Ministry of Education to add funding and extend the research to more schools that request to use the bilingual approach. A similar bilingual strategy could be adopted for Malay, taking into account the experience gained form this pilot project. However, some areas need to be examined before any such implementation can take place. Based on the Chinese experience, Goh (2007) highlighted some areas for further exploration. In particular, he indicated that if the bilingual approach were to prove viable, a number of enablers need to be put in place. These are:

- A set of differentiated teaching materials that should be developed and dedicated to bilingual use and based on students' differing ability levels. At present, the pilot project uses a standard Chinese language textbook meant for L1 students;

- Bilingual teacher training should be conducted for teachers planning to use this approach. The availability of effective bilingual teachers is important to the success of this approach. The teachers chosen must be "proficient and comfortable in using both Chinese and English" (Goh, 2007: 127);

- Class size should be smaller than the current norm so that opportunities can be given to each student to use the language at its optimum level in the classroom; and

- Schools should "organize programmes to immerse these L2 learners in a dominantly Chinese-speaking environment, either locally or overseas" (Goh, 2007: 127).

In the context of Malay, these enablers should be put in place before Malay language teaching can use this approach. Without them, the outcome desired may not be attainable.

Using Proficiency Descriptors to Motivate Progress

The report also states that

> The learning of the MTL must lead to students applying and using it in their lives. Our MTL curriculum will aim to develop students into proficient language users who can communicate in a confident, effective, and meaningful way in real-life situations. (MOE, 2011: 6)

The reference to making language teaching functional and authentic is not new but was in fact mentioned in the 2004-5 review committee's report. The difference in this review is the use of proficiency descriptors, which are meant to "help teachers tailor their teaching, classroom activities, and assessments" (MOE, 2011: 7). The proficiency descriptors will be provided by MOE, and they will clearly spell out the language skills and attainment level that students in P2, P4, P6, S2, and S4 should achieve.

The problem is how to devise these descriptors. If this is not achieved, it is possible that some students may be categorized as not having mastered the language and therefore assumed to lack proficiency in it. This suggests "mastery learning,", or the Mastery Learning Teaching Method, a learning approach whose goal is to have all students learn instructional material at a specified level. Under this method, the teacher breaks down the course content into manageable units and creates formative tests for the students to take at the end of each unit.

There are two influential models of mastery learning (Kulik, Kulik, & Bangert-Drowns: 1990). These are the classical approach, promoted by Bloom (1976), also is called Learning for Mastery (LFM), and Keller's (1968) Personalized System of Instruction (PSI). As Kulik et al. (1990) explain, even though both models are similar in nature, there are marked differences in terms of implementation:

> Lessons in LFM courses are teacher-presented, and students move through these courses at a uniform, teacher-controlled pace. Lessons in PSI courses are presented largely through written materials, and students move through these lessons at their own rates. Students who fail unit quizzes in PSI courses must restudy material and take tests on the material until they are able to demonstrate mastery. Students who fail unit quizzes in LFM courses usually receive individual or group tutorial help on the unit before moving on to new material. (Kulik et al., 1990: 265)

Bloom's classic theoretical formulation seems more in line with the Singapore model of education, whereby formative assessment is used as a tool to help the student attain a specific level of language or knowledge acquisition. Bloom also highlights the fact that in mastery learning, each student is given the right amount of instruction required in order to attain mastery of the content. This instruction also varies according to the student's needs. Bloom (1968) predicts that thanks to mastery learning, 90% of the students will perform at the level previously reached by the top 10% and that the correlation between initial student aptitude and performance outcome is near zero. Bloom (1976) later claimed that students need not put in extra hours on school work to achieve better grades by using the LFM model. Only those with weak knowledge backgrounds should devote more time at the beginning of the learning process. Subsequently, with a confident command of the fundamentals, they should be able to grasp concepts and learn at the same pace as the rest of the students.

However, what is required in mastery learning is inevitably mastery teaching, which is described by Morrison (1924: 74, cited in Laska, 1985: 307) as "pre-test, teach, test the result, adapt procedure, teach, and test again to the point of actual learning." In mastery teaching, the pre-test stage refers to diagnostic testing of the students' current ability, level of knowledge, or cognitive status. Thus, the teacher will have to craft the learning or instructional objectives of the lesson based on this finding and take into account the students' ability, knowledge, and cognitive status, and adapt teaching procedures as required. This effort by the teacher is important in mastery teaching, in which the teacher must have the willingness and be given the opportunity to help the student learn. Only then can the teacher adapt procedures and help the student achieve. Morrison (1924, cited in Laska, 1985: 307) calls these two basic principles "the willingness and opportunity principle" and "the achievability principle."

Moreover, the above-mentioned descriptors should act as motivators for students to learn the language. With clearer goals, students will be motivated to participate in authentic and functional activities in the classroom. Descriptors should also be functional pedagogically. An example will be descriptors for proficiency reading. If a student has reached the proficiency level based on the descriptors, then the outcome is successful. A problem only arises if the proficiency level is not met. Descriptors should therefore be based on level of ability, from minimal performance to basic and from proficient to advance.

If a student achieves minimal or basic performance, the teacher should be equipped with intervention strategies to ensure that the student achieves the required proficiency level. Thus, emphasizing intervention approaches should be more useful than devising proficiency descriptors.

Approaches to Intervention

There were three intervention approaches proposed by the committee with a view to nurturing active learners and proficient users of the mother tongue. These are: 1) a strengthening of interactive skills with particular emphasis on spoken interaction and written interaction skills; 2) greater use of ICT to engage students and enhance their learning experience, and 3) an approach to assessment and examinations that tests for proficiency in language use.

Strengthening Interactive Skills

The committee recommends a strengthening of interaction skills. This is in line with the emphasis on oracy skills mentioned earlier. The committee further indicated that the

> ...curriculum will emphasize spoken interaction and written interaction skills in addition to the four basic skills of listening, reading, speaking, and writing. (MOE, 2011: 7)

This is in line with the communicative approach to language teaching, which starts from a theory of language as a communication tool, which, as mentioned earlier, Hymes (1972) refers to as "communicative competence." According to Hymes, a communicatively competent person should have both knowledge and ability to use language within different situations, appropriacy and context. Therefore, a communicatively competent person is a confident user of the language and has both spoken and interactive skills, including the four language skills currently taught in schools.

Following Hymes, Halliday (1975: 11-17) outlined seven basic functions performed by language. These functions are as follows;

1. The instrumental function: using language to get things done;
2. The regulatory function: using language to control the behavior of others;
3. The interactional function: using language to create interactions with others;

4. The personal function: using language to express personal feelings and meanings;

5. The heuristic function: using language to learn and discover;

6. The imaginative function: using language to create a world of the imagination; and

7. The representational function: using language to communicate information.

These functions highlight the multi-faceted uses of language, and in order help students attain communicative competence, these functions need to be taken into account in classroom teaching.

As was discussed earlier, Canale and Swain (1980) offer a pedagogically influential analysis of communicative competence, which was divided into four dimensions, namely grammatical competence, sociolinguistic competence, discourse competence, and strategic competence. In grammatical competence the speaker is a strong user of the language in terms of linguistic knowledge and is able to use them effectively. Sociolinguistic competence refers to a persons' understanding of language use within society in terms of the community's idiosyncracy and the language nuances. Discourse competence refers to the interconnectedness of an individuals' message as well as the correlation between text and meaning. Lastly, strategic competence is a reference to how a speaker copes with the use of the language within context for his own benefit.

An emphasis on communicative language teaching should therefore apply to Malay based on the following principles:

1. Language is a system for the expression of meaning;

2. The primary function of language is to allow interaction and communication;

3. The structure of language reflects its functional and communicative uses;

4. The primary units of language are not merely its grammatical and structural features but categories of functional and communicative meaning as exemplified in discourse (Richards & Rodgers, 2007: 161).

Based on the above mentioned principles, communicative Malay language teaching should be functional, authentic, and meaningful for the students.

Greater Use of Information and Communication Technology (ICT)

The committee recommended greater use of ICT for teachers to leverage students' knowledge. Teachers will receive assistance in undertaking this initiative via a forthcoming resource package that will promote interaction skills and greater use of ICT. However, according to Petty (2007), use of ICT ranks lowest in terms of effectiveness in obtaining a higher grade. According to Petty (2007: 1), "it is not what the technology does that makes it effective, but what the student does." Petty's findings were based on the most effective teaching method based on 500,000 peer-reviewed effect sizes. An effect size of 1.0 is roughly equivalent to two grade points in the General Certificate of Education (GCE) Advanced Level Examination. Further, according to Petty, 2007, the common factors in the highest effect sizes are appropriately challenging tasks, active learning with clear purpose and strong teacher direction, and feedback given to both the teacher and the learner. Based on Hattie's (1999, cited in Petty, 2007: 2) for computer-assisted instruction, the average effect size received was a mere 0.37. Hattie indicated that it is not the computers but the teaching processes the students can mimic and enhance that creates the effect. Thus, teachers should be equipped not only with the necessary knowledge of the software but also with pedagogical content knowledge in terms of how the software, such as a social networking website, for example, can be used for teaching and learning. Pedagogical factors and task-based learning should be employed as a strategy when confronting the use of ICT.

Assessments and Examinations that Test for Proficiency

There needs to be an "alignment between curriculum and assessment" (MOE, 2011: 8). This seems to be the general concern of stakeholders during focus group discussions. There should be deeper understanding of how formative assessment can be used to analyze students' knowledge and understanding levels. Assessment of the deep learning concept (Ramsden, 1988) should be practiced. From this perspective, a deep learner is someone with an intrinsic motivation to do well in his or her studies, whereas a surface learner is someone with an extrinsic motivation. An intrinsically motivated person refers to someone who is self-motivated and self-directed in his actions, whereas in extrinsic motivation, it comes from the outside e.g. in the form of perks or prizes given.

Table 7   Differences between Deep and Surface Learners

Deep	Surface
The focus is on what is signified	The focus is on the signs (or on the learning as a signifier of something else)
Relates previous knowledge to new knowledge	The focus on unrelated parts of the task
Relates knowledge from different courses	Information for assessment is simply memorized
Relates theoretical ideas to everyday experience	Facts and concepts are associated non-reflectively
Relates and distinguishes evidence and argument	Principles are not distinguished from examples
Organizes and structures content into a coherent whole	The task is treated as an external imposition
The emphasis is internal (intrinsic), from within the student	The emphasis is external (extrinsic), from the demands of assessment

(Based on Ramsden, 1988)

As can be seen in the table above, a deep learner is a self-motivated student who relates new learning to previous knowledge and is able to organize and structure the resulting knowledge into a coherent whole. A surface learner, on the other hand, is more of a learn-what-is-required type of student, who is more interested in the assessment result rather in than the process of learning. Therefore, there needs to be a focus on developing a deep learner since it is not enough simply to aim for an alignment between curriculum and assessment, in which case the surface learner will master the content with assessment in mind and achieve high grades without being able to use the knowledge attained beyond the examination stage. Thus, in line with changes in terms of assessment, there should be changes to examination formats. These changes will come in the form of

> ...new item types (e.g., testing interaction skills), modifications
> to item types (e.g., use of video stimuli instead of line drawings
> for oral examinations), and a reduction in some existing items.
> (MOE, 2011: 6)

This should help produce deep learners as the testing of interaction skills and the use of video stimuli will test the students' relational ability, i.e. relating what they have learned to real life situations.

Enhancing Different Provisions for Learners of Different Abilities
In line with ability-driven education, in which a student should be allowed to learn Malay to the best of his or her ability, the review committee recommended additions and enhancements to facilitate more customized programs and to open these up and made them more widely available. In particular, there should also be programs catering to the needs and ability level of those who are weaker in the subject. However, the different starting points are meant to benefit not only the weaker students but also those who are linguistically inclined and show greater bilingual ability.

This proposal was to be implemented via either subject banding in primary schools, whereby linguistically stronger students would study their respective mother tongue at a higher level while weaker students would study it at the foundation level. Another initiative introduced was the school-based curriculum design concept, whereby schools would design their own curriculum to suit the needs of their students, with interventions planned for weaker students at appropriate times to ensure that sufficient scaffolding is provided. Although the objective is still that students pass the Primary School Leaving Examination (PSSLE), the process could be differentiated for each school.

Creating an Environment Conducive to Mother Tongue Use and Learning

In this respect, the committee recognized the need for a mother tongue domain out of the classroom and the school, where the language should be used. To this end, schools should be given "structured time and programmes to create an environment that encourages students to use the MTL and appreciate the culture" (MOE, 2011: 15).

Among the recommendations aiming at creating a conducive environment for mother tongue use, the committee proposed annual school-based "MTL Fortnights." These would be a joint collaboration with community organizations and key stakeholders including parents and alumni. There would also be cultural camps where students would be encouraged to learn and use the language, take part in structured reading programs to cultivate the habit of reading books in the mother tongue, and engage parents to support their children in mother tongue learning.

It is greatly hoped that with these added initiatives, the MTL-speaking domain can be enhanced and students can be given the opportunity to use the language outside of the classroom. This should help them achieve communicative competence in the language.

Deploying and Developing More MTL Teachers

With more initiatives and programmes, there needs to be a corresponding increase in the work force required to administer and ensure the continued survival of the mother tongue. Thus, the committee recommended that more MTL teachers be recruited in the coming years. According to the report, good teachers are key to the delivery of quality teaching and learning in the classroom" (MOE, 2011: 17). Consequently, MOE has decided to increase the intake of MTL teachers by a further 500 within the next few years.

In terms of Malay language teaching and learning, there should be a re-examination of the way this is taught. The old ways of teaching, using syllables at the lower primary level should be replaced by the development of Malay sight words and high-frequency words. This will help further develop reading competencies among young learners of Malay who do not speak the language at home.

Issues Pertaining to Language Acquisition Planning

In Chapter 5, which discussed language acquisition planning, there arose some issues affecting the development of new Malay language pedagogy. They are the *Arif* Budiman vision, matters pertaining to communicative competence, and revisiting some of the recommended approaches.

Arif Budiman Vision

The *Arif Budiman* vision, which was promoted by the Malay Language Curriculum and Pedagogy Review Committee (MLCPRC) report in 2005, was described by the chairperson of the committee as a holistic self-development concept based on internal and external structures. The internal structure refers to manifestations of a person's mind, emotions, and value system, whereas the external structure refers to a person's wisdom in using the language and in general behavior (Hadijah, 2008). Since the vision for Malay language teaching and learning was included in the Primary Malay Language Syllabus of 2008 and the Secondary Malay Language Syllabus of 2011, there has only been one other academic discussion on the matter, that by Azhar (2011). Azhar highlights that *Arif Budiman* is a vision of values development in Malay language teaching and learning that is meant to strengthen cultural identity and strong citizenship among Malays (Azhar, 2011: 188). Azhar also indicates that the concept should not be looked at as an academic issue but instead discussed as an integral part of social idealism and an educational vision that has an effect on the society's future (Azhar, 2011: 189). He then went further and listed and described ten characteristics linked to being an *Arif Budiman*. These were being accepting of responsibilities, seeing oneself as part of society and humankind in general, using one's intellect, being progressive, critical and creative all in one, being proud of one's heritage, accepting diversity, being steadfast in one's religious beliefs, having moral courage, rejecting moral exclusion, and having a historical mind (Azhar, 2011: 192-195).

Regrettably, however, the issue here is the promotion of the *Arif Budiman* vision to a wider audience, especially given that research on its impact remains limited. Since the vision is promoted via the teaching and learning of Malay in schools, its scope for development and outreach is limited. Beyond the scope of schooling and education, there is no mention of the vision except for the annual Malay Language Month in 2006, when *Arif Budiman* was made the theme for that year. This limited scope coupled with limited discussion of its values and characteristics, as outlined by Azhar (2011), will result in a promising vision being curtailed by implementation issues.

Communicative Competence and Authentic Situations

With the emphasis on communicative competence and assessment based on authentic situations in order to make learning come alive, there arises another problem in the Malay language situation. With the use of standard pronunciation, or *sebutan baku*, the context becomes an issue. Based on the guidelines indicated by the Malay Language Council of Singapore and adopted by the Ministry of Education, *sebutan baku* is to be used in clearly specified situations which includes classroom discourse, formal occasions and in the media. Thus the communicative competence to be achieved will be that of the formal domain rather than the informal. For authenticity's sake, the informal domain will not use the standard pronunciation because in an authentic situation, the pronunciation used is different, and this spoken variety cannot therefore be used in the classroom. This leads to a problem with communicative competence and authentic use of language in context.

Revisiting Approaches

Given some of the initiatives mentioned, including differentiated instruction, cooperative learning strategies, and the communicative approach, there needs to be more qualitative and quantitative research on their use in the Malay language classroom. This lack of classroom research in the teaching and learning of Malay will result in approaches chosen based on ideology and not necessarily on careful and systematic observation.

Conclusion

This chapter touched on language shift in terms of the changing demographics of Malay users based on the 2010 Population Census. This chapter also highlighted the latest review of the teaching of mother tongues due to these changing demographics. The review committee's recommendations which include the alignment of teaching and testing, various approaches to intervention, differentiated instruction, and creating a conducive environment for MTL learning, which together should go a long way to addressing the language shift issue. The concept of teaching for understanding and the six facets of understanding described above are important components in developing a student who not only knows the language but also understands how to use the knowledge that he or she possesses. This concept can also be linked to deep learning in that the student is a self-motivated learner whose main objective is not simply passing an examination but learning and expanding his or her range of knowledge and skills. In fact, both concepts are linked to the concept of *Arif Budiman*, the vision of the ideal Malay language learner, or a knowledgeable person who contributes to society.

7

Further Directions in Malay Language Planning

This chapter will discuss further directions in Malay language planning in a bilingual environment and recommend initiatives for facing these challenges. But first, it will be necessary to revisit the main aim of this book, which was to examine the impact of the Singapore bilingual policy on Malay language planning and subsequently answer the three questions outlined in Chapter 1. These were:

1. Has the bilingual policy in any way affected the growth of Malay in Singapore, or has the policy thwarted its use in an English speaking environment?

2. How can the language shift and changing attitudes toward Malay be addressed? What pedagogical approaches should be used to support Malay in an English-knowing bilingual context such as Singapore?

3. Can Malay still play its role as "cultural ballast" for the Malay community in the 21st century, when more Malay Primary 1 students join school with less than basic knowledge of the language?

In Chapter 1, we discussed the meaning of bilingualism based on relevant theories as well as types of bilingualism and their relationship with biliteracy. The concept of bilingual education was also explained together with its aims, types, and effects. The different frameworks for language planning and its goals were also discussed. This was followed by an outline of Singapore's bilingual policy and a discussion of the language planning structure for Malay. Chapter 2 reviewed committee reports that have had an impact on the bilingual policy and in particular on Malay. This was followed by a reexamination of studies of English-Malay bilingualism. Chapters 3 through 5 used Cooper's (1989) framework for language planning i.e., status, corpus, and acquisition planning, In essence, these three chapters analyzed the state of status planning, corpus planning and acquisition planning in Singapore for Malay language based on Cooper's theoretical framework. Chapter 6 looked at the new Malay language pedagogy that could be used in light of demographic changes in the Malay-speaking population. Chapter 7 will now begin with an analysis of Malay language planning, using Cooper's (1989) language planning accounting scheme.

An Accounting Scheme for the Study of Language Planning

Recall Cooper's (1989) view of language planning as "what *actors* attempt to influence what *behaviors* of which *people* for what *ends* under what *conditions* by what *means* through what *decision making process* with what *effect*" (Cooper, 1989:98).

Table 8   Accounting scheme for the study of language planning

I	What *actors* (e.g., formal elites, influential individuals, counter-elites, non-elite policy implementers)
II	Attempt to influence what *behaviors* • Structural (linguistic) properties of planned behavior (e.g., homogeneity, similarity) • Purposes and functions for which planned behavior is to be used • Desired level of adoption (awareness, evaluation, proficiency, usage)
III	Of which *people* • Type of target (e.g., individuals v. organizations, primary v. intermediary) • Opportunities for the target to learn the planned behavior • Incentives the target may have to learn or use the planned behavior • Incentives the target may have to reject the planned behavior
IV	For what *ends* • Overt (language related behaviors) • Latent (non-language related behaviors, the satisfaction of interests)

V	Under what *conditions*
	 • Situational (events, transient conditions)
	 • Structural
	   • Political
	   • Economic
	   • Social/demographic/ecological
	 • Cultural
	   • Regime norms
	   • Cultural norms
	   • Socialization of authorities
	 • Environmental (influences from outside the system)
	 • Informational (data required for a good decision)

VI	By what *means* (e.g., authority, force, promotion, persuasion)
VII	Through what *decision making process* (decision rules) • Formulation of problem/goal • Formulation of means
VIII	With what *effect*

From: Cooper (1989: 98)

In Cooper's (1989) framework, the actors (I) refer to people with authority who decide on the language planning process. The behavior (II) refers to the language practices targeted by the planners. This behavior can be divided into three aspects: structural, purpose, and desired level of adoption. People (III) refers to those targeted by the language change, with varying "opportunities, incentives, and disincentives" (Kaplan & Baldauf, 1997: 56). The objectives of language planning (IV) can be varied in nature as they may consist of "language purification, language regenesis, language reform, language standardization, language spread, lexical development, terminological unification, stylistic simplification, interlingual communication, language maintenance, or auxiliary-code standardization" (Kaplan & Baldauf, 1997:56). The goals are to achieve either language related behaviors (overt language planning) or non-language related behavior (latent language planning).

The fifth component (V) is that of the conditions under which language planning take place. These conditions can be further subdivided into conditions caused by situational, structural, cultural, environmental, or informational factors. A situational factor can be caused by events or transient conditions that may take place over a period of time and need to be addressed. A structural condition may be caused by political, economic, or socio-demographic or ecological reasons, whereas a cultural condition may be caused by regime norms, cultural norms, or the socialization of authorities. An environmental factor refers to outside influences whereas an informational factor refers to the need to obtain the data required to make an informed decision on a particular plan. By what means (VI) is the plan introduced either via an authoritative body, a united force of like-minded people, or campaigns aiming to promote the change and persuade speakers to adopt it. Through what decision-making process (VII) refers to the formulation of problems and goals and the means to reach the stated goals. Finally, the effect (VIII) of the language planning project will need to be analyzed. Although the determinants are not easy to access, there is a need for an audit in terms of the impact of the policy on society and to assess whether the objectives have been met.

Accounting for Malay Language Planning based on Cooper's Framework

We can now analyze Malay language planning based on the eight components listed by Cooper (1989) and divide this process into three distinct stages: pre-1956 (before the introduction of the concept of bilingualism via the All-Party Report, 1956), post-1956 (especially from 1959 onward, when Singapore achieved self-government and full implementation of the bilingual policy in 1966), and in the future. This explanation is shown in the table below.

Table 9   Accounting scheme for Malay language planning

Cooper's components	Pre-1956	Post-1956	The Future
What *actors*	Community- and race- based. Influenced by foreign elements, e.g., Chinese by clan associations, Malay by religious groups, Indians by village and family affiliation.	Based on government initiative and support. Top-down government initiatives via the ministries in charge of community affairs and education.	More community involvement. Ownership by each community – community language planning. The government plays a supportive role.
To influence what *behaviors*	The thinking and mindset of native speakers of the language for their motherland – Chinese as China-centric, Malays as Malaya-centric, Indians as India-centric.	As a language of unity and to bond the people as well as for cultural ballast, but also for achieving national interest objectives and meeting the needs of governance.	Attitudes of the community toward learning and understanding their own Asian culture.
Of which *people*	Native speakers, within their own communities and enclaves.	The majority population.	The community at large.

For what *ends*	To ensure the survival of a specific dialect group.	To help maintain Asian- ness and act as cultural ballast, and to act as a linguistic instrument to learn their culture.	Not only as a cultural repository but as a language of knowledge and commerce.
Under what *conditions*	Private school system and community- or clan-funded.	National school system based on the three phases in Singapore's education system: survival-driven, efficiency-driven, and ability-driven. English-knowing bilingualism and Mandarin-led policy.	Greater English-knowing bilingualism and Mandarin-led policy, but for Malays, a community-led approach.
By what *means*	Community-based and privately funded	Government funding and community support. Top-down, via government authority. No choice, but MTL based on paternal links.	Government and private sector funding with community support. More choice due to globalization. Widening of MTLs to not just three.
Through what *decision-making process*	Bottom up and community run	Top-down and professionally run	Democratic process and community engagement
With what *effects*	Haphazard and non-local outlook	World class education system and effectively bilingual graduates	Wider repertoire of Asian languages based on shared values.

As can be seen in the table above, Cooper's (1989) eight components of the accounting scheme of language planning can be analyzed based on three distinct eras: pre-1956, post-1956, and the future.

What actors

With regards to what actors determine the language planning, the pre-1956 era was characterized by community leaders and racial entities being linked to each language. In the case of the Chinese, they were influenced by their clan associations, the Malays by Arab traders and religious groups while the Indians through village and family affiliations. In post 1956, language planning was the purview of the government and top-down in nature. Language planning becomes a tool of unity and development. In the future it is hoped that there will be more community involvement but not necessarily racial in nature. The government's role will be more supportive in nature.

Attempt to influence what behaviours

In terms of influencing what behaviours, pre-1956 was meant to influence the thinking and mind set of the native speakers. Being an immigrant society, language planning was meant to support the struggles of their own motherland. Post 1956, with independence and the need to build a nation, language planning was geared towards bonding the people as a nation and as a cultural ballast to the widening use of English. Language planning was meant to influence behaviours to achieve national objectives and the needs of governance. For the future, Malay language planning will be tweaked towards influencing behaviours of the Malay-speaking community towards learning and appreciating their rich culture within a bigger framework of a nation.

Of which people

Pre 1956, native speakers within their own communities and enclaves was the target of this behavioural change. Post 1956, language planning was targeted towards the majority of the population especially during the early years of self-rule and independence. For the future, language planning will influence behaviours of the Malay community specifically only.

For what ends

In terms of for what ends, pre 1956 is to ensure the survival of a specific group of people e.g. a specific dialect group or to learn basic skills. Post 1956, the ends is to help maintain the Malay identity and act as cultural ballast and linguistic instrument in learning their own culture. In the future, the ends will not only be restricted to cultural repository but may include widening use in other fields of knowledge.

Under what conditions

In pre1956, the condition was community-based and privately funded language planning process. Post 1956 saw a somewhat different condition with a national school system operating within the three phases of education – survival-driven, efficiency-driven and ability-driven. In the future, conditions will be more challenging but it is hoped that the language planning will be community-led and community- centric.

By what means

How can language planning be carried out, by what means? Pre 1956 it was community-based and privately funded. Post-1956, there was much more government funding within the national school system. In the future, there will still be government involvement and funding but with more corporate funding and community support.

Through what decision making process

Through what decision-making process will this be done? Pre-1956 it was bottom-up and community-run. Post 1956, top-down and professionally run. In the future there will be more community involvement via an inclusive approach where the government and the community at large will together decide on the decision-making process.

With what effect

Pre 1956, the effect was lack of planning and poor implementation. In post 1956, with an improving education system, more students became effectively bilingual i.e. able to read and write in English and one of the three mother tongue languages. In the future, there will be a wider choice of languages to be learned especially with more immigrants coming into Singapore. Language planning for Malay will have to take into account this factor as well as the changing demographics of Malay speakers as well as language shift of Malay household.

In short, the outcome for language planning in Singapore has been relatively positive even if the communities lost their status as the actors and the government now dictates both the ends and the means. With more convergent rather than divergent language planning, Malay has been able to survive within an English-knowing bilingual environment.

Effect of Bilingualism on Malay

We will now take a closer look at the effect the bilingual policy has had on Malay in Singapore and answer Question 1: How has the bilingual policy affected the development of Malay in Singapore? This section will review both positive and negative effects of the policy on Malay.

Positive Effects of the Bilingual Policy

We will first analyze the positive effects of bilingualism on Malay.

Platform for Minority Languages

Firstly, the policy has provided a platform for minority languages to maintain their status as languages used in the education system, thus maintaining their vitality. Based on Fishman's (1991) Graded Intergenerational Disruption Scale (GIDS), there are eight levels involved in keeping an endangered language alive. Fishman indicates that a move from Stage 8 to Stage 1 is an important step in keeping an endangered language alive (see table below).

Table 10 Fishman's Graded Intergenerational Disruption Scale (GIDS)

Level	Description
1	The language is used in education, work, the mass media, and government nationwide.
2	The language is used for local and regional mass media and government services.
3	The language is used for local and regional work by both insiders and outsiders.
4	Literacy in the language is transmitted through education.
5	The language is used orally by all generations and is effectively used in written form throughout the community.
6	The language is used orally by all generations and is being learned by children as their first language.
7	The child-bearing generation knows the language well enough to use it with their elders but is not transmitting it to their children.
8	The only remaining speakers of the language are members of the grandparent generation.

As can be seen in the table above, Fishman's (1991) eight-level scale facilitates an understanding of the level of disruption faced by a particular language. The higher the level, 1 being the highest, the lower the possibility that the language will be disrupted in terms of its development and the lower the risk that it will reach endangered level. At Level 8, the most critical level, the language will be deemed to have a higher risk of being endangered if the only remaining speakers are of the grandparent generation. At the highest level of the scale, the language is used in education, work, and the mass media as well as a language of administration at governmental level. Based on this scale, Malay contains elements from Levels 1 through 4. Because Malay is taught in schools, literacy in the language is transmitted through education (Level 4), and is used for local and regional work especially in Malaysia and Indonesia (Level 3) in local and regional mass media (Level 2), and in Singapore at least, in education albeit as mother tongue school subject and to teach Civics and Moral Education at primary level. Thus the bilingual policy has helped to maintain the vitality of the language within the education system.

This view is also supported by Pakir (2004) when she highlights that the bilingual education policy has "raised the status of languages in Singapore schools," that "more time is spent teaching languages than the other subjects at primary level," and that "languages count for more in examinations and are taken into account by the gatekeepers at institutions of higher learning" (Pakir, 2004b: 262). Thus, the benefit is felt by the Malay language as well.

Providing Resources for Curriculum Development and Teacher Training Under the Mother Tongue Programme

The bilingual policy and its equal treatment for the four major languages, i.e., Mandarin, Malay, Tamil, and English has helped in providing the resources for curriculum development and teacher training under the mother tongue programme. Even though reviews of the bilingual policy were initiated by concerns for Chinese language learning, every initiative that arose out of the various review committee reports benefited the Malay language as well. As with other mother tongues, whatever is accrued to Chinese is accorded to Malay and Tamil as well. However, equal treatment, or parity, is not fully implemented in practice. For example, the Special Assistance Plan Schools, in which the government supported and financed selected schools to promote Chinese language and culture also covers Malay.

However, due to lack of numbers, there were no takers, though the potential remains, as was indicated clearly by Lee Kuan Yew, who writes that "If there is demand for it, we can start a similar scheme for students who study Malay or Tamil" (Lee, 2011: 133). Unfortunately, there has been no concerted demand from the Malay community.

Importance of Learning Culture in a Globalised World – cultural rootedness

Malay could be facing a renaissance in Singapore in the 21st century as a result of the emphasis on the learning of culture in a globalized world and the concept of cultural rootedness, which aims at ensuring the Asian identity of Singaporeans in an English-knowing bilingual setting. With the introduction of the *Arif Budiman* vision – the knowledgeable person who contributes to society – which was first introduced in the MLCPRC Report of 2005, Malay has a clear vision of what is to be achieved and what to work toward in terms of cultural achievement beyond merely passing national examinations in Malay. With the introduction of *Arif Budiman*, Malay language planning thus has a clear goal and a stated ideology. All that is required now is a clear outline for achieving this goal.

Negative Effects of the Bilingual Policy

In spite of the positives mentioned, some negatives have arisen out of the bilingual language policy.

Declining Linguistic Proficiency

As English is becoming more dominant in the life of the various communities in Singapore, more people are using the language in their everyday interactions. However, its use is spreading in other domains too, and not only in education. English is rapidly taking over the role of lingua franca that was formerly performed by Malay. More Malays are now using English. This will generally lead to a lowering in their level of Malay proficiency, especially their oral proficiency. This can be observed during formal situations, where Malays are often unable to use the standard variety of Malay although they may be proficient in the non-standard variety. This is especially evident among the younger generation of Malays, including students. This is the general perception among Malay language experts and serving and retired Malay language teachers. In this respect, the recommendation of the Malay Language Steering Review Committee that classroom teaching should give greater emphasis to aural and oral skills is both appropriate and relevant. This emphasis on basic Malay language acquisition can be seen in the new textbook for primary schools, which is aptly named *Akar*, or "Roots." Some Malay language teachers have even indicated that the new textbook is too simple. The simple nature of the book could be due to the fact that Primary l students coming into the school system do not have basic Malay linguistic knowledge, hence the need to go back to basics.

Although an oral test is one component of examinations in Malay language and students are performing well on the test, the types of oral test given need to be revised as the present oral test is neither communicative nor authentic. There is a need to test students in both giving and receiving instructions as well as in other communicative skills, not just in the reading of a text and answering a few questions about it before either explaining what they see from a picture or simply talk about a given topic. The present oral test format does not give a true picture of the students' communicative ability.

Language Shift

Another area of serious concern is the trend toward the wider use of English in the community, which may lead to the eventual loss of Malay, which originated in the Malay-medium schools being closed down as Malay parents no longer sent their children to these schools. This is evident in the 2010 population census, which recorded a 9.1% increase, the highest ten-year increase on record, in Malay households reporting English as the dominant home language. This increase is worrying as from 1990 to 2000, the increase was a mere 2.1% and from 1980 to 1990 only 4%, while the total increase from 1980 to 2000 was 15.5%. This language shift is the direct result of the bilingual language policy and the English-knowing bilingualism context it created.

Another trend that is becoming more noticeable in the Malay community is that Islamic religious teaching is increasingly being delivered in English since more children are said to be more comfortable in English than in Malay. During Friday prayers in the mosques, English is now being used, although not frequently. These two trends, in the home and in the religion, indicate that the link between language and culture in the Malay community is weakening. From the sociolinguistic point of view, a language can become endangered if there is a decreasing use of it among children (Wurm, 2002).

Changing Language Attitudes

Language attitudes are determined by a number of factors, including politics and the economy, to mention just two. Malay in Singapore is a low-status language, and it does not therefore command as much respect as it once did. In education, this attitude toward the language is evident among upper secondary and pre-university students who are learning the language. These students are aware of the low status and low economic value of the language. In general, non-Malay students have a rather negative attitude toward Malay, particularly if they are weak in the language, and consequently, they do not perform well in examinations. In a survey conducted by Forbes for MOE (2005) in 2004, a higher percentage of students at secondary level prefer to read and write in English as compared to those at primary level. This can be seen from the table below.

Table 11 Percentage of Students Who Prefer to Read and Write in English

Skills preferred	Level			
	P4	P6	S2	S4
Speaking in English	7.6	10.0	11.6	18.0
Writing in English	15.6	23.1	27.9	37.3

As can be seen in the table above, the higher the level, the greater the percentage of students preferring to use English. Compared to 7.6% of P4 students preferring to speak English, by S4, there is an increase of 10.4% in that number. The difference is even greater for writing, where it reaches 21.7%. This change in language attitudes is not helped by the fact that there is less curriculum time for Malay at the secondary level as compared to the primary level. At the primary level, students generally study 4 core subjects – English, Mathematics, Science and their respective Mother Tongue. At the secondary level, the range of core subjects increase two-fold with the inclusion of History, Geography, Physics and Chemistry which are all taught in English.

From a societal point of view, language attitudes are very much related to ethno-linguistic vitality, or a group's attitude about itself and its language, including whether the mother tongue is regarded as a core cultural value. Bradley (2002) argues that in a multilingual context, a number of factors determine the language attitude held by a minority group. Some of these factors are as follows:

1. Whether bilingualism is accepted and valued or even normal and expected;

2. How public use of a minority language in the presence of monolingual majority speakers is viewed;

3. Whether minority group members view their language as "difficult" or "hard to maintain;" and

4. Whether the society as a whole supports, tolerates, or represses language maintenance for minority languages.

Of the four factors mentioned, the first three are dependent on the Malay community. With regard to the fourth factor, Singapore society does not repress the maintenance of Malay. In addition, the Malay community is positive toward the first factor. This can be seen from the fact that the Malay community does not reject the importance of English in Singapore and sees mastery of English as enhancing their potential.

Examination-centric Learning Emphasis

Due to the decreasing domain of use for Malay, its current importance is now as an examinable subject to be learned for entry into a secondary school based on points accrued. Thus learning Malay is increasingly a matter of passing state-mandated examinations rather than of understanding and appreciating culture. Learners have become increasingly pragmatic out of necessity as well as due to the incentives offered to students who do well in their mother tongue, including Malay. The students then become disengaged learners as a result of the emphasis placed on written and spoken standards. This results in a situation of subtractive bilingualism, where the mother tongue is replaced by English in some domains of use.

Pedagogical Approach to Supporting the Teaching and Learning of Malay in an English-knowing Bilingual Context such as Singapore

With the changing demographics of Malay language learners, there is a need to review and rethink the pedagogical approach used in the teaching and learning of Malay. The MLCPRC report (2005a) outlined a broad-based approach to this issue. Among the factors that will have to be considered as part of this new approach are concepts such as differentiation, communication, authentication, functionality, and domain of use. We can therefore now answer Question 2: What pedagogical approaches should be used to support Malay in an English-knowing bilingual context such as Singapore? The present pedagogy where teaching is geared toward assessing students' linguistic competence via pen and paper end-of- year or semester examinations should be reexamined. The pedagogy should take into account the students' profile and home language use. It should be communicative and not merely focus on examinations. Content should be situational and authentic. Tasks should be functional and based on the domain of use that exists in Singapore for the use of Malay. The emphasis of assessment should also be on students' communicative competence. At present, only 10% of the assessment is based on students' oral skills. This should be increased in stages to 50% of the total assessment portfolio.

Mother Tongues as "Cultural Ballast"

We will now turn to Question 3: Is the conventional view whereby the teaching of the mother tongue in general and of Malay in particular acts as "cultural ballast" against western influence as relevant today as it was earlier?

The argument that mother tongues act as cultural ballast against western influence via English has been used repeatedly since 1956. Pakir (2004: 267) notes that "the policy of having Chinese as a Second Language (CL2), Malay as a Second Language (ML2), and Tamil as a Second Language (TL2) serving as counters to westernization and for preserving cultural roots did not work." However, with linguistic instrumentalism coming into the fore especially as a result of the awakening of China, there seems to be a need to expand the function of the mother tongues, especially for Chinese, to go beyond the traditional roles as cultural ballast and cultural repository. The emphasis on character education and value-driven education has expanded the teaching of values, which now encompasses not only mother tongue teaching but also the teaching of all subjects. This new initiative by MOE is meant to make values education a whole-school approach rather than being concentrated as a specific subject. This will challenge the status of Malay as well as that of the other two mother tongues. However, it will also limit their domain of use to simply learning culture and values via the language. It may be argued that given the changing demographic profile of Malay students entering P1, the learning of values and character education may be more effectively conducted via English in the near future.

Overall Effects of the Bilingual Policy on the status, corpus and acquisition planning of Malay

Thus we can conclude that the bilingual system has had a positive as well as a negative impact on Malay. It has provided a platform for Malay to prosper within the confines of the mother tongue framework as well as resources for its long-term development. However, the negatives threaten to outweigh the positives. Declining linguistic proficiency, language shift, and changing attitudes within the examination- centric learning emphasis are drawbacks of the bilingual policy that are impacting Malay negatively. Based on Cooper's (1989) framework, which includes status, corpus, and acquisition planning, we will now analyze the effects on Malay of the bilingual policy itself based on these three components.

Effects on the Status of Malay

The status of Malay has moved downward since the bilingual policy came into effect. When the bilingual policy, that is, the requirement to study one's mother tongue as English was granted growing emphasis, was first mooted in 1956, at a time when Malay was the lingua franca in Singapore. When Singapore achieved self-governing status Malay remained widely used among the different communities albeit in its Bazaar Malay form rather than as standard Malay. When Singapore joined Malaya together with Sabah and Sarawak to set up Malaysia in 1963, Malay became not only the National Language but also the language of even wider communication, the language of administration, and the language of unity. It was also an important language to learn in order to enter the administrative service and to obtain confirmations and promotions at work.

The position began to change when Singapore had to leave the Federation of Malaysia in 1965 to strike out on its own and become an independent nation-state. English then replaced Malay as the language of administration and the importance of Malay fell sharply from that point onward. Currently, Malay is used in the educational domain as a school subject from primary through pre-university level. However, the language is not used to teach any subject except Civics and Moral Education at the primary level, and only for those taking Malay as their MTL subject. As was highlighted by Pakir (1993: 81), "the bilingual policy has clearly raised the status of official languages in Singapore schools, although more so for English than for the three official languages." Malay has also lost its status as the dominant language and the link language in the learning and practice of Islam. This role is being taken over by English as more Friday sermons are delivered in English. Thus overall, the bilingual policy has had a negative impact on the status of Malay.

Effects on the Malay Corpus

In terms of corpus planning, Malay has progressed in tandem with the many changes planned by Indonesia, Malaysia, and Brunei under the auspices of the Malay Language Council of Brunei, Malaysia, and Indonesia (MABBIM). Having observer status, Singapore was able to tap the resources of the Council and use its many experts in an effort to understand the developments and implement changes, where required, in the education system. The bilingual language policy has not in any way curtailed the growth of the language in terms of its corpus. The issue that arises out of corpus planning for Malay is that much of it is based in Malaysia's initiative.

When Malaysia decided to implement standard spoken Malay, or *sebutan baku*, Singapore followed suit in 1992 and implemented it wholly within the education system in 1993. The need may be obvious in Malaysia due to the variety of spoken standards in the country. With Malay being the language of administration, education, and science and technology, there is a need to standardize its spoken form, especially when new terminologies are coined for new areas of study. In Cooper's (1989) corpus planning model, this form of standardization is called modernization of the language and applies to cases where the language is used for new areas of development. In contrast, in the Singapore context, there is no such need. Firstly, Singapore is a small island-state that already has a standard spoken form of Malay known as the *Johor-Riau* variety. The change to the *sebutan baku* variety saw no corresponding change in the area of use. Cooper (1989) refers to this process not as a modernization of the language but simply as renovation for non- linguistic ends. What is lost in this context is the identity of Singapore Malay speakers, who are now expected to use *sebutan baku*, especially when one of the reasons for the bilingual language policy is to imbue a strong sense of identity connected to the community's history.

As part of the bilingual policy, corpus planning for Malay has improved and kept up with the development of the language within the Malay-speaking region. However, due to the fact that the linguistic center of Malay is located in Indonesia and Malaysia, Singapore has no choice but to accept exonormative standards determined by these two majority Malay-speaking countries. As Pakir (2004) notes,

> In terms of linguistic practice, it can be said that Singaporeans accept established exonormative "standards" for the official languages often without questioning and, more significantly, without the norms being practiced by them (2004: 66).

Thus there is a need for Singaporeans to set standards they will follow in practice. This is important as it is linked to the status of languages within Singapore. As indicated above, Malay now has restricted status and functions officially as a language for learning Malay culture, that is, as a cultural repository. However, the situation is different in Indonesia, Malaysia, and Brunei, where Malay is the language of wider communication, of interaction among the different ethnic groups (the language of unity), and of knowledge. By contrast, Malay in Singapore has a far more restricted domain. Thus having their own standard will help Malay-speaking and Malay-learning Singaporeans better appreciate the language and use it fully within their own context.

Effects on the Acquisition of Malay

Acquisition planning has received the largest boost in terms of the impact of the bilingual policy. Thanks to equal treatment for all languages, Malay was able to benefit from committee reviews and recommendations and from the enhanced teaching and learning of the language thanks to additional resources and teacher support. The setting up of the Curriculum Development Institute of Singapore enabled teaching resources to be produced for the new Malay syllabus in the early 1980s. The introduction of the concept of Differentiated Instruction (DI) and the communicative language approach also greatly contributed to the enhancement of the teaching and learning of Malay. In addition, awards were given to effective teachers and incentives offered to successful students, who were given opportunities to attend immersion programmes in Malaysia, Indonesia, and Brunei. Teachers were also awarded scholarships to further their studies of Malay and increase their content knowledge on the subject.

Nevertheless, there are concerns, especially over the issue of promoting *Arif Budiman* as a vision of Malay language learning. For the past seven years since *Arif Budiman* was introduced, there have only been two academic papers published on it and none looking into its impact on Malay language development. Another issue concerns the fact that *Arif Budiman* is only promoted within the Malay language syllabus in schools and not within the larger Malay-speaking community. This limits its impact and subsequent development as a vision for the Malay community.

Conclusion

In conclusion, we need to examine the future planning for Malay. As a result of this study, a number of recommendations for possible approaches and strategies can be offered.

Firstly, a review of the *sebutan baku* policy. Singapore is now the only country in the Malay-speaking region that continues to hold on to this pronunciation system. Singapore should adopt its own standard based on its own needs since it is part of the Malay-speaking region and its local standard has a very long history. However, this is not only a question of standards but also of self-confidence. As highlighted by Pakir (2004),

> Paradoxically, for a country that invests heavily in bilingualism and language management, Singapore seems linguistically insecure, perhaps in part because the standards for its languages are derived from elsewhere: Malay standards follow those set by Indonesia, Malaysia, and Brunei; English standards implicitly comes from Britain; and Mandarin follows Beijing's standards. (Pakir, 2004: 124)

Secondly, there should be a body that oversees the development of Malay. Currently, the de-facto body consists of the Malay Language Council of Singapore and MOE, which work in tandem to decide on the policy governing the use and teaching and learning of the language. The pair also advises the government on issues pertaining to Malay and organizes the yearly Malay Language Month as well as Literary Awards. However, this constitutes the Council's main activity. In future, the Council should be more proactive and develop its expertise from within the community to engage the public and expand the use of Malay. Its activities should involve not only schools and teachers (who are already involved in the teaching and learning of the language on a daily basis) but also the Singapore community at large. The Council should also be made responsible for developing new terminologies and for keeping abreast of changes in language teaching and learning as well as disseminating information not only at school level but also at grassroots level. Organizations such as *Dewan Bahasa dan Pustaka* in Malaysia and Brunei and *Balai Pustaka* in Indonesia could be used as models for success. For example, both organizations are even involved in determining terminologies to be used for translation work and instructions in public places and are instrumental in maintaining the standard of language used in the mass media.

Thirdly, there is a need for Malay language organizations to work together in promoting the language beyond teaching and learning, working together to craft a form of community language planning that would involve promoting the use of the language outside of the classroom, especially in the public domain and within households. With more Malay households recording English as their dominant home language, parents will need to start early in exposing their children to the language. As a first step, these organizations should expand the yearly Malay Language Month to cover additional months of the year.

Fourthly, there should be a new pedagogical approach to the teaching of Malay in schools. There have been rumblings in schools to the effect that standards have dropped, and these have been echoed in the media. However, MOE statistics show that the percentage of passes for Malay in national examinations has remained high. Unfortunately, these examinations are almost entirely in written form whereas the Malay language syllabus for primary and secondary schools promotes the growing use of the language in the classroom as a communicative tool. Communicatively, students are weak. Use of the language in context is something that should therefore be examined. This new pedagogical approach should take into account the English- speaking Malay students that have entered Primary 1 as well as the foreign students, including those from The Philippines, Myanmar, India, and Indonesia, who opt for Malay as their mother tongue. Thus the bilingual approach should be given serious consideration in this respect. Via this approach, non-Malay students and students taking Malay, whose dominant home language is not Malay, will be given more time and space to develop their knowledge of the language. Exposure time to Malay will be increased and the strategy is to leverage on their dominant home language and phase in the use of the target language based on students differing needs and abilities.

Fifthly, with the rise of China, there is a need to look at Malay beyond its importance as "cultural ballast". This has happened for Chinese with the rise of China in the 1990s. Wee (2003), argued that the concept of linguistic instrumentalism, whereby a language's usefulness was pegged towards economic development or social mobility, has worked for Mandarin but not for Malay and Tamil. At present, Malay is viewed non-instrumentally i.e. as a tool in identifying one's ethnic culture or cultural identity whose existence is justified only as a symbolic value (Wee, 2003: 212). Alsagoff (2008) too weighed in on this discussion when she used the analogy "commodification of language" referring to the government's policy of looking at Mandarin, Malay and Tamil as a cultural commodity while English carries the weight of an economic commodity. Thus, there should be an expansion of Malay's commodity to go beyond that of culture but also as an instrument or tool of economic development and enhancing social mobility of its speakers. In a region surrounded by a majority of Malay speakers in Indonesia, Malaysia and Brunei where Malay is the National Language, language of administration as well as language of wider communication, finding a reason for its use as a tool of economic development and enhancing social mobility should not be that difficult. The knowledge of Malay can be useful for trade purposes with the inner region of Indonesia and certain parts of Malaysia. This knowledge should be developed and expanded upon thus making the "commodification" of Malay a reality.

Lastly, with reference to Singapore's language ideology, one of which was "prima facie parity among the official languages" (Tan, 2007: 75), it has served Malay well especially in terms of acquisition planning. Nevertheless rather than adopting a parity-at-all-cost stand there can be a more tiered approach in planning for Malay and the other official languages. In a globalized world and an ever-changing linguistic landscape a one-size-fits-all parity approach may not be the best answer for the next fifty years of Malay language planning. A three-tier approach where planning is divided to home, school and community levels be adopted. At present, the parity theory works well at the school level where Malay is given the same level of support based on the review committee reports. But the parity theory has not had the same effect for Malay at the national level as it is a minority language and the concerns generated were mainly that of English and Mandarin. Thus, in this tiered approach, a different language planning strategy will be adopted for Malay at home and community level depending on their differing needs and nuances.

# References

Abdul Rahim Bakar & Awang Sariyan (Eds.). (2005). *Suara Pejuang Bahasa.* Kuala Lumpur: Persatuan Linguistik Malaysia.

Abdullah Hassan (Ed.). (2007). *Kongres Bahasa dan Persuratan Melayu I-VI (1952-2002).* Kuala Lumpur: Persatuan Penterjemah Malaysia.

Ager, D. (2001). *Motivation in Language Planning and Language Policy.* Clevedon: Multilingual Matters.

Alsagoff, L., Chng Hung Choon, & Wee, L. (1998). *Society, Style, and Structure in Language.* Singapore: Prentice Hall.

Alsagoff, L. (2008). The Commodification of Malay: Trading in Futures. In Tan, P.K.W. & Rubdy, R (Eds.). *Language as Commodity: Global Structures, Local Marketplaces.* (pp. 44-56). London: Continuum. London.

Annaliza Bakri. (2010). *Politics of Pronunciation: Debates and Anxiety in the Case of Singapore's Sebutan Baku and Malay Language Planning.* Paper presented at the 5th Asian Graduate Forum on Southeast Asian Studies. Singapore: National University of Singapore.

Annamalai E. & Rubin, J. (1980). Planning for Language Code and Language Use: some considerations in policy-formation and implementation. *Language Planning Newsletter,* 6 (3), 1-4.

Asmah Haji Omar. (1979). *Language Planning for Unity & Efficiency: A Study of the Language Status & Corpus Planning of Malaysia*. Kuala Lumpur: UM Press.

_____. (1987a). *Malay In Its Sociocultural Context*. Kuala Lumpur: Dewan Bahasa & Pustaka.

_____ (Ed.). (1987b). *National Language and Communication In Multilingual Societies*. Kuala Lumpur: Dewan Bahasa & Pustaka.

_____. (1993). *Language and Society In Malaysia*. Kuala Lumpur: Dewan Bahasa & Pustaka.

_____. (2004a). *Muafakat Bahasa: Sejarah MBIM/MABBIM Sebagai Pembinaan Bahasa*. Kuala Lumpur: Dewan Bahasa & Pustaka.

_____. (2004b). *Penyelidikan: Pengajaran dan Pemupukan Bahasa*. Kuala Lumpur: Dewan Bahasa & Pustaka.

Asraf (Ed.). (1996). *Manifesto Budaya: Pupus Bahasa Pupuslah Bangsa*. Kuala Lumpur: Persatuan Linguistik Malaysia.

Awang Sariyan. (2006). *Warna & Suasana: Perancangan Bahasa Melayu di Malaysia* (2nd Edition). Kuala Lumpur: Dewan Bahasa & Pustaka.

Baker, C. (1988). *Key Issues in Bilingualism and Bilingual Education*. England: Multilingual Matters.

_____. (1992). Bilingual Education in Wales. In Beardsmore, H. Baetens (Ed.). *European Models of Bilingual Education*. (pp. 7-29). Clevedon: Multilingual Matters.

_____. (2000). *A Parents' and Teachers' Guide to Bilingualism*. New York: Multilingual Matters.

_____. (2001). *Foundations of Bilingual Education and Bilingualism*. New York: Multilingual Matters.

_____. (2011). *Foundations of Bilingual Education and Bilingualism* (5th Edition). Bristol: Multilingual Matters.

Baker, C. & Jones P.S. (Eds.). (1998). *Encyclopedia of Bilingualism and Bilingual Education*. Philadelphia: Multilingual Matters.

Bamgbose, A. (2004). Language Planning and Language Policies: Issues and Prospects. In Strekenburg, P.G.J. van (Ed.). *Linguistics Today – Facing a greater challenge*. (pp. 61- 88). Amsterdam: John Benjamin.

Ban Kah Choon, Pakir, A. & Tong Chee Kiong (Eds.). (2004). *Imagining Singapore* (2nd Edition). Singapore: Eastern Universities Press.

Beardsmore, H.B.(1986). *Bilingualism: Basic Principles* (2nd Edition). Clevedon: Multilingual Matters.

Bellanca, J. & Brandt, R. (Eds.). (2010). *21st Century Skills: Rethinking How Students Learn*. Bloomington: Solution Tree Press.

Bhatia, T.K. & Ritchie, W.C. (Eds.). (2004). *The Handbook of Bilingualism*. Malden: Blackwell.

Bibi Jan Md. Ayyub & Kamsiah Abdullah. (2003). Malay Language Issues and Trends. In Gopinathan, S., Pakir, A., Ho Wah Kam & Saravanan V. (Eds.). *Language, Society and Education in Singapore: Issues and Trends (2nd Edition)*. (pp. 179- 190). Singapore: Marshall Cavendish.

Bloomfield, L. (1933). *Language.* New York: Holt.

Blythe, T. & Perkins D. (1998). Understanding understanding. In Blythe, T. (Ed.). *The teaching for understanding guide.* (pp.9-16). San Francisco: Jossey-Bass.

Bokhorst-Heng, W. (1999). Singapore's Speak Mandarin Campaign: Language Ideological Debates In the Imagining of the Nation. In Bloommaert, J. (Ed.). *Language Ideological Debates.* (pp. 235-65). Berlin: Mouton.

_____. (1999). Language is more than a Language. *CAS Research Paper Series No. 6.* Singapore: National University of Singapore.

Bokhorst-Heng, W. & Wee, L. (2007). Language Planning in Singapore: On Pragmatism, Communitarianism, and Personal Names. *Current Issues in Language Planning,* Vol. 8, No.3, 324-43.

Bourdieu, P. (1977). *Reproduction in Education, Society & Culture.* London: Sage Publication

Bradley, D. (2002). Language Attitudes : The Key Factor in Language Maintenance. In Bradley D. & Bradley M. (Eds.), *Language Endangerment and Language Maintenance.(pp.1-10) London:* Routledge Curzan.

Brisk, M.E. (2006). *Bilingual Education: From Compensatory to Quality Schooling (2nd Edition).* New Jersey: Lawrence Erlbaum Associates.

Burke, L., Crowley, T., & Girvin, A. (Eds.). (2000). *The Routledge Language and Cultural Theory Reader.* London: Routledge. London.

Butler, Y.G., & Hakuta, K. Bilingualism and Second Language Acquisition. (2004). In Bhatia, T.K. & Ritchie, W.C. (Eds.), *The Handbook of Bilingualism.* (pp.114-144). Massachusetts: Blackwell.

Chaiyanara, P.M. (Ed.). (2001). *Ancangan Pengajian Melayu di Malaysia, Singapura & Selatan Thai.* Singapore: Kesatuan Guru-Guru Melayu Singapura.

Cooper, R.L. (1989). *Language Planning & Social Change.* Cambridge: Cambridge University Press.

Cummins, J. (1981). *Bilingualism and Minority-Language Children.* Toronto: OISE Press.

_____. (2000). *Language, Power and Pedagogy: Bilingual Children in the Crossfire.* New York: Multilingual Matters.

_____. (2003). Bilingual Education: Basic Principles. In Dewaele, J., Housen, A. & Wei Li (Eds.). *Bilingualism: Beyond Basic Principles.* (pp. 56-66). Clevedon: Multilingual Matters.

_____. (2008). Teaching for Transfer: Challenging the Two Solitudes Assumption in Bilingual Education. *Encyclopedia of Language and Education,* Vol. 5, No. 17, 28-38.

Cunningham, D. (2006). The Seven Principles of Constructivist Teaching: A Case Study. *The Constructivist,* Vol. 17, No. 1, 1-24.

Dewaele, J., Housen, A., and Li Wei (Eds.). (2003). *Bilingualism: Beyond Basic Principles.* Clevedon: Multilingual Matters.

Doraisamy T.R. (1969). *150 Years of Education in Singapore.* Singapore: Teachers' Training College Publications.

Edwards, V. (1984) *Language Policy in Multicultural Britain.* London: Academic Press.

_____. (2004). Foundations of Bilingualism. In Bhatia, T.K. & William C. Ritchie (Eds.), *The Handbook of Bilingualism*. (pp. 7-31). Massachusetts: Blackwell.

Fairclough, N. (2010). *Critical Discourse Analysis: The Critical Study of Language (2nd Edition)*. Harlow: Pearson.

Faiza Dekhir and Samira Abid. (2011). The Study of Globalization from a Language Planning Perspective. *Mediterranean Journal of Social Sciences*. Vol. 2, No. 1, 203-211.

Farid M. Onn. (1980). *Aspects of Malay Phonology and Morphology: A Generative Approach*. Kuala Lumpur: University of Malaya Press.

Fasold, R. (1984). *The Sociolinguistics of Society: An Introduction to Sociolinguistics Vol. 1*. Oxford: Blackwell.

Ferguson, C.A. (1996). *Sociolinguistic Perspectives: papers on language in society, 1959-1994*. New York: Oxford University Press.

_____. (2003). Diglossia. In Paulston, Christina Bratt & Tucker, G. Richard (Eds.). *Sociolinguistics: The Essential Readings*. (pp. 345-358). Oxford: Blackwell Publishing.

Fishman, J.A. (2006). *Do Not Leave Your Language Alone: The Hidden Status Agendas Within Corpus Planning in Language Policy*. London: LEA.

Fishman, J.A., Cooper, R.L. & Conrad, A.W. (Eds.). (1977). *The Spread of English: the sociology of English as an additional language*. Massachusetts: Newbury House Publishers.

_____. (2003). Bilingualism With and Without Diglossia; Diglossia With and Without Bilingualism. In Paulston, C.B. & Tucker, G. R.(Eds.). *Sociolinguistics: The Essential Readings.* (pp. 359-366). Oxford: Blackwell Publishing.

Garcia, O. (Ed.). (2009). *Bilingual Education in the 21ˢᵗ Century: A Global Perspective.* Oxford: Wiley-Blackwell.

Genesee, F., Hamers, J., Lambert, W.E., Mononen, L., Seitz, M., & Starck, R. (1978). Language Processing Strategies of Bilinguals: A Neurophysiological Study. In *Brain & Language*, Vol. 5, 1-12.

Garcia, O. & Baker, C. (Eds.). (2007). *Bilingual Education: An Introductory Reader.* Clevedon: Multilingual Matters.

George, C. (2000). *Singapore: The Air-Conditioned Nation.* Singapore: Landmark Books.

Goh Keng Swee. (1979). *Report On the Ministry of Education 1978.* Singapore: Ministry of Education.

Goh Yeng Seng. (2009). Bilingual Education Policy in Singapore: Challenges and Opportunities. In Christopher Ward (Ed.), *Language Teaching in a Multilingual World: Challenges and Opportunities.* Singapore: SEAMEO RELC.

Gopinathan, S. (1974). *Towards A National System of Education – 1945-1973.* Singapore: Oxford University Press.

Gopinathan, S., Pakir, A., Ho Wah Kam & Saravanan V. (Eds.). (2003). *Language, Society, and Education in Singapore: Issues and Trends* (2ⁿᵈ Edition). Singapore: Eastern Universities Press.

Grosjean, F. (1999). Individual Bilingualism. In B. Spolsky (Ed.), *Concise Encyclopedia of Educational Linguistics.* (pp. 284-290). London: Elsevier.

Gwee Hee Yean (Ed.). (1969). *150 years of Education in Singapore.* Singapore: TTC Publications.

Halliday, M. A. K., McIntosh, A. & Strevens P. (1970). The Users and Uses of Language. In Fishman, J. A. (Ed.). *Readings in the Sociology of Language.* (pp. 139-169). The Hague: Mouton.

Haugen E. (1953). *The Norwegian Language in America.* Philadelphia: University of Pennsylvania Press.

_____. (1983). The Implementation of Corpus Planning: Theory and Practice. In Cobarrubias J. & Fishman J (Eds.). *Progress in Language Planning: International Perspectives.* (pp. 269-290). Berlin: Mouton.

Heller, M. (2010). The Commodification of Language. *Annual Review of Anthropology,* 39, 101-114. doi:10.1146/annurer.anthro.012809.104951.

Hillerich, R.L. (1974). Word Lists: Getting It All Together. *The Reading Teacher* Vol. 27, No. 4, January, 353-360.

Ho Wah Kam & Wong, R.Y. L. (Eds.). (2003). *Language Policies and Language Education in East Asia: An Annotated Bibliography.* Singapore: SAAL.

Hornberger, N.H. (Ed.). (2003a). *Continua of Biliteracy: an ecological framework for language policy, research and practice in multilingual settings.* Clevedon: Multilingual Matters.

_____. (2003b). Literacy and Language Planning. In Paulston,C.B. & Tucker, G.R. (Eds.). *Sociolinguistics: The Essential Readings.* (pp. 449- 460). Oxford: Blackwell Publishing.

Hornberger, N. & Wang, S. (2008). Who Are Our Heritage Language Learners? Identity and Biliteracy in Heritage Language Education in the United States. In Brinton, D., Kagan, O. & Bauckus, S. (Eds.). *Heritage Language Education: A New Field Emerging.* (pp. 3-35). New York: Routledge.

Houston, S. H. (1972). Bilingualism: Naturally Acquired Bilingualism. In *A Survey of Psycholinguistics.* (pp. 203-225). The Hague: Mouton.

Irvine, J.T. & Gal, S. (2000). Language Ideology and Linguistic Differentiation. In Kroskrity (Ed.). *Regimes of Language.* (pp. 35-83). Santa Fe: School of American Research.

Ismail bin Dahaman. (1994). Sebutan Baku Bahasa Melayu. Paper presented on the Course on Sebutan Baku Bahasa Melayu for Primary School Teachers in Singapore. Singapore: Ministry of Education. Singapore.

James, E. J. (Ed.). (1996). *The Language-Culture Connection.* Anthology Series 37. Singapore: SEAMEO Regional Language Centre.

Sew Jyh Wee. (2008). Learning Malay in the Global Classroom: Mirroring Social Progress. CLS Working Papers No. 16. Singapore: National University of Singapore.

Kachru, B.B. (1985). Standards, Codification and Sociolinguistic Realism: the English Language in the Outer Circle. In Quirk, R. & Widdowson, H. (Eds.). *English In the World: Teaching and Learning the Language and Literatures.* (pp. 11-30). Cambridge: Cambridge University Press.

Kamsiah Abdullah. (2000). *Sikap, Penguasaan dan Penggunaan Bahasa Melayu di Singapura*. Singapore: ASAS50.

Kandiah, T. & Kwan-Terry, J. (Eds.). (1994). *English and Language Planning: A Southeast Asian Contribution*. Singapore: Times Academic Press.

Kaplan, R.B. & Baldauf, R.B.J. (1997). *Language Planning: From Practice To Theory*. Clevedon: Multilingual Matters.

Kasmadi Haji Nasir. (1993). Pengalaman Pembakuan Bahasa di Singapura. In *PESAN*. Singapore: Ministry of Information and Culture.

Kjolseth, R. (1978). Making Sense: Natural Language and Shared Knowledge in Understanding. In Fishman, J. (Ed.). *Advances in the Study of Societal Multilingualism*. The Hague: Mouton.

Kloss, H. (1969). *Research Possibilities on Group Bilingualism: A Report*. Quebec: International Centre for Research on Bilingualism.

Kulik, C., Kulik, J., & Bangert-Drowns, R. (1990). Effectiveness of mastery learning programs: A meta-analysis. *Review of Educational Research, 60,* 265-299.

Lambert, W.E.(1974). Culture and language as factors in learning and education. In Aboud, F. E. & Meade, R.D. (Eds.). *Cultural Factors in Learning and Education*. Washington: Fifth Western Washington Symposium on Learning.

Laska, J.A. (1985). Mastery Teaching: The Basic Principles. *The Clearing House: A Journal of Educational Strategies, Issues and Ideas*. Vol. 58, No. 7, March, 307-309.

Lee Hock Guan & Leo Suryadinata (Eds.). (2007). *Language, Nation, and Development in Southeast Asia*. Singapore: Institute of Southeast Asian Studies.

Lee Hsien Loong. (20 January 1999). Ministerial Statement on Chinese Language in Schools. Parliamentary Speech.

Lee Kuan Yew. (2011). *My Lifelong Challenge: Singapore's Bilingual Journey*. Singapore: Straits Times Press.

Lee Sing Kong, Goh Chor Boon, Frederikson, B. & Tan Jee Peng (Eds.). (2008). *Toward a Better Future: Education and Training for Economic Development in Singapore since 1965*. Washington D.C.: The World Bank.

Lewis, E.G. (1981). *Bilingualism and Bilingual Education*. Oxford: Pergamon. Lieberson, Stanley. (1969). How Can We Describe and Measure the Incidence and Distribution of Bilingualism. In Kelly, L.G. (Ed.). *Description and Measurement of Bilingualism*. (pp. 286-295). Toronto: University of Toronto Press.

Lindsay, J. & Tan Ying Ying (Eds.). (2003). *Bale or Behemoth: Language Trends in Asia*. Singapore: National University of Singapore.

Mackey, W. F. (1962).The Description of Bilingualism. *Journal of the Canadian Linguistic Association*. Vol. VII, 51-85.

Milroy, J. & Milroy, L. (2012). *Authority In Language: Investigating Standard English (Fourth Edition)*. London: Routledge.

Ministry of Education. (1991). *Improving Primary School Education: Report of the Review Committee*. Singapore: MOE.

_____. (1992). *Chinese Language Teaching & Learning In Singapore: Report of the Chinese Language Review Committee.* Singapore: MOE.

_____. (1993a). *Sukatan Pelajaran Bahasa Melayu (Sekolah Menengah).* Singapore: MOE.

_____. (1993b). *Sukatan Pelajaran Bahasa Melayu (Sekolah Menengah).* Singapore: MOE.

_____. (1999). *Malay Language Steering Review Committee Report.* Singapore: MOE.

_____. (2002). *Sukatan Pelajaran Bahasa Melayu (Menengah).* Singapore: MOE.

_____. (2004). *Report of The Chinese Language Curriculum and Pedagogy Review Committee.* Singapore: MOE.

_____. (2005a). *Report of The Malay Language Curriculum and Pedagogy Review Committee.* Singapore: MOE.

_____. (2005b). *Report of The Tamil Language Curriculum and Pedagogy Review Committee.* Singapore: MOE.

_____. (2009). *Report of the Primary Education Review and Implementation Committee.* Singapore: MOE.

_____. (2011a). *Huraian Sukatan Pelajaran Bahasa Melayu Sekolah Menengah 2011: Menengah 1 & 2.* Singapore: MOE.

_____. (2011b). *Huraian Sukatan Pelajaran Bahasa Melayu Sekolah Menengah 2011: Menengah 3 & 4/5.* Singapore: MOE.

_____. (2011c). *Nurturing Active Learners and Proficient Users: 2010 Mother Tongue Languages Review Committee – Executive Summary of Recommendations.* Singapore: MOE.

Mohamad Ali Hanifiah. (2002). *Sebutan Baku di Radio: Satu Analisis Pendekatan Fonetik Akustik.* Unpublished MA Thesis. Singapore: Nanyang Technological University.

Mohamed Aidil Subhan & Kasmadi Nasir. (2004). *Malay Language in Education Planning: Enemy Within, Enemy Without.* CRP4203MS. Technical Report. Singapore: National Institute of Education.

Mohamed Aidil Subhan & Ariyanti Sukaimi. (2009). High-frequency Words and the Impact of Teaching Reading to Struggling Readers. Paper presented at the Centre for Research in Pedagogy & Practice (CRPP) Conference. Singapore: National Institute of Education.

Mohamed Aidil Subhan. (2007). Planning for Malay Language in Education: Lessons of History and Present Ecology. In Vaish, Viniti, Gopinathan S, & Liu Yongbing (Eds.). *Language, Capital, Culture: Critical Studies of Language and Education in Singapore.* (pp. 157-176). Rotterdam: Sense Publishers.

. (2011). Bahasa Melayu Dijunjung, Bahasa Inggeris Digendong: Pengajaran & Pembelajaran Bahasa Melayu Dalam Kerangka Sistem Dwibahasa yang Berlandaskan Bahasa Inggeris. Paper presented at the 16th Malay Regional Literati Conference 2011. Singapore: ASAS50.

Mohamed Pitchay Gani. (2007). *Evolusi Bahasa Melayu 2000 Tahun: Dari Zaman Purba ke Budaya Elektronik.* Tanjong Malim: UPSI.

Muhammad Ariff Ahmad. (1990). *Bahasa Jiwa Bangsa.* Singapore: Singapore Press Holdings.

_____. (1992). Sejarah Perkembangan Bahasa Melayu di Singapura. Paper presented at the workshop on the history of the Malay Language, Institute of Language and Literature Malaysia and National University of Malaysia. November 9. Kuala Lumpur: DBP.

Nahir, M. (2003). Language Planning Goals: A Classification. In Paulston, Christina Bratt, & Tucker, Richard G. *Sociolinguistics: The Essential Readings.* (pp. 423-448). New York: Blackwell.

Norhaida Aman. (2009). The Linguistic Practices of Bilingual Singapore Malay Students: A Tale of Language Maintenance. *Jurnal E-Utama*, Vol. 2, 47-68.

Norhaida Aman, Vaish, V., Bokhorst-Heng, W., Jamaludeen Aisha, Durgadevi, P., Feng, Y.Y., Khoo B.S., Mardiana Roslan, Appleyard, P., Tan T.K. (2009). *The Sociolinguistic Survey of Singapore 2006. Final Research Report.* Singapore: National Institute of Education.

Oxford, R.L. (1997). Constructivism: Shape-Shifting, Substance, and Teacher Education Applications. *Peabody Journal of Education*, Vol. 72, No. 1, 35-66.

Pairah Satariman. (2006). *Malay Language Curriculum for Secondary Schools in Singapore: An Evaluation of its Development and Implementation.* Unpublished MA Thesis. Singapore: National University of Singapore.

Pakir, A. (1993). Two Tongue Tied: Bilingualism in Singapore. *Journal of Multilingual and Multicultural Development.* Vol. 14, No. 1&2, 73-90.

_____. (2003). Which English? The Nativization of English and the Negotiations of Language Choice in Southeast Asia. In Ahrens, R., Parker, D., Stierstorfer K. & Kwok Kan Tam (Eds.). *Anglophone Cultures in Southeast Asia.* (pp. 63-74). Heidelberg: Universitatsverlag: Heidelberg.

_____. (2004a). Medium-of-Instruction Policy in Singapore. In Tollefson, J.W. & Tsui, Amy (Eds.). *Medium of Instruction Policies: Which agenda? Whose agenda?* New Jersey: Lawrence Erlbaum Associates.

_____. (2004b). English-Knowing Bilingualism in Singapore. In Ban Kah Choon, Pakir, A. & Tong Chee Kiong (Eds.). *Imagining Singapore.* Singapore: Marshall Cavendish.

Petty, G. (1998). *Evidence Based Teaching: A Practical Approach.*

Puru Shotam & Nirmala S. (1998). *Negotiating Language, Constructing Race: Disciplining Difference in Singapore.* Berlin: Mouton.

Pohl, J. (1965). Bilinguismes. *Revue Roumaine de Linguistique.* Vol. 10. Pp. 343-49.

Lily Zubaidah Rahim. (2001). *The Singapore Dilemma: The Political and Educational Marginality of the Malay Community.* New York: Oxford University Press.

Raja Mukhtaruddin Raja Mohd. Dain. (1992). *Pembinaan Bahasa Melayu: Perancangan Bahasa di Malaysia.* Kuala Lumpur: DBP.

Rappa, A.L. & Wee, L. (2006). *Language Policy and Modernity in Southeast Asia: Malaysia, the Philippines, Singapore, and Thailand.* New York: Springer. New York.

Rassool, N. (2007). *Global Issues in Language, Education & Development: Perspectives from Postcolonial Countries.* Clevedon: Multilingual Matters.

Richards, J.C. & Rodgers, T.S. (2007). *Approaches and Methods in Language Teaching (2nd Edition).* New York: Cambridge University Press.

Riley, P. (2007). *Language, Culture, and Identity: An Ethnoliguistic Perspective.* New York: Continuum.

Rohan Nizam Basheer. (2007). *Peralihan Bahasa Melayu Dalam Domain Agama: Satu Kajian Kes di Singapura.* Unpublished MA Thesis. Kuala Lumpur: University of Malaya.

Roksana Bibi Abdullah. (2003). *Bahasa Melayu di Singapura: Pengalihan dan Pengekalan.* Singapore: Deezed Consultants.

Rubin, J. & Jernudd, B.H. (Eds.) (1975). *Can Language Be Planned?: Sociolinguistic Theory and Practice for Developing Nations.* Honolulu: University Press of Hawaii.

Sa'eda Buang. (2010). Muslim Education and Globalization: The Re-(de) positioning of Languages and Curriculum Content in Southeast Asia. In Vaish, Viniti (Ed.). *Globalization of Language & Culture in Asia: The Impact of Globalization Processes on Languages.* (pp. 34-60). London: Continuum.

Shee Poon-Kim. (1979). Singapore 1978: Preparation for the 1980s. *Asian Survey,* Vol. 19, No. 2, A Survey of Asia in 1978: Part II, pp. 124-130.

Shohamy, E. (2006). *Language Policy: Hidden Agendas and New Approaches.* London: Routledge.

Simpson, A. (Ed.). (2007). *Language and National Identity in Asia.* New York: Oxford University Press.

Singapore Government. (1956). *Report of the All Party Committee of the Singapore Legislative Assembly on Chinese Education.* Singapore: Govt. Press.

Singapore Malay Language Committee. (1992). *Ucapan dan Makalah Simposium Sebutan Baku Bahasa Melayu*. Singapore: JBMS.

Skutnabb-Kangas, T. (1981). *Bilingualism or Not: the education of minorities*. Translated by Malmberg, L. and Crane, D. Clevedon: Multilingual Matters.

_____. (2000). *Linguistic Genicide in Education – or Worldwide Diversity and Human*
Rights? New Jersey: Lawrence Erlbaum.

Skutnabb-Kangas, T. & Cummins, J. (Eds.). (1988). *Minority Education: from shame to struggle*. Clevedon: Multilingual Matters.

Spolsky, B. (2004). *Language Policy*. Cambridge: Cambridge University Press.

Tan, K.B. (2007). The Multilingual State in Search of the Nation: The Language Policy and Discourse in Singapore's Nation-Building. In Lee Hock Guan & Leo Suryadinata (Eds.) *Language, Nation & Development*. (pp.). Singapore: ISEAS.

Tan, K.W. & Rubdy, R. (Eds.). (2008). *Language As Commodity: Global Structures, Local Marketplaces*. London: Continuum.

Tan Ta-Sen. (1978). Language Policies In Insular Southeast Asia: A Comparative Study. *Southeast Asia Research Paper Series 2*. Singapore: Nanyang University.

Tan, J., Gopinathan S., & Ho Wah Kam (Eds.). (2001). *Challenges Facing the Singapore Education System Today*. Singapore: Prentice Hall.

Tan, J. & Ng Pak Tee (Eds.). (2008). *Thinking Schools, Learning Nation: Contemporary Issues and Challenges*. Singapore: Prentice Hall.

Tay, M. (1984). *Trends in Language, Literacy and Education in Singapore.* Census Monograph No. 2. Singapore: Department of Statistics.

Temple, C., Ogle, D., Crawford, A., & Freppon, P. (2005). *All children read: Teaching for literacy in today's diverse classroom.* Boston: Pearson.

Tham Seong Chee. (1990). *Multi-lingualism in Singapore: Two Decades of Development. Census of Population 1990.* Monograph No. 6. Singapore: Department of Statistics.

Tollefson, J.W. (1991). *Planning Language, Planning Inequality: Language Policy in the Community.* London: Longman.

Tomlinson, C.A. (2005). *How To Differentiate in Mixed-Ability Classrooms (2nd Edition).* New Jersey: Pearson.

Vaish, V. (Ed.). (2010). *Globalization of Language and Culture in Asia: The Impact of Globalization Processes on Language.* London: Continuum.

Vaish, V., Gopinathan, S. & Liu Yongbing (Eds.). (2007). *Language, Capital, Culture: Critical Studies of Language and Education in Singapore.* Rotterdam: Sense Publishers.

Valdés, G. & Figueroa, R.A. (1994). *Bilingualism and testing: A special case of bias in second language learning.* Westport: Ablex Publishing.

Wee, L. (2003). Linguistic Instrumentalism in Singapore. *Journal of Multilingual and Multicultural Development,* Vol. 24, No. 3, 211-224.

_____. (2011). Language Policy Mistakes in Singapore: Governance, expertise, and the deliberation of language ideologies. *International Journal of Applied Linguistics.* Vol. 21, No. 2, 202-21.

Weinreich, U. (1953). *Languages In Contact*. The Hague: Mouton.

Wiley, T. G. (1996). Language Planning and Policy. In McKay, S. L. & Hornberger, N. H. (Eds.). *Sociolinguistics and Language Teaching*. (pp. 103-148). New York: Cambridge University Press.

Williamson, R.C. (1991). *Minority Languages and Bilingualism: Case Studies in Maintenance and Shift*. New Jersey: Ablex Publishing.

Wong Hoy Kee & Gwee Yee Hean. (1972). *Perspectives: The Development of Education in Malaysia and Singapore*. Singapore: Heinemann.

Zelda Ibrahim. (2010). *Menyelongkar Ideologi & Identiti Dalam Laporan Jawatankuasa Semakan Kurikulum & Pedagogi Bahasa Melayu (2005): Satu Analisis Wacana Kritis*. Unpublished MA Thesis. Singapore: Nanyang Technological University.

www.ingramcontent.com/pod-product-compliance
Lightning Source LLC
Chambersburg PA
CBHW030425290526
45786CB00001B/138